(Ad)dressing Our Words

Aboriginal Perspectives on
Aboriginal Literatures

2001

Editor
Armand Garnet Ruffo

Theytus Books Ltd.
Penticton, BC
Canada

CANADIAN CATALOGUING IN PUBLICATION DATA

ISBN 0-919441-91-2

1. Canadian literature (English)--Indian authors--History and criticism.* 2. Indian literature--Canada--history and criticism.* 3. Native peoples in literature.*
I. Ruffo, Armand Garnet, 1955 - II. Title: Dressing our words

PS8089.5.I6A32 2001   C810.9'897   C2001-911319-6
PR9188.2.I5A32 2001

Editor: Armand Garnet Ruffo
Cover Design: Florene Belmore
Cover Art: Barry Ace, Parallel Tasking, 2000, mixed media,
Photo credit: Jeffrey M. Thomas
Composition and Layout: Judith Schmid
Managing Editor: Greg Young-Ing

Theytus Books Ltd.
Lot 45 Green Mountain Rd.
RR#2, Site 50, Comp 8
Penticton, BC
V2A 6J7

*The Publisher acknowledges the support of
The Canada Council for the Arts,
The Department of Canadian Heritage and
The British Columbia Arts Council.*

Printed in Canada

CONTENTS

Introduction

Armand Garnet Ruffo

In putting together any anthology, an editor has to make a number of tough decisions concerning inclusion and exclusion. Much of that decision making process for this anthology was made for me by the criteria that Theytus Books set in its conception of this book. (A concept, I might add, that I readily agreed with in undertaking the project.) After careful consideration it was decided that this text would be a follow-up to Theytus' 1993 anthology *Looking At the Words of Our People*. Like that collection, it was determined that *(Ad)dressing Our Words* would feature writing by Aboriginal scholars and writers working in the expanding field of Aboriginal literature. Beginning in the early seventies, a creative 'renaissance' or 'rebirth' (as it has been called at various times) had taken place. After some fifty years of being silenced by both Church and State, and marginalized by the larger Canadian society and cultural establishment, Aboriginal people were beginning to speak out. To this end, both mainstream and alternative publishers were finally publishing Aboriginal writers – recognition was being given; awards were being won. And, yet, perhaps because it was so new and unexpected, there was little critical writing attempting to provide context and analysis of the literature.

Since that time the creative and critical landscapes of Aboriginal literature have continued to change dramatically, both at home and abroad. While it can be argued that the greater part of Aboriginal cultural production is still marginalized, nonetheless, collections of poetry and short fiction, novels and plays have been coming out yearly, so much so that it is now becoming difficult to keep up with who is publishing what. In terms of anthologies, beginning with Theytus Books' *The Seventh Generation: Contemporary Native Literature* (1989), the first anthology in Canada devoted to writing by Aboriginal people, followed by Oxford UP's *An Anthology of Canadian Native Literature in English* (1992), the pace of new offerings has steadily increased to include more anthologies and special editions of journals than can possibly be mentioned in this introduction. This year alone, we have broadview press's *Native Poetry in Canada* as well as *Prairie Fire*'s special issue: "First Voices First Words."

And while the critical side of things has been slower to gain momentum, we are now also seeing academic journals actively publishing (and in some cases actively soliciting) critical writing on Aboriginal literatures. Journals such as *The International Journal of Canadian Studies* (12:1995) and *Canadian Literature* (167:2000), among others, have gone so far as to publish special editions on Aboriginal culture and literature. Furthermore, a number of critical anthologies have also been published in recent years that have either focused solely on Aboriginal culture and literature or have included it as part of a general look at 'minority literatures.' Two such anthologies come to mind, *Literary Pluralities* (broadview, 1998) and *Native North America: Critical and Cultural Perspectives* (ECW, 1999). I mention these two texts in the context of *(Ad)dressing Our Words* because in both instances the editors sought out and asked Aboriginal academics and writers to contribute something to their respective anthology. Whether a case of political correctness or a genuine conviction that Aboriginal people have something of value to say about their own cultures and literatures that 'outsiders' may not know, or cannot know, these editors nonetheless thought it necessary to include Aboriginal perspectives within their texts. For some it is only common sense; the focus on literature naturally invites a consideration of culture, as in the case of Aboriginal literature, which traditionally foregrounds cultural beliefs and values.

So why then this text? In considering *(Ad)dressing Our Words* as a follow-up to Theytus' *Looking At the Words of Our People,* we discovered in the planning that since the publication of that first critical text there has been no other collection of literary criticism solely *by* Aboriginal people, at least not here in Canada, although there have been a number *about* Aboriginal people. What this means is that the creation, publication and dissemination of such journals and anthologies have been in the hands of 'outsiders.' While they no doubt have tried to be inclusive as possible, as I mentioned earlier, anthologizing is exclusive by its very nature. In other words, who gets in? Focusing solely on Aboriginal people has allowed me to bring voices to the page that might not readily appeal to those who, despite their good intentions, cannot help but carry their own cultural/academic biases. This said, the reader will notice that some of the pieces selected are not what one would call 'academic' in the critical sense, but rather come directly out of the Oral Tradition. For those immersed in Aboriginal culture and literature, my decision should be self-explanatory. The Oral Tradition continues to influence contemporary Aboriginal literatures profoundly and has led to the development of what Thomas King calls "interfusional literature," a stylistic and thematic hybrid of the oral and written, the past and present, the Aboriginal and Western.

What I have tried to do then is open a space to publish submissions by Aboriginal people without restricting the book to one particular type of 'critical' writing. My intention was that the mix of voices be fresh and provocative. As every book has a finite number of pages so too can only a limited number of people be included between its covers. These essays therefore present but a sample of what is happening in the field today. A few of the contributors are well known. The majority is relatively new to the field, either doing graduate work or having just finished. Some are international. Some do not consider themselves academics at all (though they all have academic training) but rather poets and writers. Together the essays offer a diversity of subject and style, from the scholarly 'objective' position engaged in analyzing a particular writer's work to the writer him/herself engaged in analyzing his or her own creative process and/or interests. Yet despite this diversity a commonality is evident, and the reader will see that they are united by the common theme of de-colonization and reach out with commitment and determination to that ongoing process.

As the process of de-colonization is itself arduous (as the writing here attests to), the authors' preoccupation with it points to a range of related topics – a direct result of colonization – to which they bring their own sensibilities as Aboriginal people. In this regard, the authors tackle the subject matter from what I have previously called "inside out." This is not to advocate some kind of inherent quality that comes with being Aboriginal, an essentialism that comes hand in hand with an 'Indian Status Card' so to speak. The authors included here come to their subjects 'culturally initiated' and are thus well aware of the 'territory' of which they write. Of course, this notion of culturally initiation can be construed by some to be so vague as to have neither meaning nor validity. Whatever the implications, it entails a sense of self-awareness as an Aboriginal person and includes whatever life experience that person has had. Being adopted as a child and searching for one's roots is equally as valid as growing up at the foot of an Elder. Thus, the essays in this anthology demonstrate a wide range of interests and concerns, and provide insight into the experiences of reading, writing and living as an Aboriginal person on the cusp of the 21st century – whatever that might involve.

The contributors to *(Ad)dressing Our Words,* like the storytellers, poets, playwrights and novelists whose writing their discourse
focuses on (In some instances it is their own work.), position their
work within the genre of 'resistance' writing in that they write
from an Aboriginal perspective and address colonialism in all its
guises – whether discussing tradition, identity, language, appropriation, assimilation, self-determination or sexuality. From this
position of resistance, they raise difficult textual questions with far
reaching social-political-cultural implications. Questions, I might
add, that should interest other peoples trying to negotiate a path
through the maze of cultures and interests in which we presently
live. In her forward to *Looking At The Words of Our People,*
Okanagan writer and educator, Jeannette Armstrong suggests
"First Nations Literature will be defined by First Nations Writers
[sic], readers, academics and critics... from within those varieties
of First Nations" (7). Further in that same collection, Anishinabe
scholar Kimberly Blaeser says the "insistence on reading Native
literature by way of Western literary theory clearly violates its integrity and performs a new act of colonization and conquest" (55).
With a new generation of scholars and writers (re)searching their
traditions and applying them to literary creation and analysis, we
move closer towards the notion of a culturally centred
"ethnocriticism" (ibid 57). This does not necessarily mean dis-
counting western theory, but being cautious of its 'insistence' and
using it only where applicable and in the context of Indigenous
ways of knowing.

Pointing the way towards such a methodology of interpretation
and literary analysis, Neal McLeod grounds his essay "Coming
Home Through Stories" in the culture of the *Nêhiyawak* (Cree),
while examining of the implications of "spatial and ideological Diaspora." Drawing on family and community stories, McLeod considers the concept of storytelling and the correlation between
"hybridity and survival." For McLeod narrative is essential in that
it links one generation to the next and transmits knowledge on
many different levels. He writes that "'To come home' is to dwell
in liminal space, and the process... is not so much returning to
some "idealized location of interpretation." Rather, it is an attempt
to find a place "wherein the experiences of the present can be understood as a function of the past." To this end, he tells us that
"Our task today is to retrieve tribal narratives and paradigms, and
to reaffirm our tribal identities in the face of overwhelming pressure of Diaspora." For it is through our stories and narrative mem-

ory that we "anchor" ourselves in the world.

Like McLeod, Janice Acoose finds cultural revitalization through traditional narrative. In her essay "A Vanishing Indian? Or Acoose: Woman Standing Above Ground," she traces her own *Ninahkawewin* (Cree) family stories of her Great-grandfather Acoose (*Ekos*) and relates how these stories have been readily appropriated, rendered inaccurate, and turned into "primitive legends." Discussing traditional intellectual property in the context of the "*Wiintigo*-like consuming forces of Western imperialism," she draws the connection between literary sovereignty and political nationhood. In this context, Acoose says what is required in Aboriginal pedagogy is to become actively involved in the battle against such *Wiintigo*-like forces. She says, "when I teach Indigenous literatures I use the texts as tools for confronting colonialism and locating spaces for decolonization." She confides that this approach leaves her feeling vulnerable at times, but concludes that it is also empowering to know there are "others employing innovative methods derived from their respective cultures to interpret and analyze culturally specific literatures."

In "From Copper Woman to Grey Owl to the alterNative Warriors: Exploring Voice and the Need to Connect," Jonathan Dewar foregrounds his 'mixed blood' heritage and revisits the appropriation issue, exploring what it means to identify as Aboriginal. In situating his inquiry around Drew Hayden Taylor's *alterNatives*, Anne Cameron's *Daughters of Copper Woman* and my own *Grey Owl: The Mystery of Archie Belaney*, Dewar grapples with what he refers to as the "difficult and ambiguous nature of connection." In doing so, he poses such poignant questions as "Is respect for another culture enough to get one over the appropriation issue hurtle?" And in regard to Aboriginal people themselves, "How does one reconnect in a meaningful way to one's severed Native culture?" Concerning pedagogy, he wonders how it is possible to teach an Aboriginal text without growing up on a reserve learning one's Aboriginal language(s). Accordingly, he indicates that he finds texts that deal thematically with issues of "(re)connection" particularly useful and turns to those texts that help him "articulate his position with the discourse and navigate through the many intersecting debates."

The question of identity is also central to Rauna Kuokkanen's "Let's Vote Who Is Most Authentic: Politics of Identity in Contemporary Sami Literature." Beginning with a discussion of the stereotyping of her Sami people that is reminiscent of the experience of Aboriginal people in the Americas, Kuokkanen documents the detrimental effects that such biased views have in creating a 'false reality.' She tells us that "in many cases, the stereotypical images have functioned as a basis of defining who is Sami. This in turn has led to a controversial debate over authenticity." In response, Kuokkanen examines the work of four contemporary Sami writers (Kirsti Paltto, Jovnna-Ánde Vest, Inger-Mari Aikio and Kerttu Vuolab) in order "to dispel falsehoods and tell what it is really like." In doing so, she prefaces her work by indicating that "the writing of four Sami writers do not give a complete picture of the contemporary many-sided Sami identity. They do, however, demonstrate effectively the ways in which previous assumptions of Saminess have been misleading and limited." Echoing the concerns of her Turtle Island colleagues, she concludes by calling for a return to Aboriginal traditions, practices and epistemologies which "offer representations and perceptions created by our own people," and can be useful in "locating new ways of theorizing our own literatures."

In considering the work of Tomson Highway, Randy Lundy, in "Erasing the Invisible: Gender Violence and Representations of Whiteness in *Dry Lips Oughta Move To Kapuskasing*," tackles the issues of representation and sexism. Outlining allegations that Highway's play is misogynist and supports rather than subverts stereotypes, Lundy notes that despite various other arguments supporting the play "the question of whether or not the play reinforces stereotypes and reinscribes colonial violence and domination" has remained unanswered. Ascribing the "rupture of the relationship with women and feminine realities" to the English language itself, he says that "the solution to the social problems that the play exposes lies in the men's returning to... the internal logic of the non-gendered Indigenous languages." Lundy explains, though, that central to the complexity of the play is the premise that the imposition of English with its gender bias has served effectively to hamper a return to Aboriginal spiritual traditions. Without excusing the violent misogyny in *Dry Lips*, he concludes that the play does assign causation for this and other forms of internal oppression to colonial domination but provides no easy solutions to remedy the on going problems.

Well aware of the implications of language, Laura Ann Cranmer, in "Exploring Voice and Silence in the Poetry of Beth Cuthand, Louise Halfe, and Marlene Nourbese Philip," focuses on Nourbese Philip's concept of "l'anguish – a dead weight that sinks into the collective psyche of the colonized" – and uses it as an entry into the work of these poets in the context of her own life. Acknowledging that the "blood of the oppressor runs together with the blood of the oppressed" in her veins, she writes of the "invasion of the body and spirit" and consequently the difficulty of finding her 'voice.' Cranmer too looks to the specificity of Aboriginal culture to connect to the writing examined. She observes that "[a]ny spiritual journey demands a kind of death of an old way of being in the world owing to the transformational process and change in perspective" and reveals an interest in "the imaginative approaches and perspectives that undermine Western hegemony." Indicating new possibilities for breaking free from colonial domination, the work of these poets, she concludes, "points to the importance of journeying within to re/vision a collective past through the internal process of healing and becoming whole."

Brenda Payne, in her essay "*A Really Good Brown Girl*: Marilyn Dumont's Poems of Grief and Celebration," also identifies with the work of an Aboriginal poet. In a brief forward to her article, Payne tells us that "Dumont's poems give voice to many of my feelings and experiences of sorrow, frustration, discovery and determination. The power of Dumont's writing reinforces my belief in the significance of story and the ability to heal and be healed through creative expression and respectful acknowledgement." In a close reading of the poems, Payne traces Dumont's "experiences of loss and grief" and reveals that despite the charged emotion in the poems they rise above feelings of bitterness and cynicism. It is a teaching that Payne takes to heart, noting that Dumont "reveals a willingness to face, mourn and, eventually, recover from the losses." Like other essays in this collection, the theme of attaining spirituality is central to Payne's analysis. She concludes by referencing Dumont's use of water imagery, the connection between the human and natural world, observing that it allows the poet an avenue of "compassion for all of the Creator's children." In this manner, Payne's identification with the poet's spiritual journey reveals the power of creative expression to provide for reconciliation and healing.

In "Erotica, Indigenous Style" Kateri Akiwenzie-Damm writes of what compelled her to compile an anthology of Aboriginal erotica. Considering the role of the erotic in healing Aboriginal people from the legacy of colonialism, she tells of her search for erotica by Aboriginal writers and becoming alarmed by the realization that there was very little to be found. "There is something seriously wrong when sexuality and erotic expression are repressed. In an individual person, it might raise a few eyebrows. Amongst a whole people, it raises a red flag." For Akiwenzie-Damm erotica by Indigenous writers is "political regardless of one's personal politics" in that it rejects Western beliefs and attitudes in favour of traditional views of sexuality and thereby reclaims Aboriginal culture. She writes that "the repression of erotic art is symptomatic of our oppression and signifies a deep psychological and spiritual break between a healthy and holistic tradition and an oppressed, repressed, shamed and <u>imposed</u> sense of reality." Like others in this collection, Akiwenzie-Damm acknowledges the power of stereotypical images to create falsehoods that have lasting, negative repercussions.

Re-articulating the imagery of the 'old west,' Daniel David Moses, in his "A Syphilitic Western: Making 'The... Medicine Shows,'" recreates his experience of writing his two linked one act plays, "The Moon and Dead Indians" and "Angel of the Medicine Show." Combining elements of the oral and written, Moses' 'talk' takes the reader through the creative process as he explores the themes that emerged through the writing of the plays. Moses subverts the typology of the western by reinventing the myth of Billy the Kid from a two-spirited, Aboriginal perspective. Thus he challenges the standard idealized conventions of the genre and finds irony in the idea of an "Indian writing a western in which the genre demands that the Indians are not foregrounded." Conversely, Moses does foreground his Delaware heritage and notes the important role it plays in shaping how he writes for the theatre and relates to Western theatrical conventions. Throughout, Moses interrogates himself by constantly asking (himself and the listener/reader by extension): "Where is this coming from?" Referring to the plays themselves and creativity in general, his question is both rhetorical and literal, and it is through dream and memory that he journeys into his past to find an answer.

How the past informs the present is also central to Geraldine Manossa's "The Beginning of Cree Performance Culture" in which she "explores Native Performance Culture by examining the contemporary sociological significance between the viewer, the writer and the performer." To illustrate her position, Manossa goes to the roots of the genre and presents us with one of the earliest stories from the Oral Tradition. Relating her experience of listening with her classmates to an Elder interpret the *Wasakaychak* Creation Story, she recreates the nuances of the experience, tying them to concepts of Aboriginal performance. Citing the research of Floyd Favel Starr, she says that Native Performance Culture is the "developing practices of our ancestors," and, like Aboriginal culture(s), it is grounded in a collective experience. According to Manossa, "The collective manner through which knowledge, images, symbols, actions and humour are shared from listener to listener and from storyteller to listener is where... the essence of Native performance arises." Aboriginal performance then is not simply about copying Western conventions but entails getting to the essence of traditional sources and using them to develop something uniquely contemporary and culturally specific.

In his essay "Time is a fish: The Spirit of Nanapush and the Power of Transformation in the Stories of Louise Erdrich," David McNab analyzes the work of one of America's most prominent Aboriginal writers. Excerpted from a longer study, McNab's essay addresses the major theme of "transformation" in the context of "the place of people in the universe and the power of the natural and spiritual worlds." He notes that the concept of time being circular also informs Erdrich's work and has profound influence on both characterization and landscape in which everyone and everything is related. Noting Erdrich's own mixed Cree/Chippewa/German heritage, he indicates how the author's personal and family stories are central to her work, allowing her to incorporate an Anishinabe worldview into it, in which neither human nor the natural world is fixed but constantly in flux. As Erdrich uses vivid imagery to great effect in her writing so too does she employ startling dreams and visions that emphasize another kind of worldliness and underlie her work's essential spiritual quality.

In "Aboriginal Identity and Its Effects on Writing,' Anita Heiss considers the question of authenticity from an Aboriginal Australian perspective. Structuring her essay around a series of interviews with Aboriginal writers, Heiss gives a concise overview of the development of Aboriginal writing in Australia and the implications arising from it. She considers the 'need' of the Australian government to define Aboriginality for its own assimilative purposes in light of the push by Aboriginal people to define themselves. Referencing the recent controversy over non-Aboriginal writers passing themselves off as Aboriginal for personal gain, she poses such pertinent questions as "What makes an Aboriginal writers? Is there an Aboriginal style?" Although many of the writers claim to use "Aboriginal English," the answers she receives as expected are diverse and at times even contradictory. What does come across loud and clear is that "the term post-colonialism is meaningless to Aboriginal people." In fact, "there are few, if any Aboriginal Australian writers who agree with or use the term at all, least of all in relation to their writing." Furthermore, she indicates that the feeling among Aboriginal writers is that the discourse of post-colonialism diverges from that of Aboriginality.

Responding to the problem of authenticity raised by Heiss and others, Greg Young-Ing, in "Aboriginal Text in Context," reviews the need for Aboriginal publishing. He notes that from the colonial period to the present texts published by non-Aboriginals about Aboriginal Peoples have been rife with stereotypes and inaccuracies, which have been "degrading and offensive" to Aboriginal Peoples. According to Young-Ing, the problem of representation by non-Aboriginals continues unabated despite Aboriginal authors having developed and expressed a body of literature that now stands out as "the most culturally authentic literary expression of Aboriginal reality." To compound matters, this body of work continues to be overshadowed by non-Aboriginal writers who insist on writing about Aboriginal peoples. Raising the issue of 'Aboriginal Voice' and accessibility, Young-Ing says that "Aboriginal controlled editing and publishing is the solution to many of the problems which have held back and continue to hold back Aboriginal Peoples in the publishing industry."

Clearly, the question of accessibility is underlined by another major issue affecting the reception of Aboriginal literatures. Aboriginal writers must contend with the issue of writing from Aboriginal perspectives in countries that consider it too confrontational and offensive to raise and address the myth of Discovery and the horrific legacy of Colonialism. Say the wrong thing, write the wrong way, do not allow your readership (or audience) to have a good laugh, and your work becomes too political, too strident, and it is quietly dismissed and shelved. Out of sight, out of mind. The essays in this collection show that Aboriginal writers are gaining a readership among their own people, and perhaps this is one of the most significant developments of all in recent years. If this is any indication of things to come, this readership will see to it that Aboriginal writers continue to be read and heard despite what is officially (or tacitly) sanctioned. Although the essays in this collection range widely, reoccurring themes do emerge which deal with some of the most compelling issues facing Aboriginal Peoples today. For as a *Wiseman* once told me, without our languages, without our stories, we cease to exist.

Works Cited

Armstrong, Jeannette. (1993) "Editor's Note." in Armstrong, ed. 7-8.

Armstrong, Jeannette, ed. (1993) *Looking At the Words of Our People: First Nations Analysis of Literature.* Penticton, BC: Theytus.

Blaeser, Kimberly. "Native Literature: Seeking a Critical Centre." in Armstrong, ed. 51-62.

Hulan, Renee, ed. (1999) *Native North America: Critical and Cultural Perspectives.* Toronto: ECW.

King, Thomas. (1991) "Introduction." *All My Relations: An Anthology of Contemporary Canadian Native Fiction.* Ed. Thomas King. Toronto: McClelland & Stewart. ix-xvi

— . (1990) "Godzilla vs. Post-Colonial." *World Literature Written in English* 30(2): 10-16.

King, Thomas, ed. (2001) "First Voices First Words." *Prairie Fire.* Special Issue. 22(3).

Hodgson, Heather, ed. (1989) *The Seventh Generation: Contemporary Native Literature.* Penticton, BC: Theytus.

Krupat, Arnold. (1996) *The Turn to the Native: Studies in Criticism and Culture.* Lincoln: U of Nebraska Press.

— . (1992) *Ethnocriticism: Ethnography, History, Literature.* Berkeley: U of California Press.

Moses, Daniel David, and Terry Goldie, eds. (1992) *An Anthology of Canadian Native Literature in English.* Toronto: Oxford University Press.

Ruffo, Armand Garnet. (1993) "Inside Looking Out: Reading *Tracks* from a Native Perspective." in Armstrong, ed. 161-176.

Verduyn, Christl, ed. (1998) *Journal of Canadian Studies, Literary Pluralities.* Peterborough: broadview.

(Ad)dressing Our Words

Coming Home Through Stories

Neal McLeod

Dwelling in the Familiar

"To be home" means to dwell within the landscape of the familiar, a landscape of collective memories; it is an oppositional concept to being in exile. "Being home" means to be a nation, to have access to land, to be able to raise your own children, and to have political control. It involves having a collective sense of dignity. In a post-colonial situation, in the subversion of the stories by the colonizer, one is able to reassert one's narratives. A collective memory emerges from a specific location, spatially and temporally, and includes such things as a relationship to land, songs, ceremonies, language and stories. Language grounds *Nehiyâwiwin* (Creeness). To tell a story is to link, in the moments of telling, the past to the present, and the present to the past.

My *Nicapân* (great-grandfather) Peter Vandall used to tell stories of his uncle Big John and the Northwest Resistance of 1885. His stories were about surviving and remembering. Part of surviving is through remembrance: when you remember, you know your place in creation. Keith Basso in *Wisdom Sits in Places* uses the example of the Western Apache to discuss the importance of the relationship between narrative and space. While he notes the importance of earlier writers that discussed the importance of place names, such as Boas and Sapir (Basso 43), he extends earlier writing by showing that the narrative is an ongoing, organic activity. Basso speaks of narrative as a "spatial anchor" (91). In his view, space is more important in understanding the Apache than time. It is through memory, which is located in the landscape, that people are able to situate themselves in the world: "the meaning of landscape and acts of speech are personalized manifestations of a shared perspective on the human condition" (Basso 73).

Thus narrative memory, according to Basso, situates understanding through an interconnection between space, memory and ancestor. Essentially, Apache memory is the building of stories upon one another, and the accumulation of meaning and interpretation. Wisdom in Basso's account emerges from this layering process. Basso writes:

The commemorative place-names, accompanied by their stories, continue to accumulate, each one marking the site of some sad or tragic event from which valuable lessons can be readily drawn and taken fast to heart. (28)

Over a period of time the stories become internalized by the individual, and there is a dialectical play between tradition and the present, between individual and collective memory. Basso writes:

For the place-maker's main objective is to speak the past into being, to summon it with words and give it dramatic form, to produce experience by forging ancestral worlds in which others can participate and readily lose themselves. (ibid: 33)

In this context narratives are thus essentially maps which emerge out of a relationship to a specific area, whereas wisdom emerges from voice and memory within that landscape. Basso notes that the process of narration is as though "the ancestors were speaking to you directly, the knowledge the stones contain. Bring this knowledge to bear on your disturbing situation..." (ibid: 91). The culmination of wisdom, then, is "extremely personal" as the past is understood as a function of a person's life experience (ibid: 32), and as it used to make sense of life and to live a good life.

Diaspora

Often when one group becomes dominated by another, the dominated group tends to lose some of its narratives; history shows that the dominator imposes its narratives upon the dominated group. To describe the two groups in this dynamic I will use the term colonizer for the group that has power, and I will use the term colonized for the group which is dominated. These terms are by no means static, as many Indigenous groups which were later dominated by Europeans, were themselves colonizers in their own right. The Cree (*Nêhiyawak*), for instance, displaced other groups such as the Blackfoot and Dene in their territorial expansion of the late seventeenth to the first half of the nineteenth century.

However, while it is important to note that the *Nêhiyawak* were themselves a colonizing power at one time, the imposition of English rule altered our lives. English control over Cree territory, especially after *ê-mâyihkamikahk* ("where it went wrong" / The Northwest Resistance) of 1885, radically altered Cree ability to govern ourselves and to perpetuate our stories. The English through a systematic process attempted to alienate *Nêhiyawak* from our land and in turn alienate us from our collective traditions.

I will argue that the process of alienation occurred in two inter-related ways (and these were concurrent). First, the English gradually alienated *Nêhiyawak* from our land, a process which was accelerated with the Fur Trade winding down and also through the Treaty process (which was accompanied by increased settlement). Second, the English alienated *Nêhiyawak* from our stories and languages, and set up coercive legislation in regards to our religious ceremonies. These ceremonies were outlawed in the *Indian Act* (Section 114) and mandatory attendance to residential schools was imposed.

I define the removal of an Indigenous group, in this case the *Nêhiyawak*, from their land as *spatial diaspora*. Once *Nêhiyawak* were removed from their land and put on reserves, there was a gradual decay of the "spatial anchor" (in which *Nêhiyawak* had grounded themselves. I call the alienation from one's stories *ideological diaspora*: this alienation, the removal from the voices and echoes of the ancestors, is the attempt to destroy collective consciousness. Undoubtedly, spatial diaspora and ideological diaspora are interrelated. Both aspects of diaspora, as I have defined them, emerge from a colonial presence.

In contrast to "being home," diaspora is the process of being alienated from the collective memory of one's people. *Nêhiyawak* have been forced into diaspora in two overlapping senses: spatial and ideological. Canada has often been the land where people from around the world have come to avoid persecution and oppression in their homelands; it is my contention, however, that Indigenous people within Canada have also been placed into a state of exile within this country.

I will use the term *ideological home* to refer to the interpretative location of a people. An ideological home provides people with an Indigenous location to begin discourse, to tell stories and to live life on their own terms. An ideological home is a layering of generations of stories, and the culmination of storyteller after storyteller, in a long chain of transmission. To be home, in an ideological sense, means to dwell in the landscape of the familiar, collective memories, as opposed to being in exile. "Being home" means to be part of a larger group, a collective consciousness; it involves having a personal sense of dignity. Furthermore, an ideological home, housed in collective memory, emerges from a specific location, spatially and temporally. An ideological home needs to have a spatial, temporal home as well.

Narrative Maps

I believe that *Nehiyâwiwin* (Creeness) developed organically and will continue to develop if people choose to take the time to learn the stories and the language. However, some people such as Simon During argue against the organic development of the traditions of colonized people. During describes the post-cultural as a state of being where the "'cultural' products are not essentially bound to the life-world that produced them" (36-37). During seems to imply that attempts at recovering stories and a narrative home, essentially the attempt to move beyond the domination of the mainstream culture, are bound to fail because they are intertwined with the discourse of the colonizers.

The process of "coming home" through stories could be thought of as the experience of discerning the liminal space between Cree culture and the mainstream society. There are discursive differences between the colonized and the colonizer as they are embedded within different interpretative vantage points. The "'reality' represented... by the map not only conforms to a particular version of the world but to a version which is specifically designed to empower its makers" (118).

Trickster-Treaty Stories

It is my contention that spatial diaspora occurred first and was followed by an ideological diaspora. Frizzly Bear, an Elder from the Onion Lake Reserve in Saskatchewan, described the spatial sense of diaspora as was prophesied by the old people: "[y]ou won't be able to stop anywhere on your journeys because there will be a steel rope everywhere" (Frizzly Bear 1976). The steel rope would cut the land into different sections with a grid imposed upon the landscape. Bear noted that he thought that the "steel rope... is the wire they use for fencing" (ibid). Through the process of "fencing" the land, *Nêhiyawak* (the Cree) were marginalized. The first type of diaspora (spatial) had thus occurred.

However, despite an encroaching colonial presence, there were leaders who resisted the impending diaspora (in both senses of the word as I have defined it). Some of the strongest leaders of this resistance were *Mistahi Maskwa* (Big Bear), *Minahikosis* (Little Pine) and *Payipwât* (Piapot). There are many stories of resistance to the new colonial order. There is a story of Indigenous resistance to colonial power that was told to *Nimosôm* (my grandfather) by an Elder in Saskatchewan:

> One of the Queen's representatives had come to negotiate
> with the Indians. His aides treated him very grandly and
> even had a chair for him to sit on. A cloth was spread on
> the ground and several bags of money were placed on it.
> The representative explained through an interpreter how
> many bags of money the Queen had sent. [A Chief] was
> told this and said, 'Tell the Queen's representative to
> empty the money and fill the bags with dirt. Tell him to
> take the bags back to England to the Queen. She has paid
> for that much land.' (McLeod 1975: 6)

The story illustrates the irony in the encounter of two worldviews.
In this story, the chief, *Kawâhkatos* (Lean Man), questioned the
imposition of the Treaty in the context of his own worldview and
his concept of the land. To use Vizenor's terminology, the story
bespeaks of a Trickster encounter (1994). The Trickster-Treaty
story is about transforming assumptions: *Kawâhkatos* understood
his life through the stories and the concrete world around him,
whereas the Treaty commissioner understood the world (at least
the Treaty) within the perspective of a written legal agreement.

Another humorous resistance story exists of the Treaties. Unfortunately, the storyteller was not recorded when it was transcribed:

> So I'm going to tell a story about this woman who was
> kind of spry. She knew five dollars wasn't enough
> [amount of Treaty annuity]. So she got this notion to get
> herself pregnant as she'd get paid in advance. She put a
> pillow under her skirt; so she walked up the paymaster.
> When he saw her he said, 'So you're pregnant. Then we'll
> have to pay you an extra five dollars in advance.' When
> she received her money she fumbled a dollar bill on to the
> floor, then she bent down to pick it up. Her string bust, and
> she had a miscarriage; her pillow fell out. So this was the
> end of advances on pregnant women. They have to be born
> before they receive $5.00. This is the little story that I
> wanted to tell. (*Indian Film History Project*, IH 427)

The story is a manifestation of a hermeneutical encounter between
the new colonial order and *Nêhiyawak*: the story, while humorous,
is one of resisting the imposition of Treaty and of the reserve system. Despite having to live on reserves, *Nêhiyawak* had the power
of passive resistance. Stories, such as the ones above, in the spirit
of the Trickster, seek to transform the circumstances that the peo-

ple were living in.

Vizenor's notion of "trickster hermeneutics" is very similar to Bhabba's notion of "space of translation" (Vizenor 1994: 25). There is a need for "discursive space" to mediate these two worlds and sets of knowledge and experience. Bhabba calls such a place "a place of hybridity" (25) and offers many insights in regards to how colonized people make attempts to survive changes to their life-worlds. The strength of his position is that he does not see the various cultures as victims, but rather celebrates their ability to rec-reate themselves in the face of new circumstances. The attempt to move beyond the limitations of colonial discourse is indeed the process behind Trickster-Treaty stories.

My uncle, Burton Vandall, once told me yet another Trickster-Treaty story. At Treaty payment time, people would borrow chil-dren from other families. They would walk up to the paymaster, who was handing out Treaty annuity payments, over and over again; everyone would take turn using the same children. Eventu-ally, the paymaster caught on, and he started to paint a mark on the faces of the kids once they got their first and "final" payments.

Spatial Diaspora

The effects of spatial diaspora are devastating upon Indigenous people, and this condition of alienation exists both in our hearts (ideological diaspora) and in our physical alienation from the land (physical diaspora). Exile involves moving away from the familiar into a new set of circumstances.

Caribbean writer George Lamming, who lived for many years in England, writes of the process of diaspora:

> We are made to feel a sense of exile by our inadequacy
> and our irrelevance of function in a society whose past we
> can't alter, and whose future is beyond us. (12)

To be in exile, at least on one level, is to live a disjointed life. In this state, the discourse and the physical reality surrounding this discourse are imposed upon the people thrown into diaspora. Yet, the person in exile has no control over this imposed national dis-course and corresponding material reality. To live in exile, to live in diaspora, is to have the difficult task of keeping one's dignity, one's story, in the face of the onslaught of a colonial power.

The process of diaspora for *Nêhiyawak* (the Cree) began in the 1870s when the British Crown extended its influence into western Canada through a Treaty process. In the period after the Treaties,

1878-1885, all of the major *Nêhiyawak* chiefs on the Canadian prairies had taken Treaty. Minahikosis (Little Pine) took Treaty in 1879 and Mistahi Maskwa (Big Bear) in 1882. By this time, *Nêhiyawak* were starving, and the buffalo, their lifeblood, had vanished from the land. The diaspora was an alienation and a removal from the land. *Nêhiyawi* life-world foundations were under siege, and the ability to perpetuate *Nehiyâwiwin* (Creeness) was greatly undermined. The Treaties and the incursions of Europeans upon the Plains transformed the land: a new, colonial order had been imposed.

New Order Upon the Land

My great-grandfather, *Kôkôcîs* (Cree nickname for Peter Vandall) himself lived at the crossroads of great historical and social change, and he had the fortune of being able to sit with people who had experienced the changes of the 1870s and 1880s first hand. *Kôkôcîs* spoke of how during the time of these upheavals, the buffalo used to go to Redberry Lake, which is south of the Sandy Lake Reserve. He said that the buffalo would go out on the lake when the ice was thin. There would be thousands of them in long lines. The buffalo would then drown in the lake. My great-grandfather used the expression *ê-mistapêsocik*. The expression could be translated as "they drowned themselves." It was reasoned that they drowned themselves because the order of the land had been transformed. Instead of being able to roam the land freely, the buffalo, like the Native people, were being increasingly confined to smaller and smaller areas. It was as though the whole order of the landscape was radically changing. A word that I have heard to describe this time of massive change is *pâstahowin*. This word could perhaps be translated as "transgression" or perhaps as "when one does something wrong it comes back to them." The word was used to refer to the way in which the changes brought about by Europeans had caused the various animals and spirit beings to retreat into the earth.

Despite the efforts of *Nêhiyawak* to resist the colonial presence, the events of 1885 strengthened the colonial grip on *Nêhiyâwaskiy* (Cree territory). Because of frustration with the government, coupled with mass starvation, events culminated in the violence in 1885. Different armed conflicts, such as at Frenchman's Butte, Cutknife Hill and Batoche, broke out between Indigenous people and Canadians. In speaking of 1885, Edward Ahenakew, a Cree clergyman and for a time political activist, spoke of the "scars

[that] remain in our relationship with the white man" (71). After the troubles, the Canadians exercised their domination of the new region: they were able to impose the new, colonial order and met with markedly decreased resistance. The Cree word for all of the events of 1885 is *ê-mâyihkamikahk* "where it went wrong"; *ê-mâyihkamikahk* represents the culmination of spatial diaspora.

One of the strategies used to deal with the imposition of a colonial order is the creation of discourse within a liminal space. It is the testing of discourse and narration, the attempt to try to find the possibilities which could emerge in the face of changing circumstances. Bhabba uses the term "poetics of exile" (5) to refer to the liminal space between the colonized culture and the culture of the larger power. The space-in-between is where people make sense of their worlds; it is the location wherein they situate their consciousness, in the space wherein they try to make sense of their world. Indeed, this is the situation the Cree people were facing after 1885: the world had radically changed, and would change even more, and the collective discursive action of the Cree would reflect this.

Hybridity and Survivance

There is a trend in contemporary Indigenous discourse to create a bi-polar differentiation between colonizer and colonized: within this creation of a discursive dichotomy, the past is sometimes romanticized. Such a romanticization of the past distorts the experiences of those who lived through these times of change, and distorts present realities as well.

One reason that there was a shift in religion is due to the fact that there was widespread use of bad medicine during the time of the 1870s and 1880s. People saw how some were using the old plants and rituals to harm other people. Oftentimes people would use these powers to harm someone perhaps due to jealousy or perhaps due to anger. There was a story of Chief *Atâkahkohp* who had an encounter with a strong Swampy Cree medicine. The Swampy Cree medicine man tried to use medicine on *Atâhkakohp*; the chief in turn had to use medicine to defend himself. Edward Ahenakew notes: "... Ah-tah-ka-hoop was high in the secret society of medicine men..." (1995: 97). *Atâhkakohp* then "sang a song and chanted words that the others could not understand" (97). This song then subdued the old man and all of his negative energy fell back on himself. The Cree word to describe this is "*pâstâhowin*."

There are other stories along this line. For instance, Andrew Ahenakew notes: "There are some things about Indian custom that are not nice. Medicine Men and Cultural Doctors were the boss of people. They were taught some of the medicine that was nice, but they had some of these bad medicines" (1976). He then adds: "An old man told me once when I was visiting him, 'We were given our Indian custom ever since we've lived, to pass from generation to generation, but these old men are using these things, like medicine and visions, in the wrong way. They should use the medicine right – it was for a good purpose" (1976). Thus, Andrew Ahenakew thinks that one of the reasons why the customs were fading is that people were misusing tradition.

In the spirit of Trickster hermeneutics, one of my ancestors, Big John, adopted elements of the colonial presence and transformed them to subvert them. He was a successful farmer on the Sandy Lake Reserve in Saskatchewan, and he taught my great-grandfather *Kôkôcîs* (Peter Vandall) how to farm. In addition to being a successful farmer, and despite the difficulties many Indigenous farmers faced during this transitional time, Big John was also a photographer; Metis author Maria Campbell told me that he had a darkroom in his basement. He had a Bible in Cree syllabics which he read regularly; I have handled this book myself many times. While he adopted a hybridized form of Christianity and adopted elements of modern technology such as the camera, he was still a Cree. In the face of colonial pressure, one can struggle to retain an Indigenous identity through a process of "hybridization" (Bhabba 35). The narratives of the colonizer can be subverted through a shifting of interpretative reality and space.

In addition to being influenced by his uncle Big John, *Kôkôcîs* was heavily influenced by his grandfather, *Wîcihkos* [diminutive form of *Wîtihkokân*]. The way in which *Kôkôcîs* negotiated between the world of Christianity and the world of traditional Dene/Cree hunting beliefs is certainly an example of what Vizenor calls Trickster hermeneutics and what Bhabba calls hybridity. My great-grandfather wove the narratives of Cree/Dene hunting beliefs with those of Christianity and tried to find new ways of applying old concepts in light of new situations. While *Wîtihkokân* used dreams and intuition, Big John, his son, learned to use some of these techniques as well, but only in a new context. My father noted: "He really believed in God. Those old people who raised him talked to him about God" (McLeod 2000).

There is the interesting story of how *Wîtihkokân* would go into the Church. The word that he would say was "*sah-sîciwisiwak*. He was sitting in church and this man was preaching. He used to go there and smoke his pipe and listen. Mostly he went because the Minister at the time used to invite him. He tried to solicit him to turn to Christianity. Out of the kindness of his heart he [*Wîcihkos*] used to go to listen and smoke his pipe. He couldn't understand why they would talk about Jesus that they would save human beings yet they killed him. He used to think they were afraid that they killed him and that they would be punished. He used to think these people were afraid" (McLeod 2000). *Kôkôcîs* was raised by this old hunter who, while curious about Christianity, saw contradictions in it, and saw how it was used to scare people.

> Big John, the son of *Wîtihkokân*, was important because he represented the transitional period when people were moving from agriculture to farming. My father noted: 'At the time when people were forced to move on to the reserves he adapted quite rapidly' (McLeod 2000). My father shared the following narrative with me regarding Big John: "he used to look at the soil and he could tell by its texture how fluffed up it was, the colour of it was grey-light, it was worked properly. It had to do with circulating the soil once a year. He used to plough his land about six inches deep... no deeper than that. He would do this every year so the soil kept circulating. He studied the texture to see how much fibre there was in it. It was almost like he could feel the land." (McLeod 2000)

Big John left the earth during the sickness of 1918, the person who had bravely helped negotiate a new narrative space for Cree consciousness through his actions, farming and photography. Maureen Lux notes that "50,000 Canadians died from influenza" (4) and adds: "During the epidemic the Royal Mounted Police (RCMP) were sent to reserves to enforce strict quarantines, preventing Native people from leaving reserves" (ibid: 10). The sickness had a large impact upon the people.

Despite the shifts that were occurring in the peoples' lives, they still relied a great deal on older ways of doing things, including traditional medicinal practices. People in my family have told me that people from all over would come to see *Kwêcic* in order to get medicine for a variety of things. I have heard that people from Montana would come to see her in order to get plants to help with various illnesses. She never had children, but did raise *Kôkôcîs* for a period of time after the death of his natural mother. *Kwêcic* died when I was about seven or eight at the age of about 110.

Slowly but surely there was a shift from traditional healing to modern healing techniques; I think that one has to be careful about ascribing causation. I do not think that one can say it was simply the shift to Christianity and farming that brought about the change. With increased hospital availability people began to frequent them more often and gradually the old techniques fell out of use. I think that it would be possible to draw a comparison to the changes that occurred in the field of education, the replacement of old pedagogical techniques with new ones.

Diaspora Story

Kôkôcîs (my great-grandfather/ Peter Vandall) told this story at *Nôhkom's* (my grandmother's) funeral. It is also recorded in *The Stories of the House People* (Vandall 1987). *Kôkôcîs* opens the story:

> *aya, ê-kî-âcimostawit ôtê ohci kihci-môhkomâninâhk- nitô-têminânak êkotê itâmowak ôta kâ-mâyahkamikahk- êkwa, êwako awa pêyak nisis aya, kî-pê-takotêw tânitahtw-âskiy aspin ôma otâhk*
> It was told to me by a man from the United States – friends of ours had fled there at the time of *ê-mâyihkamikahk* – and this one was my uncle, he had come back a few years ago. (Vandall 65)

It was through the storytelling that his uncle came home from the exile caused by *ê-mâyihkamikahk*: he had managed, through stories, and the humour of the stories, to preserve his dignity as a *Nêhiyaw* person. Furthermore, it is through these stories that these people attempted to find a way home. *Kôkôcîs* reported that his uncle said, 'I do not have much to give you, but I will give this story, my nephew.'

The story is about a man who went fishing. This man liked to drink and was sipping whiskey while he was fishing. He needed bait and saw a snake with a frog in its mouth. The man took the frog out of the snake's mouth, but he had pity on the snake: he knew that the snake was as hungry as he was. This man, after having taken the frog, gave the snake some whiskey in exchange. The snake, after a while, came back with another frog to trade for a drink.

This uncle of *Kôkôcîs* had fled during the troubled times: he was forced into exile because he had made a stand for his rights and dignity. The story was given to *Kôkôcîs* and was an important element of his repertoire. The story speaks of being generous and of having pity on those with less power; it talks about the changes which were emerging, and the effort that the people were engaged in trying to negotiate this emerging space.

Old Man *Kiyâm*

The process of diaspora involves both physical and spiritual enclosement. It is the move away from the familiar towards a new alien "space." This new space attempts to transform and mutate pre-existing narratives and social structures. It was not only the old people who were imprisoned and put into diaspora, but also those who went through the residential school system. Bhabba writes: "The social articulation of difference, from the minority perspective, is a complex, on-going negotiation that seeks to authorize cultural hybridities that emerge in moments of historical transformation" (2). The story from my great-grandfather is one example of this, and so is the story of *Mistânaskowêw*. Stories are told to try to negotiate through the field of experience.

Ideological Diaspora: Residential Schools

Ideological diaspora was the internalization of being taken off the land. A central manifestation of this occurred through the residential school system, which was established as a way of "educating" Indigenous people. There were several such schools set up through western Canada, and they were operated by various Churches. Children were taken away from their homes and their communities. Instead of being taught by the old people in the traditional context, children were being taught in an alien environment which stripped them of their dignity; it was a process of cultural genocide and spiritual exile. Once put away in both an ideological and spatial sense, many children never came "home": instead they spent their lives ensnared in alcoholism and other destructive behaviours.

In the 1930s, *Nimosôm* (my grandfather) went to residential school on the Gordon Reserve which is north of Regina, Saskatchewan. At first, he was happy to go; a friend of his, Edward Burns, even remembered him clapping his hands in anticipation (Regnier 4). He was anxious to see the world beyond the borders of the Reserve: however, his experience of the school was far from what he expected.

He came back and told his father, Abel McLeod, what was going on in the school: the beatings, the naked children and the hunger. The authorities came for my *mosôm* a second time. *Nicapân* (my great-grandfather/ Abel McLeod) did not want his son to go back, but he was told by the Mounties that they would arrest his son if he resisted. The Mounties knew that *Nicapân* was a man of influence in the community, and an arrest would be difficult as the people supported him. He told the Mounties that they would also have to arrest him. He could not let them take his son again. They subsequently used force to take my *mosôm*, a boy of twelve, who spent the next three nights in jail cells throughout the province as he was taken back to the school.

This experience of residential schools exemplifies the process of ideological diaspora. Alienation from the land, political pressure and the use of force were all parts of a larger effort to destroy *Nehiyâwiwin*. The schools solidified the polarization of the entities "*Nehiyâwiwin*" (Creeness) and "Canadian." All things Cree were taken to be dangerous and not worthy to exist, whereas all things Canadian were exemplified and taken as prototypes: *Nehiyâwiwin* acted as a foil which helped to create a "Canadian" identity. The schools did much to create a sense of spiritual and ideological diaspora.

It is interesting to note how the narrative I gave of *Nimosôm* functions as a map to an old prophecy told by Frizzly Bear in 1976 (though the prophecy itself is from the late nineteenth century):

> If you don't agree with him [the whiteman], he'll get up and point at you with a revolver, but he can't fire. He'll put his gun down and everything will be over. You will agree with him and what he's going to teach you is nothing that is any good for us. (Frizzly Bear 1976)

These schools were the vehicles of cultural genocide with concerted attempts to destroy language and stories. This was forced exile, the separation from the security of culture and the wisdom of the "Old Ones." The survivors of this school are modern day *okicitawak* (Worthy Men – "warriors"). Instead of fighting in the world, they fight against the memories of these schools that linger in the landscapes of their souls.

Residential schools nearly silenced *Nêhiyawak* stories forever. In "One Generation from Extinction," Basil Johnston stresses the importance of language and stories, in the context of their fragility:

> Therein will be found the essence and the substance of tribal ideas, concepts, insights, attributes, values, beliefs, theories, notions, sentiments, and accounts of their institutions and rituals and ceremonies. (102)

Johnston comments on the effects of ideological diaspora, the alienation from collective memory: "With language dead and literature demeaned, 'Indian' institutions are beyond understanding and restoration" (103).

Tootoosis and Political Revival

John Tootoosis saw the brainwashing effects of the schools and the way that the Church was using its power to destroy traditional teachers in regard to the way we understood ourselves in the world. He often talked about how hard it was to organize people: "Indians weren't organized before. They were so damn dominated by the government" (Tootoosis 1977). People were seemingly unable to make decisions, as they had very little control over their lives. As Native people began to organize in the twenties and thirties, they began to break the yoke of domination; indeed, one of the central demands of Native political leaders and organizations was to end the domination of schooling by the Churches. Speaking of the League of Indians organized in the early 1920s, Tootoosis said: "The League opposed residential schools, the church wanted to dominate the people and keep the schools" (1977).

While there were severe pressures on our culture and on the people at that time, they found ways to preserve their identity and their place in the world. Stories and languages led some of the people back to their identities; it is only through our own stories that we can find true dignity and integrity in the world.

The late Wilfred Tootoosis, the oldest son of John, reflected on his experiences at residential school, and how he was singled out because of his father's activities:

> I had quite an experience in school. I'd get picked on. The nuns and priests spoke against my dad's movement, everywhere, in church, in the classroom. And when somebody did something wrong they ganged up and blamed me for it... They could have had my dad shot if they had a chance to. (1999: 314)

The children of activists and spiritual leaders were often hit the hardest, and they were attacked and singled out in the schools. My father told me that the priests used to call John Tootoosis' children "communists." There are many stories of John Tootoosis and his struggle to fight for the rights of the Cree people.

Coming Home Through Stories

The effects of going to school have to be understood as a radical separation with the past, as a disjunction in the daily experience of the people. People were no longer allowed to acquire language and socialization in the normal way; the economic life of the people had also changed and would in turn affect their discursive action. Bhabba calls an "unhomely moment [that] which relates the traumatic ambivalences of a personal, psychic history to the wider disjunctions of political existence" (11). He then goes on to say that "the personal is the-political" (ibid); indeed, the Crees of the twentieth century became increasingly aware of the limitations that were put upon them, and the systematic attempts that were made to wipe out their culture. The effect of being in exile and the trauma associated with it are manifested in the stories told and ensuing political action.

But our battle to survive as a people certainly goes beyond the issue of residential schools. Smith Atimoyoo, one of the founders of the Saskatchewan Indian Cultural Centre, spoke of the "new arrows" that people are presently facing (23): today we have a different kind of arrow to fight for our collective existence. Here I borrow the term "wordarrows" from Gerald Vizenor (1978): words are like arrows that can be shot at the narratives of the colonial power. Wordarrows have transformative power and can help Indigenous people "come home"; wordarrows can help to establish a new discursive space. Every time a story is told, every time one word of an Indigenous language is spoken, we are resisting the destruction of our collective memory.

Stories act as the vehicles of cultural transmission by linking one generation to the next. There are many levels to the stories, and many functions to them: they link the past to the present, and allow the possibility of cultural transmission and of "coming home" in an ideological sense. Our task today is to retrieve tribal narratives and paradigms, and to reaffirm our tribal identities in the face of the overwhelming pressure of diaspora.

Despite the fact that the original colonizing power, Britain, has been reduced in influence, there is still an attempt to maintain cultural hegemony:

> through canonical assumptions about literary activity and through attitudes to post-colonial literatures which identify them as isolated natural off-shots of English literature and which therefore relegate them to marginal and subordinate positions. (Ashcroft et al. 7)

Within this context, Cree narratives are still marginalized and kept on the periphery of Canadian consciousness. This marginalization is not only a result of canonical assumptions but also the foundation for the privileging of European narrative paradigms over Indigenous paradigms. I want to suggest that the metaphorical discursive pattern of *Nêhiyawak* needs to be taken into account in order to come to a complete phenomenological understanding of the history of Canada.

Finally, I would like to share a diaspora story which has been passed on to my family for one hundred years. It was told to my great-great-grand mother *Kêkêhkiskwêw* (Hawk Woman), then to *Nimosôm* (my grandfather), and then to my father Jerry McLeod. I have also heard elements of the story from Clifford Sanderson and Bill Stonestand. All of these people are from the James Smith Reserve.

There was a group of people from the Cikastêpêsin (Shadow in the Water) Reserve. There was a large flood on Sugar Island which is close to Birch Hills, Saskatchewan. Many people died during this flood. There was one woman who climbed up a tree with her baby; she tied a cloth around the tree and moved up the tree to escape the water. The cloth was used to hold her up there. Eventually, the flood went away, and the people left the area. Also, about eleven people from the Band had been involved in the troubles at Batoche in 1885. There were too many bad feelings associated with the land there, at Sugar Island, so they left. Some of them went to camp with the people of the James Smith Reserve. However, a group also went to the Sturgeon Lake Reserve.

The camps were close together. Back then people had pity on each other; they shared more with each other. They had pity on their fellow *Nêhiyawak*. That is why the people of *Cîkâstêpêsin* (Shadow on the Water) stayed there. There was a man who had prophecies of the *Cîkâstêpêsin* people. His name was Pîkahin Okosisa ("the son of Pîkahin"). He died about 1897, which is about 12 years after *ê-mâyihkamikahk*. My dad said that they wrapped his body up with cloths. They had a wake for him. Then, one person noticed that Pîkahin Okosisa's feet were starting to warm up, and told the others. And the man came back to life.

Pîkahin Okosisa spoke of many things. He spoke of great fires in the northern skies; also, this is what my dad told me, that there would be a great war. Pîkahin Okosisa said that families would split up more in the future. He spoke of the kind of houses that we would live in. He even foretold that people would fly in the sky.

Pîkahin Okosisa saw all of these things. He also said, "My people will have good hunting near Mêskanaw" (a town in Saskatchewan). He lived for forty more days and then he died for good. His reserve was "surrendered" in the 1890s, but before the Christmas of 1997, a letter was received stating the government would recognize the *Cîkâstêpêsin* (Shadow on the Water) claim. This is the story of Pîkahin Okosisa as I have heard it and as it has been passed on to me.

I think of *Nehiyâwiwin* (Creeness) as a large collective body. When I was born in 1970, there were so many people who knew so many beautiful things about *Nehiyâwiwin*. As *Nêhiyawak*, when we listen and tell our stories, when we listen and hear our language, we have dignity, because we are living our lives as we should. We are living our lives on our own terms; our stories give us voice, hope and a place in the world. To tell stories is to remember. As Indigenous people, we owe it to those still unborn to remember, so that they will have a "home" in the face of diaspora.

Thus, in a sense, the process of "coming home" is an exercise in cartography; it is trying to locate the place of understanding and culture. To "come home" is to dwell in liminal space, and the process of "coming home" is not so much returning to some idealized location of interpretation: rather, it is a hermeneutical act, perhaps an act of faith. It is the attempt to link two disparate narrative locations, and to find a place, a place of speaking and narrating, wherein the experiences of the present can be understood as a function of the past. At the same time, a culture is a living organism, with many layers and levels, and there will always be a manifold of interpretations of this culture. I would argue, in a similar way to David Newhouse (1999), the emerging forms of Aboriginal consciousness, including Cree forms, will be hybridized forms.

The metaphor of an anchor is helpful here in talking about narrative tradition. If a ship is tied to the anchor it will not rest in one spot forever. The ship will shift around, alternating locations. However, it will stay in the same general area, the same general location over a period of time. However, if the ship is cut off from that anchor, then it will drift beyond the known. For some time, the experiences will still be familiar; however, once the anchor is cut, and the ship moves beyond the familiar, narrative memory is lost forever.

To "come home" through stories is to anchor ourselves in the world. Many people, including my *mosôm*, John R. McLeod, and the great Cree leader John Tootoosis, survived the residential school experience and attempted to make sense of that experience and the world around them. While being thrown from their ideological home, through tremendous efforts, they were able to find their anchor again and to "come home" through stories and narrative memory. And because of them, we have that anchor today, and it is our time, it is our responsibility to keep that anchor, if Cree narrative memory is to survive through the coming generations.

Works Cited

Ahenakew, Andrew. (1976) *Kâtâayuk: Saskatchewan Indian Elders.* Saskatoon: Saskatchewan Indian Cultural College.

Ahenakew, Edward. (1995) *Voices of the Plains Cree.* Ed. Ruth Buck. Foreword. Stan Cuthand. Regina: Canadian Plains Research Centre.

Armstrong, Jeannette C. (1998) "The Disempowerment of First North American Native Peoples and Empowerment Through Their Writing." In *An Anthology of Canadian Native Literature in English.* 2nd ed. Ed. Daniel David Moses and Terry Goldie. Toronto: Oxford University Press. 239-242.

Ashcroft, Bill, Gareth Griffiths and Helen Tiffin. (1993) *The Empire Writes Back: Theory and Practice in Post-Colonial Literatures.* New York: Routledge.

Atimoyoo, Smith. (1979) Proceedings of the Plains Cree Conference. Held in Fort Qu'Appelle. October 24-26, 1975. Regina: Canadian Plains Research Centre.

Basso, Keith. (1996) *Wisdom Sits in Places: Landscape and Language Among the Western Apache.* Albuquerque: University of New Mexico Press.

Bhabba, Homi. (1997) *The Location of Culture.* Routledge: New York.

Cruikshank, Julie. (1990) *Life Lived like a Story.* Vancouver: University of British Columbia Press.

Darnell, Regina and Michael K. Foster, (eds). (1988) *Native North American: Interaction Patterns.* Hull: National Museums of Canada.

Demallie, Raymond J. (1982) "The Lakota Ghost Dance: An Ethnohistorical Account." *Pacific Historical Review.* 51(2): 385-405.

Dempsey, Hugh. (1984) *Big Bear and the End of Freedom.* Lincoln: University of Nebraska Press.

During, Simon. (1989) "Waiting for the Post: some relations between modernity, colonization and writing." *Ariel: A Review of International English Literature.* 20(4): 31-61.

Dyck, Noel. (1992) "Negotiating the Indian 'Problem'." in David Miller et al. *The First Ones: Readings in Indian/Native Studies.* Piapot Reserve: Saskatchewan Indian Federated College Press. 132-140.

Fenton, William N. (1998) *The Great Law and the Longhouse: A Political History of the Iroquois Confederacy.* Norman: University of Oklahoma Press.

Frizzly Bear (1976) *kâtâayuk.* (Ed.) Donna Phillips, Robert Troff and Harvey Whitecalf. Saskatoon: Saskatchewan Indian Cultural College.

Galbraith, John S. (1982) "Appeals to the Supernatural: African and New Zealand Comparisons with the Ghost Dance." *Pacific Historical Review.* 51(2): 115-133.

Goodwill, Jean and Norma Sluman. (1984) *John Tootoosis.* Winnipeg: Pemmican Publications.

IH-427. (Sept. 1973) "Saulteaux Elders Workshop #1." Speakers are unidentified. Saskatchewan Indian Cultural College. Part of Indian Film History, housed at the Saskatchewan Indian Federated College Library.

Johnston, Basil. (1998) "One Generation from Extinction." *An Anthology of Canadian Native Literature in English.* 2nd ed. Ed. Daniel David Moses and Terry Goldie. Toronto: Oxford University Press. 99-104.

Lamming, George. (1995) "The Occasion for Speaking." In *The Post-Colonial Studies Reader.* Ed. Bill Ashcroft, Gareth Griffiths and Helen Tiffin. New York: Routledge. 12-17.

Lux, Maureen. (1997) "The Bitter Flats": The 1918 Influenza Epidemic in Saskatchewan. *Saskatchewan History.* 49(1): 3-17.

Mandelbaum, David. (1994) *The Plains Cree: An Ethnographical, Historical, and Comparative Study.* Regina: Canadian Plains Research Centre.

McLeod, Jerry. (25 June 2000) Dialogue with Neal McLeod. Location: James Smith Reserve (Cree), Saskatchewan.

McLeod, John R. (11 Dec. 1975) Minutes from "Treaty Six General Meeting. Onion Lake Band Hall." Interpreter and Transcription: Anna Crowe. Onion Lake, Saskatchewan. From the private papers of John R. McLeod.

Milloy, John. (1990) *The Plains Cree.* Winnipeg: University of Manitoba Press.

Pflüg, Melissa A. (1997) *Ritual and Myth in Odawa Revitalization: Reclaiming A Sovereign Place.* Foreword. Lee Irwin. Norman: Oklahoma University Press.

Regnier, Robert. (1997) "John McLeod: First Nations Educator." Unpublished Paper.

Tonkin, Elizabeth. (1992) *Narrating our Pasts: The Social Construction of Oral History.* Cambridge: Cambridge University Press.

Tootoosis, John. (9 Sept. 1977). Interviewer: Murray Dobbin. Interview Location: Poundmaker Reserve. *Towards a New Past* (collection). A1178/1179. Saskatchewan Archives Board.

Tootoosis, Wilfred. (1999). In *In the Words of Elders: Aboriginal Cultures in Transitions.* Ed. Peter Kulchyski, Don McCaskill, and David Newhouse. Toronto: University of Toronto Press.

Vandall, Peter. (1997) *Wâskahikaniwiyiniw-âcimowina/Stories of the House People.* Ed. and trans. Freda Anehakew. Winnipeg: University of Manitoba Press.

Vansina, Jan. (1985) *Oral Tradition as History.* Madison: The University of Wisconsin Press.

Vizenor, Gerald. (1994) *Manifest Manners: Postindian Warriors Of Survivance.* Hanover, New England: Wesleyan University Press.

— . (1978) *Wordarrows: Indians and White in the New Fur Trade.* Minneapolis: University of Minnesota Press.

'A Vanishing Indian? or Acoose: Woman Standing Above Ground?'

Janice Acoose

Introduction

I write this essay out of the need to escape what feels like a lonely
and isolating space I work in. Currently, I am an Associate Professor of English with the Saskatchewan Indian Federated College
(SIFC) and a PhD candidate in English at the University of Saskatchewan. As the only Indigenous professor and graduate student
of English in these particular institutions, I struggle with numerous
multi-layered pedagogical and epistemological issues in my approach to Indigenous literatures. Now as I write my dissertation,
not only do I feel lonely, I feel confused and isolated. Why do I
feel lonely, confused, and isolated? First, I am working in an area
where there are few Indigenous people. Second, as both Indigenous professor and student of English, I am acutely aware, "that
the colonization process, the assimilation process is achieved
through language," as Jeannette Armstrong explains in her interview with Hartwig Isernhagen in *Momaday, Vizenor, Armstrong:
Conversations on American Indian Writing* (143). Third, as I continue to bring the experiences of Indigenous peoples which are represented through stories, poetry, drama and essays into the Department of English,[1] I feel like a parent delivering her children to the
residential school. Yet not unlike our parents who delivered us to
the keepers of those institutions I know that if our literatures are to
continue to survive they must be exposed to other ways of knowing and being in the world. However, the voices of my ancestors
become like muted echoes and my resolve to resist the ideological
influences of the colonizer becomes weaker when I come up
against the *Wiintigo*[2] like forces of Western literary criticism and
its accompanying critical language. Not unlike the contemporary
critics I mention in the pages ahead, I acknowledge that the imposition of Western oriented criticisms like postmodernism, poststructuralism, or postcolonialism enacts another form of colonialism. But what theoretical tools or critical language do I rely on for
critical analysis? As I struggle with issues of theorizing or interro-
gating Indigenous literatures from an Indigenous cultural context, I

am only too well aware of the dangers of essentialising Indigenousness. Yet, how do I approach Indigenous literatures rooted in cultures distinctly different than my own? In the discussion ahead, I review some of the theoretical positions offered by Indigenous scholars and critics. However, before I turn to my colleagues, I provide a context for my own subjectivity.

'A Vanishing Indian? or Acoose: Woman Standing Above Ground?'

I was fortunate to grow up with tellers of stories and relatives who understood the importance of the transmission of stories. My name is a daily reminder of those tellers of stories and relatives. Spoken aloud the name Acoose simultaneously connects me to *Ninahkawewin*[3] traditions of storytelling and ancestors whose legendary feats are represented by that name. I learned through story that the name Acoose[4] – or *Ekos* – (as it was historically pronounced phonetically and then translated to the page) was the name given to *Ni'meshoomis*. He was named *Ekos* (Flying Bird) in accordance with *Ninahkawewin* traditions because of his superhuman ability to run like a bird in flight. I also came to know his father *Quewitch* through story; known for his prowess as a buffalo runner, his name calls to mind the roar of thunderous buffalo stampeding across the prairies. Both the names *Quewitch* and *Ekos* connote antiquity, spirituality, cultural perseverance, and strength. Although personally unknown to my generation, *Ekos* and *Quewitch* **live** in me because my spirit was nourished by the stories told around campfires by *Ni'meshoomis* Paul Acoose. When he spoke about his own great feats as the 'running champion of the world' who beat the Onandaga Tom Longboat, *Ni'meshoomis* Paul emphasized that his name Acoose was connected to the *Ninahkawewin* oral stories of *Quewitch* and *Ekos*. According to the telling of these stories, *Quewitch* and *Ekos* were distinguished as 'men standing above the ground.' In retrospect, I realize that *Ni'meshoomis* Paul told us these stories so that we would always remember who we are. Just as they were told to us, we are expected to pass them on to our descendants so that they will know who they are. As long as we continue to pass on the *Quewitch-Ekos*-Acoose stories, our ways of knowing and being in the world will remain connected to the oral traditions and cultural heritage of the *Ninahkewewin*. For me, the stories root me in a respected family, continuing ancestral line, and vital cultural heritage that sustains my identity and influences my subjectivity.

Over the years, the stories attached to the names *Quewitch, Ekos,* and Acoose were appropriated by the Western written cultural tradition. One of the earliest re-telling of these stories was diarised in the writings of Edmund Morris. Morris, an early frontier artist, was the son of Alexander Morris the Lieutenant-Governor of Manitoba and the Northwest Territories (1872-1877) and one of the commissioners for the Western Numbered Treaties. Perhaps influenced by the *Ninahkawewin* oral stories of both *Qwewitch* and *Ekos,* Morris would come to write:

> I paint Acoose, Man Standing Above Ground. He is 61 years – his father [*Quewitch*] still lives, kept by the priests, though he is 103 years. His mind is still clear & I spoke with him in French. He is blind & his skin looks like parchment. His name was known far and wide in his time. Acoose was the fleetest of the Saulteaux. He used to compete with the whites in races & always outrun them. He went to moose hunt once & fell in with 9 elk. His bullets had slipped through his pocket so he ran them down the first day then drove them 60 miles to his own camp at Goose Lake & killed them. This brought him renown in his tribe... Acoose's son Paul is coming to the fore in races – at Winnipeg --- ran against – the Englishman. (67)

Excerpted from his diaries, this biographical piece accompanies the portrait Morris painted of *Ekos.* A reproduction of that portrait now housed in the legislative building in Regina signals the beginning of the museumization and appropriation of my family stories.

Another appropriator of my family stories was Duncan Campbell Scott, known to many in literary circles as one of Canada's most celebrated early writers. When I first read some of his literary work, I was astounded to find pieces of my family stories included in his poetry. In "Lines in Memory of Edmund Morris" he drew liberally from the oral stories of *Quewitch-Ekos.* Although the original poem is much lengthier, I quote here only the passages that directly refer to my ancestor.

> Think of the death of Akoose, fleet of foot,
> Who, in his prime, a herd of antelope
> From sunrise, without rest, a hundred miles
> Drove through rank prairie, loping like a/wolf,
> Tired them and slew them, ere the sun went/down.
> Akoose, in his old age, blind from the smoke
> Of tepees and the sharp snow light, alone
> With his great-grandchildren, withered and/spent,
> Crept in the warm sun along a rope

Stretched for his guidance. Once when/sharp autumn
Made membranes of thin ice upon the/sloughs,
He caught a pony on a quick return
Of prowess and, all his instincts cleared/and quickened,
He mounted, sensed the north and bore/away
To the Last Mountain Lake...
There Akoose lay, silent amid the bracken,
Gathered at last with the Algonquin Chief-/tains.
Then the tenebrous sunset was blown out,
And all the smoky gold turned into cloud/wrack.
Akoose slept forever amid the poplars,
Swathed by the wind from the far-off Red/Deer
Where dinosaurs sleep, clamped in their/rocky tombs.
Who shall count the time that lies between
The sleep of Akoose and the dinosaurs?
Innumerable time, that yet is like the breath
Of the long wind that creeps upon the prairie
And dies away with the shadows at sundown.

(191-193)

While one might read into Scott's poetic retelling of the 'Akoose' stories – particularly, as he wrote it in the context of his good friend's death – admiration and respect for a great man's deeds and way of life, I read his work quite differently[5]. When Scott removes the stories from their *Ninahkawewin* cultural oral traditions, he re-duces *Ni'meshoomis* 'Akoose' to a museum relic and my family stories to primitive legends. Appropriated and re-interpreted, the stories take on a Eurocentric romantic appeal as they are translated into literary form. Moreover, when Scott writes that *Ni'meshoomis* "slept forever amid the poplars.../[w]here dinosaurs sleep, clamped in their/rocky tombs" (193), he connects him to the myth of the 'vanishing Indian.'

Scott's poetic construction of *Ni'meshoomis* as a vanishing Indian made sense to me when I learned that outside of literary circles he was the superintendent general of Indian Affairs mandated "to get rid of the Indian problem" (Titley, 50). Known historically as the architect of the assimilation policy, he made clear his agenda when he proposed "to continue until there is not a single Indian in Canada that has not been absorbed into the body politic, and there is no Indian question" (50).

I came to writing, in part, as a way of reacting to the official propagandist type information about Indigenous peoples and my family,[6] as well as the fading importance of our oral storytelling traditions. In fact, the first piece I wrote came soon after the death of *Ni'meshoomis* Paul Acoose and my father Fred Acoose. In 1985, the year Saskatchewan celebrated 'Heritage Year,' I co-wrote[7] "Acoose: Man Standing Above Ground," a docu-drama for CBC radio that retold the stories of *Quewitch-Ekos*-Acoose. Attempting to recapture important elements of our oral tradition, I functioned as narrator/storyteller and utilized a medium that depended on aural skills. When the story was aired on CBC, I was told that there were numerous people with huge grins gathered around radios on the Sakimay Reserve. My immediate family, scattered throughout various Saskatchewan urban centres, telephoned after the broadcast. In cracking voices, my mom, brothers, sisters, nieces, nephews, cousins, uncles and aunties spoke with pride as they told me how they felt about hearing our family stories retold throughout Saskatchewan, particularly as our *Ni'meshoom-suk* were acknowledged as part of an ongoing way of life, traditions and family.

Sometime later, Brenda Zeman would follow in the footsteps of both Morris and Scott. In "A Song For Mooshum," she not only translated, re-interpreted, appropriated, and romanticized, my family history, she took on the guise of the *Wiintigo* when she ate my cousin Lynn Acoose's voice which she used to retell a part of my family history. Utilizing her anthropological background, her interest and experience as a long distance runner, Zeman dug up our family stories and made a connection to Scott's poem to enhance her own story. For example, she writes:

> There was a better story about Quewitch, Old Acoose's father, that Mr. Scott plain missed. Maybe Quewitch never ran down any elk; he was too busy running down buffalo in his day. The other hunters hunted on horseback, but Quewtich ran alongside the shaggy buffalo letting his arrows fly. Three times on one hunt, he lured the buffalo into enclosures by posing with a buffalo robe over him. Each time he let the lead buffalo escape so that its spirit would be protected and so the Saulteaux people would continue to have good hunts. (217)

Zeman's "A Song for Mooshum" also attempts to retell a popular oral story about Old Acoose and his two brothers, Penipekeesick and Kaypayositung who "went down into the Dakotas to steal some good horses" (217). Accordingly to Zeman's telling,

It wasn't long till they came upon a Sioux camp. Acoose
saw a horse he liked best. He was just about finished un-
hobbling it when he looked up and saw a Sioux pointing a
shotgun at his chest. The Sioux fired both barrels. All you
could see was two powder burns on Acoose's buckskin
jacket. Nothing else.

Acoose grabbed the horse, and the three brothers got out of
there fast. The Sioux were after them, he knew that. He led
them into a hollow and covered the horses' mouths so they
wouldn't make a noise. The Sioux rode right past them.
After that Acoose looked over at Penipekeesick filled his
pipe and prayed for fog. Penipekeesick was pretty strong
with medicine. He used to find missing people and horses
and he had visions. So Acoose and Kaypayositung weren't
too surprised when a dense fog started; they were able to
get out of Dakota Sioux territory and back to our people
safely. (217-218)

Because Zeman's story lacks the appropriate pedagogical approach
and removes the events from a *Ninahkawewin* epistemology, my
family stories become trivialized. And as they are "altered and in-
corporated into mainstream works of literature" (Blaeser, 54), they
become susceptible to predicted cultural vanishment.

Alex Wolfe, respected oral historian from the Sakimay Reserve and keeper of his own family stories, tells quite a different
version of this event in "The Last Raid." In accordance with oral
storytelling protocol, Wolfe contextualizes the events by rooting
them in the land:

This story recounts an event which took place on the
northeast shore of Goose Lake several winters after the Pi-
nayzitt band had made their homes on their new reserve,
which today is known as the Sakimay (Mosquito) Reserve.
Earth Elder considered this an historic event because it
was the last time such a commitment was carried out by
any of his people. (34)

Within the story, Wolfe records the challenges that faced Sakimay's people as they made the transition from hunting and gathering to reserve imprisonment during the post-treaty years. I include
lengthy passages to preserve the *Ninahkawewin* context and epistemology. He writes:

At this time a message, accompanied by a tobacco offering, was sent to every home. It said, '*Acoose*, son of

Quewich, has made a commitment to lead a group of men to challenge the unknown to the south, across the great Missouri River, to obtain horses.' Earth Elder and his four brothers, Yellow Calf, Blessed By the Sky, *Akeyhasheway mingot* (Blessed by the Earth) and *Punnichienace* (New Born Bird) received a message. Only Blessed By the Sky accepted the challenge. Earth Elder and Yellow Calf were not in favour, saying that several winters had passed since a treaty had been made, in which it had been agreed that all fighting would stop, that they should live in peace on the land they had reserved for themselves. The treaty decreed that they were only to bear arms in defence of the land they had given up. Blessed By the Sky said that he agreed with *Acoose*, that commitments made to the Creator must be honoured. Other commitments were secondary. Both men committed to this venture expected their people to approve and support them in asking for guidance and protection from the Creator as it was customary to seek and receive support. *Acoose* announced that he and Blessed By the Sky would leave when the spring break occurred and creeks began to flow. (34)

For days and days, "[t]hey traveled... the broad prairies, always keeping a watchful eye for any movement as there were already white men in the area" (35). Once the trio located a camp of many fires, they felt sure they would find the valued horses. Patiently, they watched the camp for many days, "trying to figure out the best way to approach the horses without rousing too many men from the camp" (35). They stayed so long that soon their food supplies ran out and "hunger gnawed at their stomachs" (36). After several days of watching,

[t]he time had come to make the attack. With gun in hand *Acoose* led the rush upon the wigwam. Reaching it he plunged inside. There was the sound of one shot. *Acoose* had killed the man. At that instant the woman escaped out the door, carrying a burning piece of wood which she hurled into the grass, starting a fire as a signal to those across the river. Alarmed by the sound of gun fire and the presence of the attacking men, two of the horses broke their tethers and fled beyond the reach of Blessed By the Sky and *Penipekeesik*. In a desperate attempt to prevent all their spoils from eluding them, Blessed By the Sky shot

the nearest horse, running to cut off the tail. *Acoose* already mounted on a sorrel horse, called to his companions to head north to large hill. (37-38)

Soon thereafter, they sighted many riders crossing the river in pursuit of them. And,

[a]s they stood on the hill all seemed hopeless... [because] there was no shelter...

As they looked around, Blessed by the Sky spoke, '*Acoose* we came to support you. If you fall we too shall fall. I cannot think that you brought us this far for nothing. You must know of a way to see us through.'

There were tears in the eyes of the two as they waited for a response, for they knew that *Acoose* was a man of physical and spiritual gifts.

Acoose answered, 'If both of you will be seated and hold the horse, I will seek protection.'

After they were seated *Acoose* took out a small bundle that he carried on his back and opened it. It contained his pipe, sweetgrass and a stuffed chickadee.

He lit the sweetgrass and incensed his pipe, and said, 'When I have filled and lit this pipe, I will speak to Him who made all the birds of the air, after which I will share this pipe with you. Do not move, no matter what you hear or see.'

When he lit his pipe and began his prayer a mist came upon the hill. As the pipe was passed from person to person and smoked, the mist became thicker until it was almost like night. In the distance they could hear the sound of horse hooves. As it came closer the sound became deafening. They could feel the ground shake as the riders bypassed the hill on both sides. Gradually the sound diminished as the riders raced to the west. When the quiet had returned, the mist began to lift slowly. (38-39)

After days of travelling, and "riding the horse in turns" (39) they returned home. "It is told that upon their arrival at the Leech Lake camp they were met with great joy. The horse tail that Blessed By the Sky had cut off the horse on the banks of the Missouri River was hoisted on a pole and a great victory dance was held" (41).

An apprentice/oral historian who studies with Alex Wolfe, Harvey Knight explains that there are very clear and specific rules in approaching *Ninahkawewin* oral traditions. In the preface to

Earth Elder Stories he writes, "oral tradition blends the material, spiritual, and philosophical together into one historical entity" (ix). Reiterating Wolfe's teachings, Knight instructs the readers that oral traditions are governed by principles and practices that "vary from band to band and from nation to nation. Their form and content is determined by language and environment" (ix-x). Therefore, anyone who retells oral stories "should be prepared to respect and preserve these traditions in their pure form. This can only be done if the written form is manipulated to conform to the rules, languages, and style of Indian oral traditions" (ix-x).

Ninahkawewin oral traditions, Alex Wolfe explains, "instruct a person in their identity, their purpose in life, their responsibility and contribution to the well-being of others... In later times,... the stories would be passed on to the next generation, ensuring the survival of their history and way of life (xi–xii). Wolfe, who was strictly trained in the *"Anishnaybay"*[8] traditions of storytelling, explains that his mother gave him the right to tell their family stories. But he was also cautioned by his ancestor Earth Elder that "[t]here are two things in life that must not be taken without consent. One is the family story and the other is a song. To take these without consent is to steal" (xiv).

An incident that happened to me at Wanuskewin Heritage Park brought Wolfe's words and Blaeser's 'prediction of vanishment' home to me. I overheard a tourist from New Zealand reinterpreting/translating one of the oral story about my ancestor *Ekos*. Setting it up as though it were a fairytale, he prefaced the story with "a long, long time ago" there was an old man named *Ekos*. According to his telling,

> *Ekos* ran alongside a herd of elk for several miles until they grew tired. When *Ekos* reached the Indian agency he ran inside the building and asked the agent for some bullets to slay the elk. Because he was able to slaughter the elk, the members of *Ekos'* band filled their bellies with meat. Because of his great deed, the people were saved from hunger!

When he finished the story, I felt shook up and debated about whether I should go over to introduce myself. Finally, I put one foot in front of the other and before I knew it, the words "hi, I'm Janice Acoose, the great-granddaughter of the man you were telling your son about" came rolling out of my mouth. As I extended my hand in friendship, I could feel his discomfort. A little awkward myself for a moment, I felt like 'the vanishing Indian' come to life or an archaic character spilling out from an old book.

Chasing Away the *Wiintigos*

My *Coochum* told me that the *Wiintigo* would disappear if we hid all of our valuables, or if we were brave enough to chase it away with a big stick! If she were alive now, Coochum would probably tell me that we can't afford to hide our valuables anymore – so, we have to courageously step forward with our biggest sticks!!

Because of my own connection to an ongoing *Ninahkawewin* oral storytelling tradition and the repeated appropriation of my family stories, I feel obligated to contribute to the growing body of literary criticism about Indigenous literatures. In my approach to so-called *Native Literature*, I speak from a politicized position influenced by sovereignty and self-determination. Whereas in my previous writings, I may have strategically employed the term 'Native Literature' to describe what some view as a singular **body** of stories, poems, essays, and drama, I now realize that as a term 'Native Literature' contributes to the confusion about Indigenous peoples. In the interview with Isernhagen, Armstrong explains that "Native American literatures, are lumped into one category as though there *were* such a thing, rather than many different cultures producing different kinds of literatures" (135). Here, it seems appropriate to borrow a term from Salman Rushdie who when presented with the same kind of dilemma about 'Commonwealth Literature' described it as a "chimera... a monster of a rather special type. It has a head of a lion, the body of a goat and a serpent's tail... [I]t could exist only in dreams, being composed of elements which could not possibly be joined together in the real world" (368). Like Rushdie, I suggest that 'Native Literature' will simply not do. Like Rushdie, I believe that enclosing the numerous bodies of Indigenous literatures within a singular and false category creates

> a ghetto mentality amongst some of it[s] occupants. Also, the creation of a false category can and does lead to excessively narrow, and sometimes misleading, readings of some of the artists it is held to include;... the existence – or putative existence – of the beast distracts attention from what is actually worth looking at, what is actually going on." (368)

Exercising sovereignty, we must name/define our own literatures and take control of the Indigenous-literary territory. Sovereignty, according to Patricia Monture Angus's Mohawk system of knowledge, which she articulates in *Journeying Forward*, is "defined as my right to be responsible, is really a question of identity (both individual and collective)... It is the responsibility to carry ourselves; collectively as nations, as clans, as families" (36). Because our literatures are inextricably connected to our communities, nations, clans, and families, we must acknowledge that there are numerous bodies of Indigenous literatures within Canada alone. And we must exercise our sovereign rights to take control of our own stories, define our own critical methods and language, and resurrect our respective cultural epistemologies and pedagogies.

One of the texts I continue to use to frame and enact culturally specific criticism is *Looking at the Words of Our People: First Nations Analysis of Literature.* As a critical tool, I continuously rely on it because it speaks to me of self-determination. Within the covers of the book, we[9] are Indigenous writers speaking for ourselves about our own literatures, articulating our own theories and practices on our own terms, and making connections between literary sovereignty and political nationhood. Anishnaabe scholar, Armand Garnet Ruffo calls for "a degree of cultural initiation. Those coming from outside a culture must seek out the necessary prerequisite information so that any attempt to address its literature will be more than merely superficial or, in the extreme, inaccurate" (163). Kimberly Blaeser, a self-identified mixed ancestry scholar of Ojibway and German origins, "seeks a critical voice and method which moves from the culturally-centered text outward toward the frontier of 'border' studies, rather than an external critical voice and method which seeks to penetrate, appropriate, colonize or conquer the cultural center, and thereby, change the stories or remake the literary meaning" (53). Kateri Akiwenzie-Damm, an Anishnaabe writer of mixed descent, strongly reminds us that "colonizing governments have used language and the power of words... to subjugate and control the Indigenous peoples" (11). Language, she reminds us, "has been used not only to control what we do but how we are defined" (11). Thus, she argues that "we must confront the vestiges of imperialist thought which still cling to the edges of our minds" (113). Metis poet, Marilyn Dumont challenges the "monolithic, singular images of 'nativeness' that are popularly seductive but ultimately oppressive" (49). And, in my own work, I refer to our numerous and distinct cultures which have been "transmitted from one generation to another through languages, songs, dances, traditional economic practices, and governing structures. These specific Indigenous ways continue to provide a spiritual, social, political, and economic context that... contribute[s] to the formulation of the self" (139).

I refer to this book also because one of the individuals that I respectfully acknowledge in both my scholarship and pedagogy who consistently works at 'chasing away the *Wiintigos*' is Jeannette Armstrong. As an Indigenous-Okanagan writer/critic and the editor of *Looking at the Words of Our People: First Nations Analysis of Literature* (1993), Armstrong courageously pioneered the territory of literary criticism in Canada – a territory I might add that is inhabited by the most ferocious kinds of *Wiintigos*. In the 'Editor's note,' she explains that she recognized a need for First Nations writers, readers, academics and critics to develop and strategize ways to talk about the "voices coming forward into written English" (7). Politicizing discussions of literary territory, she insists that

> First Nations Literature[s] will be defined by First Nations Writers, readers, academics, and critics and perhaps only by writers and critics from within those varieties of First Nations contemporary practise and past practise of culture and the knowledge of it. (7)

In the development of pedagogy, Armstrong maintains that we must acknowledge and recognize that there are culture-specific voices in the literatures and "experts within those cultures who are essential to be drawn from and drawn out in order to incorporate into the reinterpretation through pedagogy" (7). Naming First Nations Literatures, facets of cultural practises, she traces intersections between literatures and Indigenous political struggles. Thus, she argues that First Nations Literature[s] "contains symbolic significance and relevance that is an integral part of the deconstruction-construction of colonialism and the reconstruction of a new order of culturalism and relationship beyond colonial thought and practise" (8).

Within her own literary productions, Armstrong's work is encircled within an Okanagan epistemology. Attempting to offer some reflections of it in English, she explains to Isernhagen:

> the Okanagan person will take the spiritual, the understanding, and the connection with the spiritual, and the attempt is to materialize that, to bring that forward into the physical plane,... because it's not knowable, it doesn't

have voice in the physical plane, either through words or through movement or through carving or through paint or through social construct. (151)

During the interview with Isernhagen she diplomatically shrugs off the attempt to fix her writings within a western literary tradition of criticism. However, in the introduction to his book, Isernhagen suggests that "Jeannette Armstrong would probably be labelled a realist by most critics (at least for her fiction)" (5) because "the urgency of political questions confronting her community has made her rely on and adapt forms of referential discourse that tend to be called realistic" (7). When Isernhaagen finally asks her directly, "Do you classify yourself, as a writer, as a realist, a modernist, a postmodern writer?" (176), she attempts to diffuse the politically loaded question with humor. "I don't even know what those terms are," (176) she laughs. In the end, she takes a circuitous route to appease the interviewer; somewhat hesitantly she replies: "I'd probably say a postmodern although I really dislike that terminology and the categorization as a postmodern" (176). She also rejects the term postcolonial as a theory for analyzing Indigenous literatures. "How can there be a postcolonial literature?" (178), she queries.

> [T]he wellspring of literature and voice has been a voice of resistance and is rooted in an inner voice of resistance... resistance to colonialism and resistance to the whole culture clash that is assimilationist in nature (and aggressively assimilationist in nature), and the resistance psychologically to that in terms of the creative voice that arises out of this situation. (177)

There isn't a postcolonial literature, she convincingly argues, because "we are immersed in colonial literature" (178).

In "Godzilla vs. Post-Colonial" Thomas King humorously and in his uniquely 'Kingly' way pokes his stick at the *Wiintigo*-like forces of western literary criticism. In fact, he steadfastly stands his ground against the *Wiintigo* manifestation – post-colonial – when he declares outright: "As a contemporary Native writer,... I am quite unwilling to use these terms" (343). King rejects the term post-colonial and its imperialist imposition because "it demands that I imagine myself as something I did not choose to be, as something I would not choose to become (348). Never just a reactionary, he articulates his reasons for rejecting the term post-colonial.

> While post-colonialism purports to be a method by which
> we can begin to look at those literature which are formed
> out of the struggle of the oppressed against the oppressor,
> the colonized against the colonizer, the term itself assumes
> that the starting point for that discussion is the advent of
> Europeans in North America... And, worst of all, the idea
> of post-colonial writing effectively cuts us off from our
> traditions,... which have come down to us through our cul-
> tures in spite of colonization. (342-343)

Not unlike other Indigenous scholars, critics, and writers mentioned herein, King suggests that we need a critical language and
appropriate methodologies to describe "the various stages or
changes in Native literature[s] as it has become written, while at
the same time remaining oral and as it has expanded from a specific language base to a multiple language base" (343). In terms of
a critical language for Indigenous literatures, King offers the
terms: tribal, polemical, associational, and interfusional.

He refers to the term 'tribal' literature as literature that is com-
munity/tribally specific and 'polemical' literature as that written in
Indigenous languages as well as English or French. Whereas
'tribal' literature is shared only amongst its members, preserved
within an Indigenous language, and centers on a tribally-specific
community, 'polemical' literature gives voice to conflicts between
Indigenous and non-Indigenous cultures. When he employs the
term 'interfusional,' King uses it to refer to Indigenous literatures
that blend the oral and the written. Comparatively, the term
'associational' literature refers to most contemporary Indigenous
writers' whose work generally centers the story in an Indigenous
community. For Indigenous readers, 'interfusional' and
'associational' literature encourages a valuing of cultures that are
rooted in meaningful histories and oral literatures.

Like King, Craig Womack rejects the imposition of western
literary criticism albeit he pokes his stick at the *Wiintigo* manifestation postmodernism. In *Red On Red: Native American Literary
Separatism*, he suggests that "Native literature and the criticism
that surrounds it, needs to see more attention devoted to tribally
specific concerns" (1). Thus, he announces his intention to negotiate a space in literary criticism for his own Creek approach to literature and criticism. Locating himself in Creek-Cherokee epistemology, Womack maintains that he has a responsibility to critique
Native literatures from his own tribal-specific perspective.

In the introduction to the book, he explains that his purpose in writing the book was to open up a "dialogue among Creek people, specifically, and Native people[s], more generally, regarding what constitutes meaningful literary efforts" (1). Despite the fallacy that Indigenous peoples have only recently become active constructors of our world through a singular *body* of *literature*, Womack makes it abundantly clear that, "Indian people have authored a lot of books" (2). Indeed, we have a history with the written tradition, that "reaches back to the 1770s in terms of writing in English, and hundreds of years before contact in terms of Mayan and Aztec pictoglyphic alphabets in which were written the vast libraries of Mesoamerica" (2).

Because of our history with the written tradition and our own culturally rich resources, Womack recommends that we harvest our own epistemological and pedagogical systems to guide our work. He also reminds writers, critics, and scholars of our responsibilities to pass on the traditions of our respective nations to the future generations (15). Indeed, he insists that "[p]erhaps it is time to really dig in, to entrench ourselves with what we have inherited from our home cultures" (15) because there are valuable sources of literary ideas to be gleaned from past generations of Indigenous writers and thinkers.

Tracing intersections between literature and political struggles, he maintains that "[t]he ongoing expression of tribal voice, through imagination, language, and literature, contributes to keeping sovereignty alive in the citizens of a nation and gives sovereignty a meaning that is defined within the tribe" (14). As his words suggest here, we can develop critical methodologies for Indigenous literatures by breaking "down oppositions between the world of literature and the very real struggles of American Indian communities" (11). Collapsing oppositions between the world of literature and the political struggles of American Indian communities, Womack formulates a politicized criticism that emphasizes autonomy, self-determination, and sovereignty. And, he announces his intention to seek out a literary criticism that focuses on "Native resistance movements against colonization, confronts racism, discusses sovereignty and Native nationalism, seeks connections between literature and liberation struggles, and, finally, roots literature in land and culture" (11). Following the example of nineteenth century Creek anticolonial resistors, Womack names this critical method the 'Radical Red Stick' approach, and he makes clear that it privileges unique Indigenous worldviews and political realities. Delineating the 'Radical Red Stick' approach to literature, he writes:

> the assumption that Indian viewpoints cohere, that Indian
> resistance can be successful, that Native critical centers are
> possible, that working from within the nation, rather than
> looking toward the outside, is a legitimate way of examin-
> ing literature, that subverting the literary status quo rather
> than being subverted *by* it constitutes a meaningful alterna-
> tive. (12)

Like Womack, I also believe that we need to make connections between literary sovereignty and political nationhood.

Thus, when I teach Indigenous literatures I use the texts as tools
for confronting colonialism and locating spaces for decolonization.
In looking at the process of colonization through the experiences of
some of the events or characters in the literatures we read, I encour-
age students to make connections between their own lives, their
own communities, and their own nations. In the process, I suggest
that they might carefully and thoughtfully examine our histories and
"culturally affirm toward a new vision for all our people in the future" (Armstrong 241).

"How Do I Fight The Enemy When The Outposts Are In My Head?"[10]

In my approach to Indigenous literatures, I attempt to collapse
boundaries between text and self. I believe that "empowerment cannot happen if we refuse to be vulnerable while encouraging students
to take all the risks" (hooks, 21). Like hooks, I also believe that
"linking confessional narratives to academic discussions... shows
how experience can illuminate and enhance our understanding of
academic material" (21).

The roots of my reality are reflected in the following passage
that I quote from Emma LaRocque's "Tides, Towns, and Trains."

> The third tidal wave, which continues to affect my genera-
> tion, took place soon after World War II. This wave was the
> modernization movement, in which various white agencies
> seemed driven to whip Indian and Metis in white, middle-
> class, 'ordinary' Canadians... This is the wave in which dis-
> orientation, grief, fear and internalized rage grew among us.
> (80)

For me, disorientation, grief, fear and internalized rage grew because "I was heavily indoctrinated by the power of white european
christian patriarchal institutions," as I wrote in *Iskwewak Kah' Ki*

Yaw Ni Wahkomaknak: Neither Indian Princesses Nor Easy Squaws (19). For me, not unlike many other Indigenous writers, those colonial institutions have "long been a source of ideological confusion, economic oppression, social disparity, and political confusion within my family, community, and nation" (10). One generation after another, my family was exposed to "cruelty, manipulative controls, segregation through the reserve system and the Halfbreed" [colonies]... dehumanization, despiritualization through the christian residential schools, and other less overt but just as genocidal assimilative programs" (12).

Like so many other writers, such as Emma LaRocque, Howard Adams, Maria Campbell, Beatrice Culleton, I too internalized the 'white ideal.' My parents, siblings, and extended family too learned to internalize the 'white ideal,' and because "we were socialized to the image that we were inferior, stupid, lazy" (Adams 7), we became statistics represented as "the 'social problems' of Native people" (Armstrong 239). Hidden in the shadow of those statistics however is the nightmarish years in which my family "for generations, were seized from our communities and homes and placed in indoctrination camps until our language[s], our religion[s], our customs, our values, and our societal structures almost disappeared" (239). Hidden in the shadows of those statistics are the generations of my family who

> returned to communities and families as adults, without the necessary skills for parenting, for Native life style, or self-sufficiency on their land base, [and] deteriorated into despair. With the loss of cohesive cultural relevance with their own peoples and a distorted view of the non-Native culture from the clergy who ran the residential schools, an almost total disorientation and loss of identity occurred. (239)

Not surprisingly, as Armstrong points out, "the disintegration, of family and community was inevitable, originating with the individual's internalized pain [and consequently] the [i]ncreasing death statistics from suicide, violence, alcohol and drug abuse and other poverty-centred diseases" (240). As I make clear in my discussions with students, for me colonization is not merely a theoretical concept that I can intellectualize to frame my work. It is a reality that I live with every day![11] And, unlike those literary critics or scholars who naively refer to a postcolonial Canada, for me colonization is a reality that shadows me in the classroom as a professor/graduate student.

Conclusion:

Given my own connection to *Ninahkawewin* oral traditions of storytelling and the subsequent appropriation of my family stories, I have thought long and hard about approaches to Indigenous literatures. I have thought long and hard because our stories are being transplanted into the Canadian literary landscape and subject to the *Wiintigo*-like forces of Western literary criticism. However, as a *Ninahkawewin-Metis* scholar and professor of Indigenous literatures, I will continue to speak out and 'chase away the *Wiintigos*' – in whatever manifestations they may appear! And, I feel empowered knowing that there are others employing innovative methods derived from their respective cultures to interpret and analyze culturally-specific literatures. Indeed, as Craig Womack explains: "Native literature[s], and Native literary criticism[s], written by Native authors is part of sovereignty: Indian people exercising the right to present images of themselves and to discuss those images" (14).

Notes

1. While I cannot claim total responsibility for Indigenous-literatures being present within the Department, my voice and actions have encouraged non-Indigenous professors to turn their attentions to Indigenous authored works.

2. In my home territory of Southwestern Saskatchewan, the *Wiintigo* is known as an anthropomorphic giant canibal. Feared by everyone, the *Wiintigo* is known for its insatiable greed!

3. *Miigwetch* to Dr. Cecil King for helping me with *Ninahkawewin* spelling and grammar.

4. There are numerous variations for the spelling of Acoose [*Ekos, Akoos, Akoose*] and *Quewitch* [*Quewich,* Q'wich]. I use Acoose and *Quewitch* unless quoted from a text.

5. Herein, I do not intend to critically analyze this poem or any of the other re-tellings of my family history in any kind of meaningful way. I intend to save that for a future critical essay.

6. In official reports during the early 1900s, the Department of Indian Affairs refers to the name Acoose in a pejorative way, and attaches to it labels such as pagans, devil worshippers, outlaws, and resistors.

7. Throughout the writing/research process for the radio docu-drama I came to meet Brenda Zeman, a Saskatchewan writer. She co-wrote the script for the radio docu-drama "Acoose: Man Standing Above Ground."

8. Wolfe footnotes this word in his text and explains that it refers to the word Indian in singular form.

9. The book includes the following Indigenous writers and scholars: Kateri Akiwenzie-Damm, Janice Acoose, Marilyn Dumont, Kimberly Blaeser, Duane Niatum, Gerry William, Victoria Lena Manyarrows, Armand Garnet Ruffo, Greg Young-Ing, and D.L. Birchfield.

10. In borrowing these words, I gratefully acknowledge the authors of *The Circle Game: Shadows and Substance in the Indian Residential School Experience* in Canada [Penticton: Theytus Books, 1997] – Roland Chrisjohn and Sherri Young with Michael Maraun – for succinctly describing what I feel during this frustrating period in my life/scholarly work.

11. As I write this paper, my family is entangled in a very painful process. Because of years of drug and alcohol abuse, my youngest sister's six children were apprehended by the Department of Social Services. Ironically, it was one of my former students of 'Literature for Decolonization' who rescued my nieces and nephews. And, I am thankful that between my two sisters and me, we could provide safe and loving homes. Unfortunately, my baby sister is not so lucky for she remains a shadow hidden in the statistics of the 'social problems' of Native peoples.

Works Cited

Acoose, Janice. (1995) *Iskwewak Kah' Ki Yah Ni Wahkomakanak: Neither Indian Princesses Nor Easy Squaws.* Toronto: Women's Press.

Adams, Howard. (1975) *Prison of Grass: Canada From a Native Point of View.* Saskatoon: Fifth House Press.

Armstrong, Jeannette. (1998) "The Disempowerment of First North American Native Peoples and Empowerment Through Their Writing." *An Anthology of Canadian Native Literature in English.* Ed. Daniel David Moses and Terry Goldie. 2nd ed. Toronto: Oxford University Press. 239-244.

Armstrong, Jeannette, ed. (1993) *Looking at the Words of Our People: A First Nations Analysis of Literature.* Penticton: Theytus Books.

Blaeser, Kimberly. (1993) "Native Literature: Seeking a Critical Center." In Jeannette Armstrong, ed. 51-62.

Chrisjohn, Roland and Sherri Young with Michael Maraun. (1997) *The Circle Game: Shadows and Substance in the Indian Residential School Experience in Canada.* Penticton: Theytus Books.

hooks, bell. (1994) *Teaching to Transgress: Education as the Practise of Freedom.* New York: Routledge.

Isernhagen, Hartwig. (1999) *Momaday, Vizenor, Armstrong: Conversations on American Indian Writing.* Norman: University of Oklahoma Press. 135-183.

King, Thomas. (1997) "Godzilla vs. Post-Colonial." *New Contexts of Canadian Crticism.* Eds. A. Heble, D. Palmateer Pennee, and J.R. Struthers. Toronto: Broadview Press. 241-248.

LaRocque, Emma. (1990) "Tides, Towns, and Trains." In *Living the Changes*. Ed. Joan Turner. Winnipeg: University of Manitoba Press. 76-90.

Monture Angus, Patricia. (1999) *Journeying Forward: Dreaming First Nations Independence*. Halifax: Fernwood Press.

Morris, Edmund Montague. (1985) *The Diaries of Edmund Montague Morris: Western Journeys 1907-1910*. Trans. Mary Fitz-Gibbon. Toronto: Royal Ontario Museum.

Rushdie, Salman. (1998) "Commonwealth Literature" Does Not Exist." *Concert of Voices: An Anthology of World Writing in English*. Ed. Victor J. Ramraj. Peterborough: Broadview Press. 366-373.

Scott, Duncan Campbell. (1916) "Lines in Memory of Edmund Morris." *Lundy's Lane and Other Poems*. Toronto: McClelland, Goodchild & Stewart.

Titley, E. Brian. (1986) *A Narrow Vision: Duncan Campbell Scott and the Administration of Indian Affairs in Canada*. Vancouver: University of British Columbia Press.

Wolfe, Alexander. (1988) *Earth Elder Stories*. Saskatoon: Fifth House.

Womack, Craig: (1999) *Red on Red: Native American Literary Separatism*. Minneapolis: University of Minnesota Press.

Zeman, Brenda. (1988) "A Song For Mooshum." *To Run with Longboat. Twelve Stories of Indian Athletes in Canada*. Edmonton: GMS Ventures Inc.

From Copper Woman to Grey Owl to the alterNative Warrior: Exploring Voice and the Need to Connect

Jonathan R. Dewar

It can be argued that Drew Hayden Taylor's play *alterNatives* covers too much ground; many issues are glossed over, although this is in keeping with the superficiality of the dinner conversation. It is also controversial, as Taylor himself points out in his introduction, with something to annoy everybody. Nevertheless, *alterNatives* is a worthy text to teach in a Native literature or a Canadian literature course. It should fit in nicely with the curricula already being taught *ad infinitum* in English departments, including works such as George Ryga's *The Ecstasy of Rita Joe*, W.P. Kinsella's *Dance Me Outside*, and Duncan Campbell Scott's "Indian poems." I would never argue for the rejection of any of these texts (except in a course on Native literature – that is, literature by Native writers) but would insist on teaching them within the proper context, including the role these texts have played in confusing the notion of Native voice in literature. Proceeding from a discussion of Taylor's *alterNatives* and the central issues that the text raises, I will move to a discussion of a troublesome text I encountered a few years ago in a course on Commonwealth women writers, Anne Cameron's *Daughters of Copper Woman*, and a text I brought to the classroom, Armand Garnet Ruffo's *Grey Owl: The Mystery of Archie Belaney*. As a person of mixed heritage, I have often turned to texts that deal thematically with issues of (re)connection to culture to help me articulate my position within the discourse and navigate my way through the many intersecting debates. Both of these texts, Cameron's and Ruffo's, are two such books, although they may initially seem worlds apart. Cameron, a White woman, immerses herself in a Native narrator/alter ego, and Ruffo, an Anishnaabe writer, presents a fictionalized and stylized biography of Canada's famous Indian impostor, Grey Owl, problematizing both the notion of voice and connection.

In Hayden Taylor's *alterNatives*, six characters engage in a lively, spirited, no-holds-barred "debate" that covers more ground than your average short play, but not nearly the amount of ground covered by your average treaty. This 'punny', 'jokey' opening is liable to be read in a few different ways, perhaps as offensive, perhaps not. And it is this writer's amateurish attempt to convey the spirit of Taylor's tone: *alterNatives* is funny, but it is also challenging, deeply personal (although Taylor provides a similarly humorous caveat in his introduction: "Any resemblance to people, dead or alive, is purely coincidental. Honest Injun!" (6)), and, by his own admission, "unsympathetic." He says,

> While writing this play, I was fully expecting to become the Salman Rushdie of the Native community, for I'm sure there is something in this play to annoy everybody. Part of my goal was to create unsympathetic characters right across the board. And to do this, as the saying goes, I had to break a few eggs. A close friend, a Native woman, came up to me quite angry and said, 'So this is what you really think of Native people!' Then some time later, one reviewer referred to it as "witless white bashing." Evidently I have become a racist! (ibid)

And there is definitely some White baiting, if not White bashing, but I wouldn't call it entirely witless; Taylor is no Oscar Wilde, but he should share with Wilde, or any other playwright, the conceit of authorial distance any well-written play – or short story or novel – deserves from the outset. That is, if characters express outrageous, outlandish, racist, or otherwise controversial opinions, we should not assume that particular character is a mouthpiece for the writer, any more than a play or novel is a vehicle for the promotion of the writer's personal agenda.

Yet, although it is necessary for the audience to buy into such a writerly conceit, one would have to be terribly idealistic to believe that some literature and drama has not served as issue-driven sermons, propagandizing a person's or group's position. This is what drives Taylor's play. Each character, more or less, speaks from a particular ideology (including some hilarious Star Trek philosophy), some more eloquently than others, some more venomously than others. But has Taylor succeeded in creating largely unsympathetic characters? Or, has he created characters who deserve both scorn and sympathy? The latter would be the more successful reading, at least in terms of objective literary criticism. This play works on many levels, including the subjectivity of opinion. It is intended to poke fun, in a meaningful way, at a fractured debate, particularly the question of voice in art and academia, and

Native literature in particular.

It may not be too great a stretch to argue that Taylor sees part of himself in each of the characters, with the exception perhaps of Michelle Spencer, the unflinching vegetarian who is the main target of the alterNative warrior ("a new breed of warriors who have an allegiance to the truth, rather than tradition" (Taylor 57)) and the sarcastic s.o.b. Bobby Rabbit. His attacks on the strictness of that particular dogma and his joke-at-any-cost attitude contribute to the initial humour of the play and serve to fire up the emotions of the characters and catapult the evening's conversation into outright hostility. This eruption results in the exits of both host – Colleen Birk – and her guests. They are Yvonne Stone and the aforementioned Bobby Rabbit, the alterNative warriors and childhood friends of co-host Angel Wallace, and non-Native Michelle and her partner Dale Cartland. Only Angel, Ojibway science fiction writer and ambiguous urban Indian, remains. That is until "innocently" ignorant Dale returns for more moose meat and conversation. The play closes with Dale, a fellow Trekkie and lover of sci-fi, looking past (or failing to see) the Native "issues" broached earlier in the evening, concentrating instead on Angel's writing, as Angel himself argued should be the case. But the story Angel closes with is certainly not devoid of "issue":

> There's this Native astronaut and he's cruising at the edge of the solar system in his space ship. And he's in a bad mood because back on Earth everybody is celebrating. The biggest party since... whenever, because the very last land claim has finally been settled... He picks something funny up on his scanners and goes to investigate. As he approaches the far rim of the solar system, in uncharted territory, he discovers a big space... thing... The astronaut's sensors are going nuts... [G]radually, the thing understands that the astronaut speaks English and in translation the thing begins to spell out a message... This big flashing thing suddenly says, in English, "For Sale." You get it, it's a huge interstellar billboard. Evidently the solar system is up for sale. The astronaut stares at it in disbelief. Then suddenly the sign slowly begins to change. It now says "Sold." Somebody's just bought the solar system. The Native astronaut mutters to himself "Not again." The end. (143-4)

Angel and Dale clink glasses and the lights go down. So, some of the ground covered in the play includes just that, ground, or land, and communication – or lack thereof.

The play, though, is not without its controversy. Racism, White guilt, appropriation, stereotype – these are not easy topics. As a mixed-blood scholar of Native literature, I read with both sympathy and something far less than scorn the character of Jewish Canadian professor of Native literature Colleen Birk. I realized from the outset the direction Taylor's play would take. I did not see this telegraphing as a fault of the play in my initial reading; rather, I was prepared to find my own position as both a scholar and person of mixed blood heritage challenged. And I like to believe I was up for the challenge, even if Colleen was not (although to be fair, she did not know she was entering such a charged arena – if that makes a difference). But the challenge is, nonetheless, deeply personal. Because of my "connection"/interest into the so-called issues, I found myself wanting to pick sides but realized, ultimately, that although I've come to terms with my voice having a place within the discourse, that placement must be interrogated. The play doesn't pull any punches in this regard, although it starts slowly with Bobby referring to the bookshelf full of "Native" literature, including texts both by and/or about Aboriginal people:

Bobby:	"Hey Angel, nice collection of books. Yours?"
Angel:	"What do you think?"
Bobby:	"I didn't think so."
Angel:	"Colleen's."
Yvonne:	"Wannabe?"
Angel:	"Literature professor."
Yvonne:	"Almost as Bad."
Angel:	"Yeah."
Yvonne:	"She any good?"
Angel:	"She has her strengths." (45-6)

From the outset, Angel's relationship with non-Native Colleen is destabilized. Although he has not derided her position openly, apart from jokingly putting her copy of *How A People Die* in the freezer ("Where else would you put a dead people but in a freezer?" 37), he has switched "allegiances" upon the arrival of his Ojibway friends. Or perhaps this is making too strong a case at this point, because allegiance is an issue of debate as well. Bobby and Yvonne see Angel's position – his relationship with a White woman, his disconnectedness from his past, his culture, his friends – as a change of allegiance. Angel feigns ambivalence, preferring to define his own identity, but his position – even his relationship with Colleen – is psychologically complicated, if we believe Bobby and Yvonne, and intentionally orchestrated. The penultimate revelation in the play, which serves as the impetus for the mass exodus of Colleen and her dinner guests, is that Angel orchestrated his meeting with Colleen months earlier because she interviewed Bobby and Angel for a book called *Legends of the Ontario Ojibway* when they were just children. Bobby and Angel had, of course, made up most of the stories. Bobby is thrilled, but Angel is deeply troubled by this fact. Angel says, "This book is in its seventh printing. This book is also on the reading list at five other universities that have a Native literature course. Native teachers are teaching this book to Native students" (130). Bobby replies, "If it will make you happy, I promise I won't tell any more fake legends. At least not for fifty cents." To which Angel replies, "I just don't want to be an alterNative warrior any more. You've come to enjoy this too much. Too many people get hurt. As a result, they're missing your point... It's not the message I don't support, it's the medium" (131). And to Colleen he says,

> When I was seventeen my Grandfather died. He had been a wonderful storyteller and we had been very close... That night, after the funeral service, I had a dream. It was my Grandfather, he told me about the importance of stories, of how often they're more important than the storyteller. He knew I had been up to mischief, and had not respected the art of storytelling. He told me I had to correct my mischief if I wanted to honour his spirit. I guess that's why I'm here. (136)

Colleen asks in disbelief, "Is that true?" and, narrowly avoiding some serious melodrama, Taylor has Angel reply, "No, but you were willing to believe it. Weren't you?" (137)

This exchange is the beginning of the end for Colleen and Angel and for the play. It is also, as a friend of mine – a Metis woman and fellow scholar of Native literature – pointed out in a conversation, the beginning of an even more problematic dynamic, one that all scholars and educators should be aware of when teaching Native literature: respect. Picking up on Yvonne's "wannabe" comment, Angel and Colleen have the following exchange when Colleen asks Angel if he still loves her:

Angel: "In Ojibway, how do you say what time is it?"
Colleen: "What does that have to do with anything?"

Angel: "I'll explain later. How do you say it?"

Colleen: "I believe it's... *aani epiijiyaag?*"

Angel: "And 'I'm glad to meet you'?"

Colleen: "This isn't the time..."

Angel: "Humour me."

Colleen: "I'm glad to meet you. I think that's *Nikichinen dam nakweshkonaan*. Does that humour you enough?"

Angel: "One more. 'I'm sorry.'"

Colleen: "Oh for Christ's sake..."

Angel: "I'm sorry."

Colleen: "Well that depends on who's sorry. And for what."

Angel: "I'm sorry."

Colleen: "*Ndimijinwez.*"

Angel: "Now say those three sentences in Hebrew. I'll even accept Yiddish."

    Colleen is silent.

Angel: "I think that says it all."

Colleen: "Is it so wrong to want to share?"

Angel: "I don't think that's sharing. You want to be more Native than I do." (137-9)

As my friend pointed out, while Angel may have a point, he, like Bobby, chooses to attack rather than engage in a discourse based on any healing principle. He has certainly failed to live up to the spirit of his admonishment of Bobby's "medium" or the spirit of truth at the heart of the alterNative warrior. Perhaps this is why he has rejected the movement. Earlier, Yvonne accused Colleen of being a "woman in search of a culture," saying, "You're Jewish, yet you're not. That explains the teaching of Native literature. It's almost like you want to establish a connection to a culture to fill a vacuum" (112). Yvonne's response then, which should still resonate with the listener/reader, especially after her final exchange with Angel, was "I am a Jew. I am proud of that. My personal connection to my people and religion are my business and not subject to your sophomoric psycho-babble" (113). However, after her exchange with Angel, it would appear that he considers her personal "connection" to Native literature as invalid because she is not Native, and despite her vast knowledge of culture and language, she is merely appropriating a culture to fill a void. This may be a standard form of the appropriation debate, but Angel's equation of her inability to speak Hebrew or Yiddish with a lack of respect for Native culture is flimsy logic. Perhaps, in the heat of the moment, Angel did not think out carefully what he wanted to say. There has been no mention of whether or not Angel speaks Ojibway, just that it is wrong that Colleen does. Maybe there is an unseen internalized debate raging here within Angel in which he asks of himself, What does it mean with regard to my identity as a Native person that I, unlike Colleen, cannot speak my own language?

My Metis friend and I found ourselves asking the same question, specifically in regard to our roles as scholars, students, readers and teachers. How would we respectfully teach a Native text, despite not having been raised on a reserve, learning "our" language(s) at our grandparents' knees? Taylor both perpetuates and questions stereotypes, ultimately asking what it means to be an authentic Indian. When I initially tried to make sense of *Daughters of Copper Woman*, I turned to Linda Alcoff's article, "The Problem of Speaking for Others," which addresses many of the problems prevalent in both postcolonial and feminist theory, with a particular focus on the study of Native literature. I was immediately struck by the simple (but not simplistic) and straightforward way in which Alcoff poses many probing questions regarding often contentious issues of authenticity and appropriation. She asks, "Is my greatest contribution to move over and get out of the way? And if so, what is the best way to do this – to keep silent or to deconstruct my discourse?" (8). As a young scholar, I was, like many young people, looking for a comfortable place to stand within the field of study, and trying to find the appropriate place for my voice. I found myself actively engaged in a deconstruction of my own discourse as well as some of the important questions encompassed by the title of Alcoff's article.

Although vastly different, both *Daughters of Copper Woman* and *Grey Owl* deal with the need to connect to a culture that is not one's own. These differences do not polarize the texts; rather, they serve to elucidate the ambiguous nature of connection and the need for the kind of discourse that questions what it uses and uses what it questions. Satya Mohanty writes, "What better way of ensuring the equality of cultures than to assert that, since all explanations of the other risk repeating the colonizer's judgements, we should simply refuse to judge or explain, forsaking understanding for the sake of respect" (111). Mohanty's comment is delivered with a sizable degree of irony and is the sort of problematization of issue that prompts Victoria Boynton to position herself as reader. I echo that declaration here because it rings true to my own sense of the problems with navigable/unnavigable boundaries and because it serves as a useful introduction to Anne Cameron's *Daughters of Copper*

Woman: "I don't want to colonize through reading. I don't want to steal, appropriate, lay claim to what is not mine, impose what [Paula] Gunn Allen refers to as a 'Western technological-industrial' mentality on the story, make a reputation off of somebody else's culture" (54). These are the two poles of my ideology, and my personal relationship to both Ruffo's *Grey Owl* and Cameron's *Daughters of Copper Woman* necessitates my need to similarly position myself as a reader.

I return to Linda Alcoff's article, "The Problem of Speaking for Others" because it offers a good set of parameters for such an engagement. Alcoff cautions against "retreating into an individualist realm" (21). She writes: "A further problem with the retreat response is that it may be motivated by a desire to find a method or practice immune from criticism. If I speak only for myself it may appear that I am immune from criticism because I am not making any claims that describe others or prescribe actions for them. If I am only speaking for myself I have no responsibility for being true to your experience or needs" (22). I could very well have qualified the preceding section on *alterNatives* with a statement amounting to an 'in-my-opinion-and-my-opinion-alone-the-play-is-about...' as a pre-emptive deflation of criticism but that would have been as transparent as it is here. This is not to say that I believe my reading to be immune to criticism, just as I would expect some readers to disagree with Ruffo's decision to write about an impostor. Okanagan writer, Jeannette Armstrong has been criticized and lauded for her use of a male title character in *Slash*. Patricia Morley, an early reviewer of *Daughters of Copper Woman*, called Cameron's text "a strong feminist statement [that] reminds us of a part of our history we have preferred to forget. Her work compels attention, calling out for social justice and spiritual healing" (43). But it remains appropriative. As a reader, perhaps as one who professes a 'connection' to Native literature, perhaps as a man, this kind of reading, and Cameron's own statements that the stories in *Daughters of Copper Woman* are relevant to her, connected to her, because she is a woman, seems suspect. But Cameron is simply positioning herself.

Alcoff rejects a general retreat from speaking for others, but qualifies it, saying, "I am not advocating a return to an un-self-conscious appropriation of the other, but rather that anyone who speaks for others should only do so out of a concrete analysis of the particular power relations and discursive effects involved" (24). The parameter that is key to this discussion is the second in a list of four: "We must also interrogate the bearing of our location and context on what it is we are saying... One deformed way in which this is too often carried out is when speakers offer up in the spirit of honesty autobiographical information about themselves usually at the beginning of their discourse as a kind of disclaimer" (25). I have already engaged in just such an endeavour, although my positioning, vague though it was, cannot be said to be the sort of apology for being non-Native that Alcoff's definition alludes to. My claim of mixed heritage could be seen as an attempt to consciously occupy both insider and/or outsider positions (although we could argue which half is inside and which is out, depending on the forum). In this article it is more likely that the mixed claim will be seen as a not-so-subtle leaning toward insider Native status. I need not make such a claim, except that I have chosen to talk about the personal reading experience and what better way to inform such a subject? The paradox here, of course, is that in most discussions of non-Native literature, I would likely not make any such claim. In positioning myself I could simply be following the lead of many of the critics I have already quoted, as well as Julia Emberley in the introduction to her book, *Thresholds of Difference: Feminist Critique, Native Women's Writing, Postcolonial Theory*, and Cameron herself: "The question that gets asked most about [the book] is 'Is this history or is this fiction?' Nobody ever stops to ask if the crap they push down your throats in school is history or fiction... this book, for me, as a person who was born on this island, and certainly as a woman, has more truth than anything the school system ever came up with" (Twigg 38). But is my positioning any different than Cameron's, articulated here in the preface to *Daughters of Copper Woman*?:

> For years I have been hearing stories from the native people of Vancouver Island, stories preserved for generations through an oral tradition that is now threatened. Among the stories were special ones shared with me by a few loving women who are members of a secret society whose roots go back beyond recorded history to the dawn of Time itself. These women shared their stories with me because they knew I would not use them without their permission. (7)

This last part is important and respectful, but it is likely the kind of statement Taylor is lampooning in *alterNatives*.

I study Native literature and culture because I want to connect

with my Huron-Wendat ancestry, a connection that is made difficult by the fact that my maternal grandmother did not grow up in
Wendake, the Huron-Wendat community in Lorrette, just outside
of Quebec City. Even if she had, the strong traditionalist movement that I have come to know is relatively new. Add to that the
literal distance between my long-established family home in Ottawa and the long-since-separated (in the Huron dispersal of 1650)
Wyandot nations of Kansas, Oklahoma, Michigan, and Southern
Ontario. And, while Bill C-31 retroactively reinstated status rights
to those disenfranchised by earlier acts, it did not and could not by
its very nature repair any of the real damage of severed connection.
And, what of those people attempting to (re)connect, albeit with a
respectful acknowledgment of vastly different experience? Where
are the real rules and parameters that instruct people on how to
connect or reconnect? This is precisely where individual decisions
and experiences come into play, further blurring or greying lines of
authenticity and appropriation.

It is out of a desire to show the proper amount of respect for
that cultural heritage that I have imposed certain boundaries on
myself, including an approach that, at times, is more academic than
personal. Although that in itself has become a personal journey. I
relate to Archie Belaney/Grey Owl, perhaps even envy him, and
struggle with feelings of being an impostor, especially when con-
fronted with questions of the hotly debated pan-Indian identity.
That is why I felt such a connection to Ruffo's *Grey Owl*. But,
when I first read *Daughters of Copper Woman*, I was similarly
moved by Cameron's very powerful, compelling, and beautifully
crafted narrative. I found myself asking difficult questions. What is
my connection to a text that announces itself as being for women?
What or who is it that I connect with – the Native subject matter or
Anne Cameron, the White woman who, like Belaney, had access to
a culture not her own? When my initial reaction was to say "White
people can't do that" or "I wish a Native woman had written this,"
what was I really saying in regard to an already difficult discourse?
When I read that the royalties from the book go not to Cameron
but to the community from which she received many of the stories
and that she did indeed "move over" when asked by a group of Native Canadian writers,[1] I found myself softening my initial negative reaction. I was thus forced to ask where my opinion fit into
this whole mess and for the first time forced to consider the possibility that my opinion did not fit or matter at all, a telling admission for a male scholar discussing a decidedly feminist text.[2]

I initially embraced Cameron's book because of what it provoked in me as an academic. With the inherent objective distance of scholarship, I was able to say that Anne Cameron was wrong because appropriation is a philosophical issue, and she had appropriated what was not hers to use for her own means. Her end goal was not to promote Native women but to use them, to syncretize and primitivize. However, upon further research into the criticism of Cameron's work and the broader issues that necessarily developed, I began to see that my own struggle with the theme of the impostor was not far removed from issues of appropriation, authenticity and positionality. Many of Cameron's critics, Native and non-Native alike, have raised the issue of authenticity of voice. Christine St. Peter provides an interesting twist on the authenticity of genre: "On one level, *Daughters of Copper Woman* will only be considered authentic by ethnographers if Cameron has operated as a transparent medium, recording word-by-word transcriptions of Native stories" (503). And she adds, "I doubt that Cameron has done this, because the powerful filter of her own style appears to have given the stories their shape" (503).

St. Peter relates an anecdote that reveals the problems associated with *Daughters of Copper Woman*. "Many of the students in my women's studies course have insisted that this book was our most important reading, and they are suspicious of some local anthropologists who insist that Cameron has falsified the ethnographic tradition in her discovery of lost sources of female power. To their credit, the same students are disturbed to hear that some Natives also reject the book" (501). She rightly points out, however, that since many Native men and women admire it we can hardly reject it on their behalf. She asks, "If the writer is a woman intent on sharing knowledge of a hidden women's culture, can she assume a privileged position as transmitter for the sake of other women, even though not born to the racial heritage she recounts? (501)." This notion of accepting and/or rejecting is a privilege itself, and we must not lose sight of that. Alcoff concurs, saying that "we have to acknowledge that the very decision to move over or retreat can occur only from a position of privilege" (24). In fact, this discussion too is privileged in so far as it takes the form of a critical study of issue(s).

The point I am trying to make is that this is a worthy context in which to situate the teaching of *Daughters of Copper Woman*. However, in a classroom it may be more useful to turn this notion of privilege on its head and to re-use the word in another way: to make the point that it is a privilege to be welcomed into another's realm or sphere of experience and understanding. There is certainly an inherent "invitation" to engage in any published material. However, that material must be properly contextualized and interrogated. If we believe Cameron, she rightly and genuinely entered the circle of Native tradition because she was invited in, purportedly given permission to reproduce and interpret stories, and lastly, but no less importantly, because she is a woman. Some critics will see the use of the Kiki narrator/alter ego as a disguised (although not necessarily well disguised) appropriative voice and statements like the following one by Granny as that sort of pre-emptive deflation of criticism. Cameron writes: "There's gonna be women jump up and start tryin' to make a religion out of it and tryin' to sound like experts and tryin' to feel big and look clever in front of other women. And they'll get tired after a while, and give up, but the truth will still be there for the ones who keep lookin' for it" (144). The truth is, it is not just women who have jumped at these stories, specifically to criticize. St. Peter is correct in her assessment of the situation. She says, "Different people hear differently; more pertinently here, different searchers – and this definitely applies to [Ron] Hamilton [a grandson of one of Cameron's primary informants] and Cameron" (502). She says of Hamilton that it can no longer be ascertained "to what extent he is defending his territory, or his grandmother's stories" (ibid). The point is that it is his right to criticize and defend what he perceives as cultural appropriation or invasion. But his sphere of understanding does not encompass the whole of his grandmother's. There are portions that are unknown to him, but, and this is merely speculation for the sake of argument, perhaps not unknown to Cameron.

In another article, "Fringes, Imposture, and Connection: Armand Garnet Ruffo's *Grey Owl: The Mystery of Archie Belaney* and "Communitist" Literature," I have written at length of Jace Weaver's notion of "communitism... a combination of the words 'community' and 'activism'" because literature "is communitist to the extent that it has a proactive commitment to Native community" (xiii). Again, speaking from the perspective of an engaged reader, that article discusses how *Grey Owl* serves a decidedly utilitarian purpose by thoughtfully examining the need to connect to a culture that is not one's own. Thus, in considering the positioning of Cameron in *Daughters of Copper Woman*, I now turn to *Grey Owl* in order to show how that text consciously addresses notions of cultural appropriation within the central theme of imposture, something *Daughters of Copper Woman* – without the proper contextualization – certainly lacks.

Growing up, I knew Grey Owl in the same way that I knew my Huron-Wendat great-grandfather: through photographs. In Grey Owl's case, there was the famous Karsh photo that hung in the Chateau Laurier's Karsh collection. As for my great-grandfather, there were the many pictures my family had of him. And, like Grey Owl, there were also the many newspaper articles, for he had had a somewhat public profile as Prime Minister Louis St. Laurent's personal aide; he had been known as the Indian who accompanied a Prime Minister around the world. The photographs were, as my family often said, unmistakably Indian; he was, in fact, lovingly referred to as the Cigar Store Indian whenever someone attempted to describe him without the aide of those photographs. But I never saw the Cigar Store Indian in him. He was always the gentleman wearing a three-piece suit in those photos. A wholly costumed Grey Owl, on the other hand, seemed truly unmistakably Indian despite the fact that I knew he was not. He fit the stereotype.

It was this connection to the Grey Owl myth that initially drew me to Ruffo's book. Having read many of the biographies, I was anxious to read a Native perspective. I was pleasantly surprised by Ruffo's approach. As a child I remember struggling with the problem that, though a fraud, Grey Owl had made the transition I could only imagine – to go Indian. That was my first, childish approach to connection to culture. Ruffo hints at possibilities of finding a deeper connection to a culture one may be only tenuously connected to, and this a worthwhile avenue for Native and non-Native scholars alike, but, most importantly, for those readers who turn to literature by Native and mixed-blood Native Canadians for insight into so-called Nativeness. The article explores the important role Grey Owl plays for readers looking to understand their own feelings of imposture when attempting to connect to some aspect of Native culture. Was Grey Owl the ideal Indian, or was it his ability to "go Native" that is the ideal for contemporary Native and mixed-blood Native Canadians? Or, is the message more akin to the repeated offer of kinship proffered by Natives in Ruffo's *Grey Owl*: "Dance with us as you can." (146)?

Working with both archival records and the oral history of his own family's connection to Belaney, Ruffo re-constructs a historical figure in a text that is part fact, part fiction. Ruffo subtly subverts a historically problematic genre: the Indian autobiography or biography. While clearly not autobiography, *Grey Owl* readily employs the actual writings of Belaney/Grey Owl and others, but we are not meant to confuse *Grey Owl*, the object, as writing by Grey Owl or any other of the first person voices within the narrative. However, the prominence given to Grey Owl's writing in the first of the book's two epigraphs is meant to serve as a validation of his role as text-producer and rightfully places him "in the pantheon of nature writers... with Henry David Thoreau, John Muir, Aldo Leopold, and Rachel Carson" (Brower 74). Ruffo's subversion of the Indian autobiography, while not necessarily overt to those unfamiliar with the history of Native literature as a distinct category, is evident on one basic level even before an engagement with the actual text. A quick glance at the author's bio and photo immediately following the narrative's close allows one to pick up on the fact that in this case the author is Native and his subject is non-Native. While Louis Owens has been critical of this extra-textual departure with regard to reviews of his own novels, saying "Do we really need to go beyond 'END' and consider photograph and bio blurb to decide the authenticity of a fiction" (14), I argue that in this case it is a worthy exercise and one that adds, deliberately, to the flavour of the "mystery." The Native writing the story of the non-Native is an immediate send-up of the conventional early Indian biography, and, although Ruffo did not actually converse with Belaney for the book, he does employ excerpts from his journals and gives fictional voice to other undocumented events and so approximates what Arnold Krupat termed the "bi-cultural composite authorship" (262) or co-authoring of the Indian autobiography.

The Indian autobiography has essentially been ignored by literary scholars because, as Krupat notes, "[they] have been presented by the whites who have written them as more nearly 'scientific' documents of the historical or ethnographic type than as 'literary' works" (261) and do not conform to the accepted definition of autobiography as a narrative of a person's life written by that person. Krupat correctly notes that the Indian autobiography is a contradiction in terms. They are "collaborative efforts, jointly produced by some white who translates, transcribes, compiles, edits, interprets, polishes, and ultimately determines the 'form' of the text in writing, and by an Indian who is its 'subject' and whose 'life' becomes the 'content' of the 'autobiography' whose title may bear his 'name'" (262). On a very simple level, since the methodology of autobiography and even biography is limited to the telling of a story, the distance between the White culture's definition of history and a Native definition of history in so far as it applies to these genres should not be too great. After all, the exchange of personal "histories" is an integral part of Native cultural interaction. For example, a traditional greeting ceremony between the Mohawk and Ojibway nations would necessarily involve the exchange of stories that make up each respective group's history. However, because Native cultures do not see history as necessarily progressive and linear or "evolutionary, teleological, or progressive" (Krupat 261) and did not traditionally engage in a written tradition of recording stories as empirical data, the Indian "autobiography" is flawed at its roots because it cannot convey the necessary sense of mutability of story and even personal history. Krupat's essay concerns itself with the importance of treating the traditional Indian autobiography as literature rather than science and it is an important point. His principle of bi-cultural composite authorship at least acknowledges that there was a Native voice despite its diminishment through translation and transcription and the culturally biased notion that the story of one's life as told by oneself (whether independently or in conjunction with another) can be used as historical fact. Whether White or Native, though, the voice can only approximate a perspective.

This issue of voice is an important one to Ruffo's *Grey Owl* because Archie Belaney as Grey Owl was the Native voice in the 1930's, at least to the White world on whose fringes Indians remained. His was an accepted point of view. And although not truly Native, he is essentially the embodiment of Krupat's bi-cultural composite authorship even though he did not work in conjunction with someone who actually belonged to the culture he spoke of – unless we count his relationship with Ruffo's family at Biscotasing and his numerous relationships with women of Native heritage. His life as Grey Owl had no ethnographical or anthropological significance because it was a fiction. As history, too, it is flawed because it necessarily demands that one choose a perspective. In this way, Belaney/Grey Owl, despite the openness with which his fraud is treated by Ruffo, is treated historically in much the same way as many famous Native North Americans. Consider the stories of Geronimo, Sitting Bull, or Cochise, whose words Belaney memorized as a child ("Influences" 2). Only until recently with the advent of revisionist movements, the kind that would see the influential Canadian poet Duncan Campbell Scott as a racist assimilationist and necessitate a re-examination of his poetry (specifically his "Indian" poems), have these stories been told from a Native perspective.

While there was considerable scandal concerning Belaney's unmasking ("Since the death of Grey Owl a remarkable conflict of opinion has arisen over his parentage, particularly regarding his Indian blood. *London Times*, April 21, 1938" (Ruffo 207)), he has been treated relatively kindly by history, even by those who insist on concentrating on his ruse. Consider the excerpts from news reports that Ruffo closes with: "The chances are that Archie Belaney could not have done nearly such effective work for conservation of wildlife under his own name. It is an odd commentary, but true enough. *Ottawa Citizen*, April 20, 1938... What, after all does his ancestry matter? The essential facts about his life are not in dispute, for as a conservation officer under the Canadian Government, and as a lecturer and broadcaster in Great Britain, he worked unceasingly for the protection of wild life. *Liverpool Daily Post*, April 21, 1938... His attainments as a writer and naturalist will survive and when in later years our children's children are told of the strange masquerade – if it was a masquerade – their wonder and their appreciation will grow. *Winnipeg Tribune*, April 23, 1938" (Ruffo 207). This last passage is particularly telling and no surprise that Ruffo ends with it. It is surprising, however, that the conservative *Winnipeg Tribune*, like the *Ottawa Citizen* and *London Times*, should justify his fraud at all, but not surprising that they do so in this manner. His deception is acceptable, they imply, because it was for a good cause. Only the *Winnipeg Tribune* alludes to what Ruffo has similarly been alluding to all along: "if it was a masquerade," or, more succinctly put, if it was simply a masquerade. Now, of course, this passage has been taken out of context and the original did not have the benefit of some sixty years of hindsight, but the reference to "children's children" is important. Ruffo is one of these children as it was his great-grandparents' families that "adopted" Belaney. However, the newspaper article's reference to children was likely to those of its White readership and not inclusive of Natives. Throughout, Ruffo has subverted this and has made the last line a link to the Grey Owl epigraph that opens the book:

> The trail then is not merely a connecting link between widely distant points, it becomes an idea, and a symbol of self-sacrifice and deathless determination, an ideal to be lived up to, a creed from which none may falter.

Within the context of its original, this reference to "the trail" is a concrete one, although it is certainly mystified by Grey Owl.

Here, though, as the textual introduction to Ruffo's narrative, it must be read in a different light. The fact that the word connection appears here is immediately significant, and the trail as symbol of the need to find one's way between two points – places, states of being – resonates heavily within the text where this subject matter is more overtly verbalized. Even the use of the word "distant" carries weight. It echoes the distance Krupat notes exists between the White and Native cultures.

Like Krupat's definition of the Indian autobiography, Grey Owl's life and writing live up to the notion that, as Bill Ashcroft et al. write, "the text creates the reality of the Other in the guise of describing it, [and] although [it] cannot operate as ethnography,... the literary text... is not the site of shared mental experience and should not be seen as such" (59). However, Ruffo's narrative, despite spending little time on Belaney's life within the Native community at Biscotasing, subtly works to show the kinship between Belaney's perception of the Indian and Ruffo's own. This is accomplished by Ruffo's piecing together of authentic Belaney/Grey Owl writings and fictionalizing others. Except in Belaney's own mind, the severity of his fraud is never truly played out within the narrative. One would assume that his fraud would elicit a much stronger response from both the Native and non-Native camps. One might at least expect Native groups to have voiced concern as it is made clear by Ruffo that "an Indian can tell who's Indian" ("John Tootoosis, 1936" 128). But Ruffo takes a distinctly different direction with *Grey Owl* in two sections, both titled "John Tootoosis, 1936": "An Indian can tell who's Indian./Grey Owl can't sing or dance./But he's doing good/and when we meet/I call him brother" (128) and, later:

> We know Wa-Sha-Quon-Asin is not born of us, and we say nothing. For us it is of no importance. We do not waste our words but save them, because we know in this struggle of generations they are our strongest medicine. The man flies for us true and sharp, and we are thankful he has chosen our side. While we cheer, and the elders nod in approval, we can see the light shine in his face. We can see he feels better about himself than before. This is good. This is how it should be, to feel good about yourself and your duty in the honourable way. Wa-Sha-Quon-Asin, we say, dance with us, as you can. (145-6)

Voice is further complicated by an extra-textual, untitled poem that follows the book's two epigraphs but precedes the section titled

"Beginning"; it contains the first example of Ruffo's use of the second-person, "you," which here seems not to be an address to the implied reader as within the text but rather to a writer, historian, storyteller that may or may not be Ruffo. It begins:

> Archival memory.
> Paper brittle as autumn, unearthed
> across the desk, files scattered.
> Words floating like smoke
> smell of moccasins you are wearing
> warming of the bright neon,
> carrying you on
> to the beginning
> It is past midnight, everyone
> is gone, except uniformed security
> and you – What is it you are digging for
> exactly? (iv)

This an interesting decision by Ruffo, who is otherwise absent in the tradition of the biographer or Krupat's autobiographer. Clearly, though, we are meant to see that there is a connection between author and subject. When that unspecified narrator says "one day/you will catch him," the "you" could apply to anyone who has been introduced to the Archie Belaney/Grey Owl mystery and who has seen the photograph of Archie as a child, or to this persona in charge of putting together the story. Similarly, when Grey Owl says, "You in the audience who sit in expectation cannot know./This fear, this inexorable fear, I take with me" ("Grey Owl, 1935" 104), the address could be to the implied reader of his journals or could be seen to be working on another level, with Ruffo, or the narrator of that prefacing poem, again addressing his implied reader. The real, historical connection between Ruffo and Belaney and a story about Belaney's need to connect with the culture of Ruffo's heritage is a complicated and cleverly disguised examination of his own or any connection to cultural heritage. His ambiguous address to an unspecified "you" allows other like-minded readers to explore the troubling issue of connection to Native heritage. A truly cultural component exists, then, to Krupat's bi-cultural composite authorship. Ruffo has made the making of Belaney's story his story. As such, this narrative line can be seen as an example of what Weaver defines as "the struggle to be self-defining" (44) in that Ruffo's use of Belaney's "history" as an exploration of a theme – connection to culture – speaks directly to a Native experience.

To many young people of Native heritage, Grey Owl was more successful as an authentic Indian than they could ever imagine themselves to be. Of course, the question of authenticity is further complicated in that Grey Owl is part of Ruffo's heritage; it was his Ojibway family that "adopted" Belaney. Why should he, then, or we, not look to Grey Owl as both a professional and cultural example? The answer for both may be because Belaney was an impostor. But it is this notion of impostor that Ruffo deconstructs. That feeling of not belonging or being an impostor is a real and valid emotion that contemporary Native writers deal with regularly, particularly with regard to the mixing of White and Native cultures and the issue of mixed cultural backgrounds.

We can complete the circle here with a return to Drew Hayden Taylor and his "Pretty Like a White Boy," a personal essay that deals with the difficulty of growing up as a status Indian who looks White:

> In this big, huge world, with all its billions and billions of people, it's safe to say that everybody will eventually come across personalities and individuals that will touch them in some peculiar yet poignant way. Individuals that in some way represent and help define who you are. I'm no different, mine was Kermit the Frog. Not just because Natives have a long tradition of savouring frogs' legs, but because of his music. If you all may remember, Kermit is quite famous for his rendition of 'It's Not Easy Being Green.' I can relate. If I could sing, my song would be 'It's Not Easy Having Blue Eyes in a Brown Eyed Village.' (436)

While I may be guilty of continuing the cycle of turning every issue into a philosophical debate by using *Daughters of Copper Woman* and its peripheral issues as pieces in a larger puzzle, there is a personal investment in this endeavour. Others may find varying degrees of use for such a discussion, in the same way that my symbolic connection to Grey Owl pales (pun intended) in comparison to Ruffo's own. What I have tried to illustrate is the difficult and ambiguous nature of connection. No matter how useful my model is, it still is limited in its scope. It does not allow me, my mother, or my grandmother to navigate the boundaries imposed by ourselves or by others any easier. What I have come to realize is that I am beginning to become comfortable "moving over" when my circle of experience and understanding no longer overlaps those that inform a particular discourse. So, rather than being an unconscious (or, more dangerously, a conscious) decision to act from a position of privilege, it is a respectful act. That does not mean it is a permanent action. If anything, it is simply a resistance to give in to the impulse to "teach rather than listen" (Alcoff 24). These are hard lessons to be learned from an even more difficult, but rewarding, obstacle course. While of extreme importance to know one's own position and positionality, it is as necessary to know and attempt to understand others,' and not just to survive one of Angel and Colleen's dinner parties.

Notes

1. Lee Maracle makes a similar demand in her article "Moving Over." See Work Cited.

2. Again, Alcoff's parameters are extremely useful. The other three are: "1. The impetus to speak must be carefully analyzed and, in many cases (certainly for academics!), fought against... 2. Speaking should always carry with it an accountability and responsibility for what one says... 3. In order to evaluate attempts to speak for others in particular instances, we need to analyze the probable or actual effects of the words on the discursive and material context" (25-6).

Works Cited

Alcoff, Linda. (Winter 1991-92) "The Problem of Speaking for Others." *Cultural Critique*. 20: 5-32.

Ashcroft, Bill, Gareth Griffiths, and Helen Tiffin. (1989) "The Empire Writes Back: Theory and Practice." *Post-Colonial Literatures*. London: Routledge.

Boynton, Victoria. (Spring/Summer 1996) "Desire's Revision: Feminist Appropriation of Native American Traditional Stories." *Modern Language Studies*. 26: 2-3, 53-71.

Brower, Kenneth. (Jan. 1990) "Grey Owl." *Atlantic Monthly*. 74-80.

Cameron, Anne. (1981) *Daughters of Copper Woman*. Vancouver: Press Gang Publishers.

Dewar, Jonathan R. (2001) "Fringes, Imposture, and Connection: Armand Garnet Ruffo's *Grey Owl: The Mystery of Archie Belaney* and 'Communitist' Literature." *Creating Community: A Roundtable on Canadian Aboriginal Literatures*. Brandon, Manitoba: Bearpaw Publishing.

Emberley, Julia V. (1993) *Thresholds of Difference: Feminist Critique, Native Women's Writings, Postcolonial Theory*. Toronto: U Toronto Press.

Krupat, Arnold. (1983) "The Indian Autobiography: Origins, Type, and Function." *Smoothing the Ground: Essays on Native American Oral Literature*. Ed. Brian Swann. Berkeley: U California Press. 261-282.

Maracle, Lee. (Spring 1989) "Moving Over." *Trivia*. 14: 9-12.

Mohanty, Satya. (January 1995) "Colonial Legacies, Multicultural Futures: Relativism, Objectivity, and the Challenge of Otherness." *PMLA*. 110(1): 108-118.

Morley, Patricia. (February 1982) *"Daughters of Copper Woman."* *Quill & Quire*. 48: 43.

Owens, Louis. (1998) *Mixedblood Messages: Literature, Film, Family, Place*. Norman, OK: U Oklahoma Press.

Ruffo, Armand Garnet. (1996) *Grey Owl: The Mystery of Archie Belaney*. Regina: Coteau Books.

St. Peter, Christine. (1989) "'Woman's Truth' and the Native Tradition: Anne Cameron's *Daughters of Copper Woman*." *Feminist Studies*. 15(3): 499-523.

Taylor, Drew Hayden. (2000) *alterNatives*. Burnaby, BC: Talon Books.

— . (1998) "Pretty Like a White Boy: The Adventures of a Blue Eyed Ojibway." *An Anthology of Canadian Literature in English*. Ed. Daniel David Moses and Terry Goldie. Toronto: Oxford University Press. 436-439.

Twigg, Alan. (June 1982) "Nanaimo's Favorite Daughter: Eloquent and Immovable." *Quill & Quire*. 48: 38.

Weaver, Jace. (1997) *That the People Might Live: Native American Literatures and Native American Community*. New York: Oxford University Press.

Let's Vote Who is Most Authentic!
Politics of Identity
in Contemporary Sami Literature

Rauna Kuokkanen

Introduction

In mainstream literature, the well-known image of the Sami[1] has been created by non-Sami writers. Since the 18th century, explorers, scientists and other adventurers have been visiting *Sápmi* (Samiland) and other northern areas in Europe, and have written books about their experiences. They have described both the fabulous nature and the people living in the region. According to these books, the Sami are small, dark, filthy and ugly with slanted eyes, flat noses and high cheekbones. They are as calm as their reindeer, hospitable, frank, modest, healthy and happy people whose only bad habit is drinking too much alcohol. By these explorers, the Sami were admired for their freedom and unspoilt nature, reflecting Rousseau's notions of "the Noble Savage." These descriptions by non-Sami visitors also created the persistent myth that only the reindeer herding Sami are the real Sami (see e.g. Nousiainen).

Even in Finland, school children were reading similar stories about the Sami as late as the 1950's and 1960's. Sakari Topelius, the respected 'story-teller of all Finland,' described the Sami in his famous book *Maamme-kirja* (1954, Our Land), which was used as a text book in all Finnish primary schools, as follows:

> In summer time, a Lapp village is not a pleasant sight. Everywhere on the ground one can see fish bowels, fish scales, rotten fish and other garbage, which contaminates the air. From the low doorways of the tents crawls a group of people covered by dirt. They themselves are not bothered at all... [the] Lapp's body is short, the forehead low, eyes small and cheekbones prominent. By nature he is slow, melancholic and morose. He is blamed to be envious, relentless and shrewd, but others thank his good heart, his hospitability and chaste behaviour, when he is not tempted by alcohol. (Topelius 118-9)[2]

These images based merely on the physical appearance of the Sami and quick notions of their nature after a short acquaintance have spread all over the world and are still the basis of stereotypical attitudes and biased views of the Sami, even in the countries within whose borders the Sami live today. These stereotypes are not only incorrect but they may also have an impact on the formation of a person's Sami identity by creating false demands of 'authenticity.'

Due to the powerful stereotypes, the images of the Sami people created by Sami themselves are overlooked. In this article, my intention is to study the representations of Sami identity in contemporary Sami literature, as it both reflects and creates reality in various ways. For this study, I have chosen writings from four Sami writers: Kirsti Paltto, Jovnna-Ánde Vest, Inger-Mari Aikio and Kerttu Vuolab. Three of the writers are female and one is male. All are from the Finnish side of *Sápmi* and three are from the Deatnu Valley. These divisions effectively represent the current situation in Sami literature: most contemporary Sami writers come from the Finnish side of *Sápmi*, particularly from *Vuovdaguoika* in the Deatnu Valley. This might be the result of the strong and lively storytelling tradition of the region and also thanks to the influence of Hans-Aslak Guttorm, a writer who also taught at the local school.

Definitions of Literature

Literature is the storage of human being's knowledge, understanding and inventiveness. It is also the foundation stone of humanity, survival, language and learning skills. Outsiders used to think that the Sami did not have literature before our first books were published. But we have had our own literature since time immemorial and we still have a rich oral storytelling tradition. (Kerttu Vuolab 1995:27)

One of the most persistent prejudices in the Western literary canon is that only certain categories of experience can be recognized as 'literature' (Ashcroft et al. 88). We have learned that literature means written books and that the existence of literature is a sign of a 'civilized' people. For peoples on the margins, writing has often been a political and social act and its collective dimension has been significant. Minority and Indigenous writers have often stressed their critical and oppositional relationship towards mainstream societies. Paula Gunn Allen, a Pueblo-Laguna writer, has said that

> literature is one facet of a culture. The significance of a
> literature can be best understood in terms of the culture
> from which it springs, and the purpose of literature is clear
> only when the reader understands and accepts the assump-
> tions on which the literature is based. (Allen 54)

Within the Western tradition, written literature is regarded as a crucial step towards 'a civilized society' entering the sphere of
'culture.' What precedes written literature is only the folklore of a
'people of nature.' For many Indigenous scholars, however, using
the concept 'literature' to refer only to written texts implies judging everything else – the whole storytelling tradition – as being
subordinate to written forms. If literature is to be redefined from
the Indigenous point of view, oral traditions must be included since
they play a crucial role also in contemporary writing. Agnes Grant
for instance defines North American Native literature as "Native
people telling their own stories in their own ways, unfettered by
criteria from another time and place" (Grant 124).

Evolving Sami Literature

> When we speak of Sami art, it's worth remembering that
> we have our own cultural background, but that we have
> adopted a quantity of words from neighbouring nations –
> words like war and hell – and art and artists... Walls used
> to be unknown in the Sami culture, and nobody hung up
> pictures. When you think how heavy books are, they're not
> the first thing one puts into one's supply bag when one
> heads for the mountains to herd reindeer. (Valkeapää 58-9)

Sami literature has always reflected, in its own specific ways, social phenomena and responded to them. In the history of Sami literature, two upward trends can be seen which are clearly connected to historical events of Samiland. The birth of written Sami
fiction and the press occurred in the early 20th century when the
actions of the states and the pressure of dominant societies aroused
tensions between settlers and the Sami. The Sami writers of that
time, such as Anders Larsen, Matti Aikio, Johan Turi and Pedar
Jalvi described the prevailing conditions of Samiland in various
ways (Lehtola 40).

In the initial stages of written Sami literature, the Sami lan-
guage has been crucial in the struggle against cultural alienation.
For some writers, it has been the most important reason to write.
According to the late writer and teacher Hans-Aslak Guttorm, it is

possible to describe Sami culture *only* in the Sami language, because an individual's experience 'lives' in the words of the person's mother tongue (ibid. 49). Most of today's Sami writers could
not agree more with Guttorm who is considered a connecting link
between Sami oral and written traditions. Thus, contemporary
Sami literature is still written in the Sami language (with the exception of few writers) despite all the odds the writers are faced
with.[3]

Since most current Sami writers did not receive their education
in Sami, they have been forced to learn to write in their mother
tongue in later life. Their readership is quite small (although eager)
because many Sami are not able nor used to reading their Sami; a
factor complicated by the fact that a common North Sami orthog-
raphy was not established until 1979. The few Sami publishing
houses (Davvi Girji, Dat and Sámi Girjjit) that exist are so starved
of funding that some of the *Sápmi*'s best known writers are forced
to publish their own material. Lack of funding makes the publishing process very slow, as writers usually have to wait a year or two
to see their manuscripts realized as books. In spite of the difficulties Sami writers experience writing in their mother tongue, there
is no indication that they are willing to change their language of
expression. The reason for writing in Sami is the maintenance of
the Sami language as a strong and living language. There have also
been some institutional attempts at improving the current situation:
the Sami Council, for instance, has an on-going campaign to en-
courage people to read more Sami literature. Moreover, Sami educational institutions have also arranged courses for Sami adults to
learn reading and writing in their mother tongue.

Sami women were at the vanguard of the breakthrough in contemporary Sami literature in the 1970's and the 1980's. The first
Sami woman writer was Kirsti Paltto with her short story collection based on traditional storytelling called *Soagŋu* (1971, Marriage Proposal). After her, many other Sami women started to
write, particularly poetry and stories for children. The most prominent Sami woman writers include Kirsti Paltto, Rauni-Magga Lukkari, Elle-Márjá Vars, Inger-Mari Aikio and Kerttu Vuolab. The
first Sami novel, *Árbeeatnan luohti* (The Yoik[4] of the Inherited
Land) was published in 1981 and was written by Eino Guttorm.
Until then, Sami writers were educated people who left their
homes to go to study in larger towns in the south, and thereby were
forced to negotiate their Saminess in new ways and to find new
ways of expression. Eino Guttorm was the first writer who stayed

in his own environment and started to write from that position (ibid. 48).

Nils-Aslak Valkeapää also started writing in the early 1970's. He has written several poetry collections which have been translated into many languages (Finnish, Norwegian, English, German). He is also a musician and visual artist, a 'multi-artist' who does not want to be put into any particular category. *Beaivi, áhčážan* (*The Sun, My Father* 1997), which is a collage of poems and historical photographs, was published in 1988. For six years, Valkeapää collected photographs of Sami from museums across Europe and America for the book, which is a conscious attempt to create a Sami national epic. It can also be read as a creation story; the poems and pictures start from the time before the existence of human beings and ends with death. Moreover, it is a polemical statement on Sami rights and a Sami history and interpretation of colonialism.

Kirsti Paltto: Let's vote who is the most authentic!

Since the early 1970's, Kirsti Paltto has written poems, short stories, stories for children, theatre and radio plays and other writings concerning many different elements of Sami culture. In 1987, she published her first novel *Guhtoset dearvan min bohccot* (Pasture in Peace, My Reindeer), which tells about a Sami village just before the Second World War. The Finnish translation *Voijaa minun poroni* (1986) was shortlisted as a candidate for Finlandia literature prize in 1986. The sequel novel *Guržo luottat* (Tracks of the Omen, translated in Finnish *Juokse nyt naalin poika* 1993) came out in 1991.

Paltto's books are deeply rooted in Sami traditions. They are based on description of a whole community. For this kind of storytelling, common amongst Indigenous peoples' literature, she has been criticized for 'fragmented' and 'unfinished' works (Aikio 1987). On the other hand, it has been claimed that Paltto's novels are structured like a Western novel "and thus falls much more easily into a class of European literature than just Sami literature" (Dana 1995:8). According to the writer herself, it is only the structure which might resemble Western models; otherwise the novels clearly follow the Sami storytelling tradition (personal comment 1995; see also Dana 8).

Paltto's novel *256 Golláža* (1992, 256 Golden Coins) is a satirical work of fiction about a people who call themselves '*orbbežat*' (Orphans) and who live far up north beneath Ursa Major[5] on an island called *Goddesáhpánoaivi* (Lemming Top). According to one anthropologist, they call themselves 'orbbežat' because they feel like lonely orphans on that far north island, in the middle of the Arctic Ocean's floating ice. Near *Goddesáhpánoaivi*, there are three other islands which are also inhabited by *orbbežat*. These four islands are not independent states as larger states have already marked each island to themselves a long time ago. These four states are called *Hoašša* (*Equisetaceae* species, cf. Sami word Ruošša for Russia), *Suorbma* (Finger, cf. Sami word Suopma for Finland), *Ruolla* (Evil, cf. Sami word Ruotta for Sweden) and *Nordalas* (Nudger, cf. Sami word Norga for Norway).

256 Golláža is a detective story set at the end of the 20th century and as the prologue tells it, it is a story about money, or rather about the lack of it, and what happens when the big world starts roaring in *Bollomohkki*, a village on *Goddesáhpánoavi* Island. One November morning a young man called Bieraš is woken up early in the midst of winter's darkest and coldest season. The phone call is from the panic stricken municipality treasurer Begá claiming all the municipality's savings have been stolen. Only the empty box where the 256 Golden Coins were held has been found in the middle of Begá's office. Bieraš is asked to work as a detective to find the thief – according to Begá, the police cannot be brought in yet, as there are important guests from *Ovttastuvvan Jurohpa Stáhtain* (Integrated European States)[6] visiting *Bollomohkki* and the ensuing public chaos would have a negative impact on the guests.

The tone of the story is highly sarcastic and critical of both home and the 'big world' outside. At the same time, the story is overtly humorous: some of the characters gain comical features and the central theme of the novel, the search for the 256 Golden Coins, becomes a farce: the money was eaten by the cleaner's dog. But there are also serious, sorrowful elements in the story. It represents the current situation in *Sápmi* in a very straightforward way covering issues such as self-determination, the expansion of tourism onto the traditional reindeer grazing lands, the language, land title and human rights, nature conservation, use of natural resources, the activities of researchers, the controversial role of Christianity and the exotic 'Wild North.' There are (at least) two groups whose interests clash: those "backward fanatics who want to be even more backward" and those who run after development and money – themes in many Indigenous peoples' societies. Moreover, as it becomes clear in the book, the division is not simply a Sami – non-Sami one.

Saminess in Paltto's novel *256 Golláža* is extremely multifaceted: on one hand, there are old people who are afraid of "Natural Development:"

> You need to believe that we orbbeš people won't exist anymore in this world, if we don't start protecting and defending ourselves. I don't like this tourism nonsense. They don't belong here. I'm already an old man and I know how orbbeš people used to live in a way that they survived in this tough world. Our life is in peace, in the lap of the forest, the hills, the rivers and the lakes. The big world will drown us and our life. They coach us into a too easy life and we won't go up to the mountains as we used to. In the cold weather, young people don't dare to go outside the house. And without a snowmobile they can't get anywhere no matter how good the weather is. They can hardly ski. That's why I hold a different opinion. (68)

On the other, there are the modern, educated 'traditionalists' who promote the culture, language and Sami values and who demand land rights and public services in their mother tongue. Some even dream about their own state:

> I know that some dream about an independent orbbeš state, Begá flared up. I guess you too. But we can't push time backwards, whatever comes. We will stay within the Suorpma state and other orbbeš will stay within the states where they belong. A new time has arrived – also for Goddesáhpánoaivi and orbbeš fanatics shouldn't try to get us back into the goahti[7] time. Do you understand? (*Paltto* 44)

There are also those like *Begá*, 'red apples,' according to whom the orbbeš language is not worth the paper it is written upon (*Paltto* 161). There are also non-Sami 'wanna-bes' who want to learn the language, probably even find a reindeer herding man and start making Sami handicrafts and helping at the reindeer round-ups. There is an interesting conversation between Bieraš and two non-Sami women one night after coming from the bar:

> 'Are orbbeš language and orbbeš life so holy that no outsider can touch them?' Pirjo got annoyed.
> 'Oh no, for my part I don't mind!' Bieraš waved with his hand. 'Dear Pirjo, for my part you can be whatever you want. But wouldn't you let me also be what I want? If you want to be orbbeš, nobody will prevent that.'

'That's not true! There are also those who don't want us to become orbbeš,' said Ánná-Liisse.

'Like who?' Bieraš doubted.

'Those model orbbeš people who have one suorbmalaš parent or grandparent.

Those types who try to watch orbbeš people's blood.'

'Do those kind of people exist?' Pirjo asked.

'They do!' Ánná-Liisse was getting angry.

'I say only that our language and life aren't toys which can be grabbed when you feel like and then thrown away when not interested anymore. At least my language and life are one with my blood and the whole body. That is not anything that can be dragged around or traded, that's all I can say.' (*Paltto* 129-130)

As Paltto suggests in her novel, Sami society is not homogeneous nor is it without conflicts. The Sami are not a peaceful, humble people living in harmony with nature or with each other. She also discusses the 'right' Saminess: through the character of Bieraš, she considers what it might be and asks "why don't they organize an election on who is the most authentic orbbeš" (*Paltto* 32). Bieraš himself is an unemployed young man who has been living away from his hometown and has returned only recently. Back home, he feels he is an outsider, a strange bird, although according to himself, he is a frank person who neither schemes nor pretends. In *Bollomohkki*, he has few upon whom he can rely; there are too many who just want to trade gossip about your property or your family – it seems that everybody is a product of one's family and tied to those qualities forever. According to him, people in the village do not seem to care much about other people's thoughts, feelings and values or if someone is in trouble or hurt by the cold-hearted world. What really matters is physical appearance. In *Bollomohkki*, your value depends on your clothes and your car – even owning a house is not considered as important as owning a car.

Paltto's novel is a realistic representation of Sami society. After coming out, it was considered by some critics a protest against the European Union. For others, the story was too critical and too close to the bone. Yet as Paltto points out, the reality is often more complex than the idealistic and sometimes even romantic notions of harmony. Perhaps the best strategy of resistance in Paltto's novel is a certain kind of double communication: a reader can take it as an entertaining story that makes fun of municipality and EU politics and their politicians (both Sami and non-Sami), as a joke about the prevalent situation of Sami society or as protest literature and an oppositional stand against the current state of affairs.

Paltto is critical towards everyone by using the power of laughter. Many Indigenous writers maintain that a unique sense of humour, scintillating satire and dry understatements combined with a twinkle in the eye are the strongest weapons in the cultural struggle against assimilation (e.g. Awiakta 210-1). We have to learn to laugh at our oppressors but also at ourselves, even in grief.

Jovnna-Ánde Vest: The Big World Makes You Excited

Jovnna Ánde Vest was born in Roavvesavvon, in the Deatnu Valley but currently lives in Paris. His first autobiographical novel *Čáhcegáddái nohká boazobálggis* (The Reindeer Path Ends by the River) was published in 1988. In the novel, Vest describes his family and particularly his father from the 1950's to the 1970's. Central to the novel is the writer's examination of the father-son relationship. Everyday life on the Deatnu River is also represented in a very vivid manner. Veli-Pekka Lehtola writes:

> Where 'people of nature' have been seen especially in ethnographic and ethnologic descriptions as solidly traditional and practical, even one-sided people, Vest draws an entirely opposite picture of his father. His hero, 'Little-Vest' is a Deatnu Sami, who instead of everyday work, gets excited in everything new and unpractical like a child. (67)

Through his father and the rest of his family, Vest describes the modernization of *Sápmi* after the Second World War. Vest's father is the first one to buy a tractor in the region. Later the motorbike and the camera also come into the picture. The change from a traditional way of life to a modernized one was not easy in *Sápmi* and, in his novel, Vest illustrates clearly how it was faced by one family (ibid, 67-8).

His second novel, *Kapteainna ruvsu* (The Captain's Rose), which I have chosen for this paper, was published in 1991 and differs radically from Vest's first novel. *Kapteainna ruvsu* is located far away from Samiland, in the 'New World' behind the 'Big Ocean.' It is a story about Kapo, a Sami man, who as a child dreams of going to see the big world. Kapo is a descendant of the famous *Guovža-Dávvet* who had arrived in Kapo's home region from the East and gradually gained wealth and fame as a healer. During fishing trips with his father, young Kapo loves hearing everything about his great-grandfather but also his father's stories from abroad which he has learnt during his times on a fishing boat. A strange longing fills young Kapo's mind when he hears about people living on other continents on the other side of the world. He decides that one day he will leave *Dávvetnjárga*, his home, and its simple life (Vest 18).

When that day finally comes, he signs upon an old ship called the Esmeralda. He spends a few years working hard and sometimes even doubting whether he has made the right decision in leaving his home. Later, he ends up in a city in the 'New World,' not really knowing what he will do on this new continent. He ends up in a cozy little guesthouse called Madam Sally's Oasis. Madam Sally, a friendly woman feeling sorry for this strange backpacker, helps him adjust to his new life. She easily arranges citizenship for him, helps him with shopping and gives him a job as the guesthouse janitor:

> That man has lots to learn, the hostess thought. First, he has to buy proper city clothing and leave those ugly patched rags behind. And if he just takes care of himself a bit, it might even be possible to make a man out of him.
> Well-meaning Sally wanted to help the permanent guest even more when she saw how unskilled and incapable he was. He was not like the others who came from beyond the seas who immediately started looking for work and worrying about the future. But Kapo – the poor fellow was like God's bird who does not worry about the next day. (Vest 49)

At the guesthouse there is also a cook, a young woman called Nelly McCullish whose parents came to the 'New World' when she was very young. She is a lively, cheerful red haired woman and a hardworking and diligent cook, whose presence in the guesthouse is received with great pleasure. Since their very first acquaintance, Nelly makes Kapo feel restless and soon he is in love with her. After some problems with Sally, who behaves possessively as if Nelly was her daughter for whom only the best man was enough (and Kapo is definitely not that), Nelly and Kapo get married and start the family life. For many years, Kapo has dreamt of having a son who will be named Paul David, after the Captain of the Esmeralda and Kapo's great-grandfather *Guovža-Dávvet*. He has also thought of speaking his mother tongue to his son in order to have proper chats without the need of trying to remember strange words. Life does not however give him a son, but rather a daughter named Sally Elisabeth to whom, for some reason, Kapo does not speak his own language. One day, he thinks, he will teach her a few words.

In the 'New World' Kapo also learns the meaning of money. With the help of money, Sally arranges his stay in the country. "Money is so powerful here that you can get almost everything" Sally explains to Kapo (Vest 51), teaching him to take his savings to the bank:

> He flips it, wonders at the stamp with an eagle's picture. And that strange number. Into that fit everything he owned. For the first time in his life he wanted to become rich. Get rich! Get rich! there was a voice in his mind. Lots of money and possessions! Kapo was also caught by the lust for money, which made people run. (Vest 54-55)

Saminess is not mentioned once in *Kapteainna ruvsu*. Kapo, the main character, does not speculate about his identity nor do others ask him about it. Kapo does not miss his home back in *Dávvetnjárga*, yet he is not fully satisfied with his present life either. He does not complain, but he thinks that it would be nice to have somebody to speak with in his own mother tongue. Despite this, he does not teach the language to his child which is probably because of the outside pressure felt by many Sami in non-Sami speaking environments. There are, however, a few glimpses of Kapo's 'difference' from city people:

> But there was one thing on which they could not agree. The woman was a city person and as such she used to rambling in all kinds of shopping malls and shops. There she used to look at nice things, compare prices and consider if it was worth buying or really needed. It could take hours in a large shopping mall. At the end, Kapo felt dizzy, his knees became sore and his eyes could hardly see the bright beauty. (Vest 129)

Instead of nicknacks in the shopping malls, Kapo pays attention and recognizes people's moods and their physical condition. These skills seem to be inherited from *Guovža-Dávvet* who paid attention to every small landmark in order to survive in nature. From nature, he used to read directions and was also able to see from other small things whether it would be sunny or rainy (Vest 94). Kapo has left his Saminess behind but nevertheless has retained some characteristics which remind him of his background. His Saminess resides in his traits and in his outlook. Others consider him to be 'different,' a simple and unmannerly man who first is under Sally's and later under Nelly's control.

Vest's novel is storytelling without extraordinary events. It could be considered a self-conscious, self-healing story for the writer himself living far from *Sápmi* as he does. In many ways, Kapo is an example of an urban Sami living outside Samiland. Others struggle with their identities asking and questioning their Saminess, others become assimilated and do not want to identify themselves as Sami for various reasons. In a way, assimilation could also be seen as a survival strategy, a response to the outside pressures particularly if they become too overwhelming to resist.

Inger-Mari Aikio: Words are Nourishment

Inger-Mari Aikio was born in *Buolmatjávri*, the northernmost village within Finnish borders. Her first poetry book *Gollebiekkat almmi dievva* (Sky Full of Golden Clouds) came out in 1989. Since then she has published two poetry collections: *Jiehki vuolde ruonas giŋŋa* (1992, The Green Spring Under the Glacier) and *Silkeguobbara lákca* (1996, The Cream of a Silky Mushroom). Her poetry is concise and it rarely deals directly with questions of Saminess. Like Jovnna-Ánde Vest, she has admitted her inability to reflect traditional Saminess and values (Lehtola 71).

In Aikio's poetry, nature's presence is palpable. The way she deals with the surrounding environment is one of the most striking features of her writing. Taking a closer look at a few poems from her collection *Gollebiekkat almmi dievva,* I will particularly consider the relationship between the poet and nature and how her words evoke nature. The first poem is both a wish and a love poem, where creatures of nature are part of the two people's relationship. *Bižus* (Golden Plover, *Pluvialis apricaria*) is a common bird up in the cloudberry swamps of Sápmi, whose whistle follows you everywhere:

vare moai oktii	if we once
salošeimme duoddar alde	could embrace atop the fell
allin ja áidna olmmožin	high and as a single person
boaimmáža biškkanas	scream of eagle
guhkes máidnasa álgun	beginning a tale
bihčosa luohti viidnin.	yoik of bižus like wine
njála suollemas geahčastat	sly look of Arctic fox
bálggisin vilges balvvaid	pathway to the white clouds'
čábbaseamos máidnasii.	beauteous tale. (8)

In this poem, the central element is a wish to become one with the person she loves. Despite the theme of love between two human beings, nature plays a significant role in this relationship. The poet wants to become *as a single person*. Although the reference is made to a human being, there is also the possibility of a desire to become one with nature. Different elements of nature are part of her experience and feelings of love; they also show the *pathway to the white clouds' beauteous tale*.

The following poem is a critique of the disastrous effects on the land caused by human beings:

jurddašmeahttun giehta	thoughtless hand
gaikkoda soahkelastta.	rips off a birch leaf.
gihpu coahkká	pain pulses
rukses bárrun.	like a red wave.
oasážat gahččet eatnamii	little shreds fall onto earth,
isket njammat goiki suonaide	try to suck into their drying veins
beaivváža dálkkodan suolnni	dew which the sun has healed. (22)

In the poem, a person deliberately violates nature: a human hand rips a leaf from a birch. The pain caused by this act is illustrated in a very tangible manner: it is a red wave, like blood bleeding from a wound. It is the concrete pain of nature which we often ignore although we can see it. This reflects the idea that human beings are hurting nature with their actions, ignorance, pollution and technology. The only cure nature can receive is the sun's medicated dew. Although Aikio does not consider herself an activist in the traditional sense (Kailo & Helander 78), she can still sympathize with the pain caused to nature. Perhaps her accusations are hidden; without finger pointing the reader can still sense nature's pain.

The following poem is about *skábma*, the winter season when the sun does not rise above the horizon, and about the seemingly quiet nature:

seavdnjadasa gufihtariid	candles in the eyes
čalmmiin gintalat	of the *gufihtars* of darkness
dorkkas skilžžit.	ice drops in fur.
geahppa skilla	a light tingle
duottarravddain.	in the fells.
násttit savkkástallet	stars whispering
gižahit buollaša.	creaking the cold.
lihkastat bulžu	movement freezes
varra jávohuvvá	blood quiets down
dušše vuorddanas coahkká.	nothing but expectation pulsating. (26)

The poem is visually very intense. It is not difficult to see the image she is drawing in front of the reader's eyes or even to hear the light tingle or feel the cold. She also makes a reference to Sami oral tradition, to *"gufihtars,"* who are the underground people who resemble the Sami in many ways.

In these three poems by Inger-Mari Aikio, the permanent presence of nature is outright. It is expressed in the atmosphere and images that she creates, but also through her use of words: they are natural and concrete. Her poems are sprinkled with only a few abstract words and only a few words refer to human beings. In most of her poems, nature's presence is an inseparable part of the atmosphere she creates. Many times, her writing resembles a certain kind of animism where nature and the human being become one, or at least the border between these two elements is very vague. In Aikio's poems it is difficult to say where nature ends and the human being appears: "movement freezes/blood quiets down/nothing but expectation pulsating" (26). She discusses nature through her own experiences and feelings and vice versa. The images she reveals are not merely metaphors or observations but events of which she is a part. She does not have to step into nature from the outside, she is already there with her poems. The vicinity of nature and Saminess intertwine; nature is the everyday life through which she lives.

Her use of words reflects the traditional Sami way of life; she does not want to waste words but uses them only as much as is needed. In many poems, she discusses the ways in which words are nourishment for her and the very act of writing is an inner cleansing process. The power of words is strongly connected to nature: single words are like visual tracks leading the reader's mind to create their own images; she 'drops' highly visual words onto a page for a reader to pick up. Thus she invites the reader to become a part of the poem as well as a part of her experience in nature.

In Western literary tradition, nature writing has been defined as a distinctive genre emanating from essays describing the surrounding nature. In Indigenous writing, however, it is not limited to a specific genre; nature is present in almost all the literature. Indigenous peoples' relationship with nature and land is interdependent and continuous throughout annual cycles rather than dominant and objectified, as it has often been in Western tradition springing from Biblical authority (Schweninger 47). Despite her own comments that she does not deal with Saminess in her writing, Inger-Mari Aikio discusses one of the most important elements of Sami culture – the land. This demonstrates the way in which core elements of Saminess stay close and bear significance, no matter how a person feels estranged or alienated from 'traditional' values or Saminess.

Kerttu Vuolab: School as a Source of Insecurity and Emptiness

Kerttu Vuolab was born in *Vuovdaguoika*, in the Deatnu Valley. Her first book *Golbma skihpáračča* (Three Friends) came out in 1979 and the second, *Ánde ja Risten jagi fárus* (Ánde and Risten along with the year) in 1990. They are both children's books illustrated by the writer. Her latest book, *Čeppari čáráhus* (1994), is a novella, a story about a young Sami girl starting school. *Čeppari čáráhus* is set in the late 1960's. Máret's experiences and feelings resemble those of the writer's: after starting school, she feels increasingly estranged from home as she has to stay in the residential school for most of the year. In the residential school, she misses the security of home, yet at home, she feels alienated. Therefore, she often has the feeling that she does not properly belong anywhere (Vuolab, 1994: 5).

The story begins with Máret packing her clothes in order to get ready for the first trip to school. She is slightly afraid of her forthcoming life and wonders whether she will learn anything there at all. Her family escorts her to the post bus, which takes the children to school. On the bus Máret checks out the other children: "Nobody has a Sami hat. Only me. And those big girls have such nice curly hair. If only I had the same…" (Vuolab, 1994:12). Máret quickly learns that school life is full of orders and restrictions and that timekeeping is particularly important. She is roomed with an older Finnish girl called Tuulikki. Tuulikki is disappointed to get her as a roommate as she wanted to share a room with her own friends. From the very beginning Tuulikki and her friends tease and mock Máret. They also forbid her to speak Sami. The girls pick on her clothes and once they rush into Máret's and Tuulikki's room and start messing up Máret's closet. They pull all her cloths down from the shelves and laugh at what they see:

'You have forgotten your lasso and the hay for your shoes!' Hannele cackles. 'And where are you going when wearing that gákti[9]?' Ulla giggles.
'Maybe you're going to dress up so that the teachers also from the South can see a real Sami girl,' Tuulikki starts.
'That will make our school real fancy and even the tourists will find it worth seeing! There is a student in this school

who is such an authentic Sami that her clothes still smell of
smoke!' The girls start laughing together.
'Perhaps you don't even have a real house as a home. When
your father brought you here with reindeer bulls, which
mountain goahti did your family stay at?' (Vuolab, 1994:25)

Máret's hiding place is the washroom where she runs away from
the girls. Behind the locked doors, she cries until she falls asleep.
She often escapes to the forest where she can talk with the creatures of nature; once when lost, she suddenly realizes that she can
understand the crow's croaking and the languages of other creatures as well, who tell her how to get back to the school. Only in
the forest Máret has friends to whom she can talk:

'I don't want to go back to the residence. It is much nicer
here. Here I have friends. In the residence I'm so lonely and
others mock me all the time!'
'I also used to be very lonely in this swamp in the beginning
and I used to think that everybody is in my way. But then I
started to practice to stretch towards the sun. So that's how I
started to get on. If you don't get on with yourself then you
won't get on with anybody. But it is also true that nobody
gets on alone. I would have been taken by the wind a long
time ago already if I hadn't friends helping me to hold onto
the ground,' the hay tells. (Vuolab, 1994:67)

In the forest she also runs into a young reindeer herding man who
used to think that attending school is much easier than working
hard in the woods, but who changes his mind after hearing Máret's
story. Máret is also teased as Čeppari čáráhus,[10] a swot who is the
teachers' favourite. Máret herself is happy to hear somebody prais-
ing her after all the mocking:

Serves them right! Now you see that I also understand
things although I know only standard Finnish from the
books, Máret thinks very contently. Now they probably do
not dare to tease me anymore because I am so clever.
(Vuolab, 1994:37)

But it is not the case. Bravely, Máret goes to the girls during the
break and asks if she can play with them. Full of spite, the girls tell
her to go and read her grammar and other textbooks. Máret realizes
that they have just gained another reason to mock her. Things get a
little better when she changes rooms and gets a new room-mate
Kirste, who is Máret's relative and much nicer than Tuulikki. After

that, Máret's life becomes easier. Her second semester is not as bad, but she still does not have any good friends. Finally Máret finds a friend in Láilá who is another shy little girl. Unfortunately her new friend moves to southern Sweden with her family after the spring semester. By the end of that semester, Máret has already learned to defend herself quite well against the bullies and to hold her own.

Gradually Máret's life at school becomes easier although she still feels lonely. She has grown up enough to be bored at home with her younger siblings. Eating becomes her new way to escape loneliness. Sweet cakes that she bakes sweep her along like a stream and the further she goes, the more she eats until she feels ill and throws up. She sees herself as too round and large, and she is concerned about the fact that she can never become a model. Towards the end of the story, Máret is going to the fifth class, and there are two different voices talking inside her: one child's and one adult's voice.

Čeppari čáráhus is a story about the change which Sami children had to face in the 1950's and the 1960's. It is also a story about the painful experience of attending school – a traumatic experience that marked a whole generation. Sami children were teased for being Sami, strange people with all those 'funny clothes' as Tuulikki and other girls point out. Vuolab herself describes the situation as follows:

> After the Second World War, lots of babies were born. First as little kids, we filled all the rooms at home. When I was at school, all the residential schools were full because of us. After the school, we filled all the jobs. Because we were so many, the competition over managing in life was tough. For my generation, not many could gain a living from the traditional livelihoods. Grazing lands would have not taken all our herds. Farming offered a living only for one child in a family. Bits of land would have not given a living for anybody if they had been divided any further. To get a job or go to school meant that many of us had to leave our home region. That caused feelings of insecurity and emptiness. (Vuolab, 1994: 5-6)

In *Čeppari čáráhus*, Vuolab demonstrates the ways in which pressures of racism and assimilation are a part of the Sami identity. Even today, people bear marks of (continued) colonialism such as feelings of inferiority and shame. Many times a person is caught between two opposing worlds like Máret at the end of the story: she has a dream where she is skiing up in the mountains and carrying a big bag with her. This Máret is the young one and the adult one is waiting on the top of the mountain. The adult Máret gets angry when she sees what the young Máret is dragging with her – why does she not have a backpack? And what is she doing with high-heel shoes and make-up in the mountains? According to young Máret, they are a good shield behind which it is easy to hide (Vuolab, 1994: 105).

Multidimensional Identities

Obviously, the writings of four Sami writers do not give a complete picture of the contemporary, many-sided Sami identity. They do, however, demonstrate effectively the ways in which previous assumptions of Saminess have been misleading and limited. Out of such various identities, we can sketch a picture where every part of Sami literature contributes uniquely to the Sami continuum.

In her novel *256 Golláža*, Kirsti Paltto describes both the positive and negative aspects of contemporary Sami society; one could say that she represents it as it is. There are those who feel strongly about their Saminess and want to maintain it through the language in particular. There are also co-opted Sami who do not regard Sami culture or language as having much worth but who rather pursue economic development and want to catch up with the 'big world.' Paltto's way of telling is at once joyful and serious so each reader can perceive it differently. Paltto's style is bitingly sarcastic which may bother some readers. Nevertheless it is a literary strategy as well as one of the most useful survival skills. Although the image of Saminess she gives is diverse, her central message to the reader is to emphasize the significance of laughter. As she herself puts it, "*juos ii leat leaikkastallan, dalle ii leat ii ilbmi iige álbmi*" ("if there is no humour, there will be no air nor nourishment").

Jovnna-Ánde Vest is writing outside Samiland which is also part of the contemporary Sami reality. Many Sami are living outside the Sami region; Oslo, the capital of Norway, for instance, is claimed to be the biggest Sami village with 5,000 Sami! This is the situation for many other Indigenous peoples as well. It is important to take their realities as seriously and as 'authentic' as those living in 'traditional' areas (which is, in terms of history, also a relative concept). Vest's main character Kapo starts a new life in the 'New World' and while not really longing for his previous life, he still has retained some Sami features. Sometimes assimilated Indigenous persons like Kapo are rejected and ignored by their own people. The important question would be whether it is really possible to fully get rid of your ethnic identity and its manifestations. No matter how difficult it is for most of us to respect the choice of these people, we should remember however that assimilation can also be a response to outside pressure,[11] one survival strategy among others. As Paula Gunn Allen notes:

> The crucial factor in the alienation so often treated in American Indian writing is the unconscious assumption that Indians must ally with one particular segment of their experience and not with another. The world is seen in terms of antagonistic principles... For many, this process has meant rejection of Indianness. (Allen 134)

Inger-Mari Aikio represents the younger generation in contemporary Sami literature. She has said herself how her writing is not involved in promoting Sami culture, but that the act of writing is rather an inner cleansing process for her (Kailo & Helander 79). Yet she admits that the Sami language is an important basis of the culture: according to her, without Sami language there would be nothing to distinguish us as a people (ibid). Despite her personal comments, a reader can sense a worry about the future of many elements in Sami culture. Instead of direct statements, her opinions are expressed through feelings and visual images linked closely to the presence of nature. In many poems, the writer becomes one with her environment; her feelings and nature's feelings enmesh. Despite her claims of alienation from the traditional Sami values, she still is in the midst of the most important element of Sami (and other Indigenous too) culture, i.e., nature and the land.

Kerttu Vuolab is one of the writers who describe the situation experienced by Sami children in schools in the 1960's and the 1970's in a very open and honest way. As Vuolab illustrates, school attendance was a traumatic experience for many Sami and the ramifications are still with us in many ways. The sense of inferiority and shame involved in using one's own language has not completely disappeared. Many also have difficulties in finding a place in the society, since they feel that they do not adequately belong anywhere. There are also many people like Máret who feel that they are struggling between two worlds and between two sets of traditions and values.

The main purpose of this paper has been to demonstrate the way in which contemporary Sami literature reveals multiple and complex representations of Sami identity. Representations of the Sami created by non-Sami explorers and others have usually been very limited and stereotypical and have perpetuated discrimination and racism. In many cases, these stereotypical images have functioned as a basis of defining who is Sami. This in turn has led to a controversial debate over authenticity. The writings of the four contemporary Sami writers studied in this paper clearly show however that there is no single representation or identity of the Sami that could be termed 'real' or 'the most authentic.' These writings also indicate that Sami identities are a long way from the stereotypical images of Topelius, as described earlier. As with any contemporary identities and representations, Sami identities are expressed in numerous ways. They are not fixed nor are they without contradictions, as the selected texts demonstrate.

It is important that while discussing Indigenous identities, we look at the diverse representations and perceptions created by our own people rather than lapsing into stereotypical notions created and perpetuated by outsiders. Oral traditions and written literatures offer powerful insights into the ways in which Indigenous identities have always been diverse and multidimensional. As scholars of Indigenous literatures, it is however critical that we pay attention to the theories and methodologies we apply to our research. Analyzing Indigenous peoples' literatures through Western literary theories may violate the integrity of these literatures, as Western literary theories tend to dismiss non-Western literatures as 'primitive,' 'child-like,' 'overpopulated' or as 'having no clear plot.'

In my view, it is crucial that we consider and remain open to new models of theorizing that particularly derive from our own traditions, practices and epistemologies. I have suggested elsewhere (Kuokkanen 2000) the development of an 'Indigenous paradigm,' a perspective and a framework of concepts based on Indigenous peoples' systems of knowledge and cultural practices. In my view, a conscious attempt to create a closer connection with the subject is needed in order to avoid misinterpretations. Another important task of an 'Indigenous paradigm' would be to challenge often subtly racist, dualist notions still prevalent in much of Western scholarship, according to which the world is divided along lines of Western high culture and non-Western folkloric traditions. An 'Indigenous paradigm' may also introduce new perspectives to research by challenging dominant values, worldviews and epistemologies. Last but not least, a point particularly relevant to this paper: an 'Indigenous paradigm' can offer a new set of tools for analyzing non-Western cultures which, for its own part, may diminish the dangers of misinterpretation of our cultural expressions.

Notes

1. The Sami are also known as the Lapps or Laplanders, terms created by outsiders, which today are increasingly considered derogatory and outdated. The Sami are an Indigenous people living today in the northern parts of Norway, Sweden, Finland and the Kola Peninsula, Russia. There are approximately 75,000 – 100,000 Sami, most of them living in Norway. (For further information about the Sami people, see for instance Kailo & Helander 1998.)

2. All English translations are by the author of the article unless otherwise indicated.

3. Currently, there are a few books on Sami literature available in English. See the list at the end of the article.

4 A yoik is a Sami way of communication in a special form of singing. Traditionally, it is also an identification of a person; a child did not fully become a part of her/his society until she/he received her personal yoik. The Christian missionaries banned yoiking as a sinful activity. Today, there are many well-known (also internationally) Sami yoikers.

5. This is an interesting reference to the Sami anthem Sámi Soga lávlla, which starts with the words Guhkkin davvin Dávggáid vuolde (far up north beneath the Ursa Major).

6. This is a playful reference to the European Union.

7. The Sami 'teepee,' a temporary dwelling.

8. A traditional Sami costume.

9. Čáráhus, as Vuolab explains in the preface, is a traditional creature in Sami stories who used to tease people in their dreams. Čáráhus is both a trouble and a strain (Vuolab, 1994:5).

10. There is also, of course, the possibility of assimilation without apparent pressure.

11. It can of course be argued that not only the Indigenous peoples are close to nature but for Indigenous peoples nature and the surrounding land is the first condition for survival as distinct peoples.

Works Cited

Aikio, Annukka. (1987) "Suullinen perinne kaikuu Kirsti Palton romaanissa. Vielä joikataan ja tarinoidaan." Uusi Suomi, January 7th.

Aikio, Inger-Mari. (1989) *Gollebiekkat almmi dievva*. Vaasa: Dat.

Allen, Paula Gunn. (1986) *The Sacred Hoop: Recovering the Feminine in American Indian Traditions*. Boston: Beacon Press.

Ashcroft, Bill, and Gareth Griffiths, and Helen Tiffin. (1989) *The Empire Writes Back. Theory and Practice in Postcolonial Literatures*. London: Routledge.

Awiakta, Marilou. (1993) *Seeking the Corn-Mother's Wisdom.* Golden, Colorado: Fulcrum Publishing.

Dana, Kathleen. (1995) "Literary Voice and Cultural Identity: Sami Creative Literature." Unpublished paper presented at the ICASS II, Rovaniemi, Finland.

Grant, Agnes, ed. (1991) *Our Bit of Truth. An Anthology of Canadian Native Literature.* Toronto: Pemmican Press.

Kailo, Kaarina, and Elina Helander, eds. (1998) *No Beginning, No End. The Sami Speak Up.* Edmonton: Canadian Circumpolar Institute/ Sami Institute.

Kuokkanen, Rauna. (2000) "Towards an 'Indigenous Paradigm' from a Sami Perspective." *The Canadian Journal of Native Studies.* 20:1.

Lehtola, Veli-Pekka. (1995) "Saamelainen kirjallisuus vanhan ja uuden risteyksessä." *Marginalia ja kirjallisuus. Ääniä suomalaisen kirjallisuuden reunoilta.* Ed. Matti Savolainen. Helsinki: SKS. 36-89.

Nousiainen, Pentti. (1983) *Anglosaksisten matkakirjailijoiden Lapin kuva 1799-1860.* MA Thesis. Oulu University.

Paltto, Kirsti. (1992) *256 Golláža.* Ohcejohka: Gielas.

Schweninger, Lee. (1993) "Writing Nature: Silko and Native Americans as Nature Writers." *Multi-Ethnic Literature Journal.* 18:2. (Summer).

Topelius, Sakari. (1954) *Maamme kirja. Lukukirja Suomen alimmille oppilaitoksille.* 54., muuttamaton painos. Porvoo: WSOY.

Valkeapää, Nils-Aslak. (1971) *Greetings From Lappland. The Sami-- Europe's Forgotten People.* London: Sage Publications.

Vest, Jovnna-Ánde. (1991) *Kapteainna ruvsu.* Kárášjohka: Davvi Girji.

Vuolab, Kerttu. (1994) *Čeppari čáráhus.* Kárášjohka: Davvi Girji.

—— . (1995) "Riggodagaid botnihis gáldu – máidnasiid mearihis mearkkašupmi..." *cafe Boddu* 2. Ed. Harald Gaski. Kárášjohka: Davvi Girji.

Sami Literature available in English

Gaup, Ailo. (1992) *In Search of The Drum.* Fort Yates, ND: Muse Publications.

Gaski, Harald, ed. (1996) *In the Shadow of the Midnight Sun. Contemporary Sami Prose and Poetry.* Kárášjohka: Davvi Girji.

Lukkari, Rauni Magga. (1999) *The Time of the Lustful Mother.* Trans. Kaija Anttonen. Kárášjohka: Davvi Girji.

Valkeapää, Nils-Aslak. (1994) *Trekways of the Wind.* Trans. Ralph Salisbury, Lars Nordsträm, and Harald Gaski. Guovdageaidnu: Dat.

—— . (1997) *The Sun, my Father.* Trans. Harald Gaski, Lars Nordström and Ralph Salisbury. Guovdageaidnu: Dat.

Sammallahti, Pekka, and Anthony Selbourne, eds. & trans. (1996) *Beyond the Wolf Line. An Anthology of Sami Poetry.* Guildford, Surrey: Making Waves.

Erasing the Invisible: Gender Violence and Representations of Whiteness in *Dry Lips Oughta Move To Kapuskasing*

Randy Lundy

The invisibility of Whiteness is an enabling condition for both White supremacy/privilege and race-based prejudice. Making Whiteness visible to Whites [and to the oppressed] – exposing the discourses, the social and cultural practices, and the material conditions that cloak Whiteness and hide its dominating effects – is a necessary part of any anti-racist project.

> (Wray and Newitz, *White Trash: Race and Class in America*, 3-4)

In 1989, Tomson Highway followed up the considerable success of *The Rez Sisters* with a second play, the equally successful *Dry Lips Oughta Move to Kapuskasing*. Jennifer Preston observes that those involved with the production "were a little worried about the reception of the play as it dealt with some very difficult issues... [and they] wondered if people would be able to accept the way Christianity and its effects on Native people were portrayed" (149). However, Highway's second *Rez* play soon received critical praise and awards:

> *Dry Lips Oughta Move to Kapuskasing* was nominated for six Dora Mavor Moore Awards and won four... The play also won the 1989 Floyd S. Chalmers Award for Outstanding Canadian Play performed in the Toronto area. The text was published in 1989 and was one of three plays shortlisted for the Governor General's Literary Award for Drama in that year. In the fall of 1990 *Dry Lips* was produced by the Manitoba Theatre Centre... [and went on to be produced] at both the National Arts Centre in Ottawa and the mainstream Royal Alexandra Theatre in Toronto (Preston 149-150).

From the overwhelmingly positive narrative Preston presents, it would seem that Tomson Highway and these two plays epitomize successes to be celebrated.

However, Preston neglects to acknowledge that, in 1991, performances of Tomson Highway's play *Dry Lips Oughta Move to Kapuskasing* drew plenty of angry criticism from women, particularly Indigenous women. In the pages of *The Globe and Mail*, Marion Botsford Fraser, a non-Indigenous woman, writes "The two central events in the play are horrible abuses of women, unmitigated by compassion... *Dry Lips* is not only about misogyny but is a drama studded with misogyny" (17 April 1991, C7). Two of the most damning responses to the play are those of Anita Tuharsky and Marie Annharte Baker, both Indigenous women. In a letter to the editor published in *New Breed* (April 1991), Ms. Tuharsky writes that the play "terribly misrepresented the Aboriginal peoples... [and] only represented a dysfunctional sector of any community... The play did nothing to balance the negativity being presented about life on the reserve and the attitudes prevailing there... the playwright and play clearly misrepresented the Aboriginal women, Aboriginal men, life on the reserve, and the Spirit Wesakaychak" (5). Ms. Tuharsky expresses her particular concern regarding the representation of Indigenous women:

> Aboriginal women were portrayed as loose, unfaithful, sleazy, [sic] drunks with no respect for human life and childbirth. The women in the play were nude and showed no modesty for their body but allowed it [sic] to be portrayed in a degrading manner. I, for one, would like to tell Mr. Highway, that Aboriginal women are not like this... This is pornography, this disrespectful portrayal, [sic] only reinforces damaging stereotypes against our women. (5)

Furthermore, Tuharsky is quite correct when she observes that in the play "Aboriginal men fared no better. They were portrayed as unfaithful drunks, uneducated, slovenly in dress, uncaring, selfish and self-absorbed failures. The men had no respect for women" (5). In Ms. Tuharsky's opinion, "Mr. Highway's images only open the wounds and adds [sic] salt to them. He does not go far enough because he does not help the audience to overcome the obstacles, to heal the wounds of the past and develop directions for building stronger spirits in our people and acceptance and responsibility by the institutions and Europeans for the damage they have done to us" (6). Her observations about the play lead her to the conclusion that "It is images such as this play which breed oppression, racism, and disrespect for the Aboriginal peoples and their culture, traditions, and spirituality" (6).

Most of the concerns raised by Ms. Tuharsky, an unknown commentator, are very similar to those voiced by well-known Indigenous writer Marie Annharte Baker. In her article "Carte Blanche: Angry Enough To Spit But With *Dry Lips* It Hurts More Than You Know" published in the *Canadian Theatre Review* 68 (Fall 1991), Baker begins with a reference to "the perpetuators of racism and sexism" (88), presumably implying that Tomson Highway and his play are among those perpetrators. She also makes reference to "Our internalized racism and sexism [that] seems to get financial rewards, literary or artistic awards" (88), again with the implication that Highway's play and the success it has enjoyed are representative of such internalized racism and sexism and the positive attention their manifestation can attract. That this implication is clearly Baker's intention becomes obvious when she writes that "Now it is even fashionable to sit and watch plays written 'for' us and 'about' us. We even find excuses to praise our further degradation on stage or screen" (88). In the published version of the play, Highway has included a quotation from Lyle Longclaws "before the healing can take place, the poison must first be exposed," (6) and Baker tells her reader that the same quotation was printed on the playbill for the performance she attended. However, far from finding any solace in the quotation, Baker responds to it in quite another way: "It is convenient to make enough commentary to be unaccountable for any inadvertent racist or sexist imagery. But it arouses my suspicion about the audience because it is not popular to attend 'politically incorrect' performances that might *intentionally* endorse racism or sexism. I worry about the unintended" (89). It is clear that Baker believes that the play, even if unintentionally, promotes the same racist and sexist stereotypes that Ms. Tuharsky writes about in her letter to the editor of *New Breed*: "A Yuppie would go home feeling relieved that Indians live on the rez and in the other part of the city. For Whites and white-nosers, the play is a wonderful revelation about the contradictions in Indian lives. But to a young Native person, the play might be another affront to one's identity" (Baker 89). Just as Ms. Tuharsky is concerned that the play does not assign responsibility to non-Indigenous people and institutions for the damages they have caused in our communities, Baker voices the same concern:

> I wanted to see that the average white Canadian gets a bit of responsibility. It is obvious that white guilt is milked to what I may guess is the consistency of cottage cheese, but

would the average Native woman or man walk out of the theatre with a greater understanding of either racism or sexism? Would our Yuppie boss or co-worker find anything in the play to better understand the inequity of the workplace where racism and sexism is [sic] a structural and hierarchical reality? (89)

It is clear that for Marie Annharte Baker, as for Anita Tuharsky, the answer to these questions is a resounding no.

While women such as Ms. Tuharsky and Annharte Baker charge that Highway's work supports rather than subverts the stereotypes of Indigenous peoples and women held by the dominant and overlapping White and patriarchal cultures, non-Indigenous, theatre critic Alan Filewood makes an equally damning argument that the plays reinscribe White colonial domination. Filewood begins his article, "Averting the Colonising Gaze: Notes on Watching Native Theatre," with the following assertion: "I can't write about native theatre; all I can write about is my response to it. When I watch native theatre I see my own gaze returned; my watching is an appropriation, even when it is invited. *As the coloniser I am the invisible presence in these plays*" (17, emphasis added). He proceeds to a discussion of Tomson Highway's work, refers to the long list of awards the plays have received, and then suggests,

> The [positive critical] response is... problematic because this celebratory response erases the politics of the play and re-establishes the narrative as a generalised statement of anticolonialism, permitting the coloniser to assume the posture of the colonised. It is inevitable that we should come to Highway's plays through an identification with the oppressed characters rather than an awareness of our place as coloniser. (21)

In these statements there is, again, an emphasis on the *invisibility* of the coloniser, and this emphasis continues when Filewood states that "not only do we erase our own culpability in Highway's plays, but we reconstruct their cultural patterns to serve our own cultural project – a project that has historically erased native peoples" (21). He goes on to note that "*Dry Lips* has been picked up by a major commercial producer."

> The anger in the play... is transformed through a change in material conditions and audience into sentimentality. Put simply, it lets the Anglo audience off the hook. If it didn't,

it could scarcely appeal to a commercial producer... it is regression when that redefinition upholds the cultural myths by which Anglo Canada excuses its marginalisation of native Indians. (22)

Perhaps because of his confidence in the invisibility of the coloniser in Highway's plays, Filewood is fearful of the message they promote: "My fear is that so long as Highway narrates the native struggles as a process of spiritual regeneration audiences will be less accepting of an angrier voice that narrates the struggle in terms of political action" (22). Speaking for non-Indigenous audiences, Filewood asks, "Do we applaud Highway's plays because we can write into them the image of the native that makes us most comfortable?" and then answers his own question by asserting that "we are comfortable with what we hear" (23). Filewood's charges against the play are related to charges such as Tuharsky's and Annharte Baker's in that all of these critics argue that the play reinscribes, rather than challenges, the dominant White and patriarchal ideologies.

Unfortunately, those critics who have identified and focussed on the merits of the play have failed to deal with the angry criticisms in any substantial way. Critical reaction to *Dry Lips* has been largely polarized with little carefully reasoned dialogue between those who have condemned the play and those who have responded more favourably, with Sheila Rabillard's essay being a significant exception. As long as this is the case, the question of whether or not the play reinforces stereotypes and reinscribes colonial violence and domination will remain unanswered. However, in a twist that is appropriate to a work as complex as *Dry Lips*, the answer to the angry criticisms of the play lie not in a direct analysis of the images of Indigenous peoples alone. The response to such criticisms lies in an examination of the representations of Whiteness and what these representations reveal in relation to representations of Indigenous identities. Contrary to Filewood's comfortable assertions, the colonizers' invisibility is erased by Highway's representation of Whiteness. Thus, it is to an examination of Whiteness as represented in *Dry Lips* that the critical gaze must now turn.

In the stage directions that precede the opening of Act One of *Dry Lips*, the description of the set includes the following: "Prominently displayed on one wall is a life-size pin-up poster of Marilyn Monroe" (15). In his article "White" Richard Dyer makes the following observations regarding Marilyn Monroe, the Holly-

wood icon: "the codes of glamour lighting in Hollywood were developed in relation to White women, to endow them with a radiance that has correspondences with the transcendental rhetoric of
popular Christianity. Of no woman star was this more true than
Marilyn Monroe, known by the press at the time as 'the
Body'" (160-161). Dyer's remarks are significant in an informed
reading of *Dry Lips* because female bodies, as objects of desire as
well as fear and loathing, are an almost constant preoccupation of
the male characters in the play. In a brief discussion of Monroe's
film *The Seven Year Itch*, Dyer argues that the film "lets on it
knows about male fantasy and its remote relation to reality. Yet it
is also part of the Monroe industry, peddling an impossible
dream... White women are constructed as the apotheosis of desirability, all that a man could want, yet nothing that can be had, nor
anything that a woman can be" (161). If this male construction of a
specifically White ideal of female sexuality is something White
women cannot achieve, the question must be asked: how much
more unrealistic is the ideal in relation to Indigenous women?

The internalized racism and sexism, the obvious misogyny,
that the male characters of Wasaychigan Hill display must be read
in the context of the presence of the male fantasy Monroe represents. The men's behaviours and attitudes towards women in the
play must be considered in relation to the prominently displayed
poster of Monroe, the single dominant image of Whiteness in *Dry
Lips*. Furthermore, an investigation of the representation of Whiteness in the play must also consider how this dominant image of
Whiteness relates to the two other major themes of the play,
namely the language and the spiritual tradition of the colonizers,
since "Highway more than hints at an association between opposition of the sexes and White oppression" (Rabillard 15). What the
play suggests is that the male construction of a specifically White
ideal of feminine sexuality as an object of male desire, as a male
fantasy, is enabled and perpetuated by the discourses of the English language and the Christian spiritual tradition of the colonizers.

The play, which opens with the exclamation "Hey
Bitch!" (16), makes it clear that much of the men's confusion, anger, general feelings of powerlessness, and dislocation from their
people's spiritual traditions arise from a lack of understanding of,
or a rupture of the relationship with, women and feminine realities.
The first dialogue in the play is an indicator of the attitude toward
women that is prevalent; the first words are spoken by Big Joey,
the most violent misogynist in the play and also the owner of the

Marilyn Monroe poster. Much later we learn of the source of Joey's fear and hatred of women. Big Joey refers to the violent confrontation between Whites and Indigenous peoples at Wounded Knee: "Wounded Knee, South Dakota, Spring of '73. The FBI. They beat us to the ground. Again and again and again. Ever since that spring I've had these dreams where blood is spilling out from my groin, nothin' there but blood and emptiness. It's like... I lost myself. So when I saw this baby comin' out of Caroline, Black Lady... Gazelle dancin'... all this blood... and I knew it was gonna come... I... I tried to stop it... I freaked out. I don't know what I did... and I knew it was mine..." (120). Robert Imboden suggests,

> Big Joey, in attempting to flee the fate of misery on the reservation, goes to Wounded Knee in 1973. But instead of finding liberation from his fate, he finds murder and assassination. When he returns to the reservation, he brings with him the hatred and violence of the South Dakota site. Seething in hatred and despair, he becomes responsible for the three strikingly tragic events of the play: the damaged birth of his son, Dickie Bird, whom he refuses to recognise, the brutal crucifix rape of Patsy by Dickie Bird, and the subsequent accidental, suicidal death of her lover, Simon. His hatred has both caused and allowed Black Lady Halked to drink constantly for three weeks preceding Dickie Bird's birth. The same hatred allows him to watch silently as Patsy is raped. Every one of these events can be seen as one of the steps that binds Big Joey and his people more securely than ever in their agonising fate of impoverishment. (116)

When Zack asks Joey why he allowed the rape to happen, Joey responds: "Because I hate them! I hate the fuckin' bitches. Because they – our own women – took the fuckin' power away from us faster than the FBI ever did" (120). As Sheila Rabillard observes, Big Joey's words "make an explicit association between political domination and male/female antagonism... Big Joey appears to assert that the women – who, offstage, have intruded into an exclusively male sport – and the agents of White domination both emasculate" (15). The association Rabillard identifies becomes clearer if one understands the patriarchy that many see as characteristic of the American Indian Movement. Lee Maracle writes that "sexism... was inherent in the character of the American Indian Movement" (137) and that "culturally, the worst dominant, White male traits were emphasised. Machismo and the boss mentality were the basis for choosing leaders. The idea of leadership was essentially a European one promulgated by power mongers" (126). Thus, in Big Joey's mind, non-Indigenous males and Indigenous females are characterized as threats to Indigenous male longing for political power.

Big Joey's sense of himself and his identity as an Indigenous person are heavily formed by the conflict between White and Indigenous men. Big Joey's dream – nightmare might be more accurate – is a dream of castration or emasculation, making it clear that his understanding of power is based upon his penis. In other words, his understanding of power is phallocentric, meaning that social and political power are the domain of men. In her book *Yearning: Race, Gender and Cultural Politics*, bell hooks writes:

> The discourse of black resistance has almost always equated freedom with manhood, the economic and material domination of black men with castration, emasculation. Accepting these sexual metaphors forged a bond between oppressed black men and their white male oppressors. They shared the patriarchal belief that revolutionary struggle was really about the erect phallus, the ability of men to establish political dominance that could correspond to sexual dominance... Sexism has always been a political stance mediating racial domination, enabling white men and black men to share a common sensibility about sex roles and the importance of male domination. Clearly both groups have been socialized to condone patriarchal affirmation of rape as an acceptable way to maintain male domination. It is this merging of sexuality with male domination within patriarchy that informs the construction of masculinity for men of all races and classes. (58-59)

Her words might be applied directly to the Indigenous men in *Dry Lips*. However, in considering the ways in which bell hooks' words can be applied to men such as Big Joey, we must remember that "Viewing Aboriginal men as dysfunctional (and not, for example, oppressed), and Aboriginal women as inherently rapeable confirms the superiority of white men" (Razack 69), thus maintaining both racial and gender hierarchies. We must also remember that "many of these wrongs [suffered by women at the hands of men] work in concert with other systems of oppression [such as racism], systems that benefit some women at the expense of others" (95-

96). In other words, to consider Highway's work as emphasising gender concerns alone is to ignore the ways in which interlocking systems of domination converge: "The dictates of patriarchy demand that beneath Native man comes the female Native. The dictates of racism are thus that Native men are beneath white women and Native females are not fit to be referred to as women" (Maracle 17-18). On the other hand, to emphasise racial concerns alone would be to deny that the male characters are complicit in the oppression of a segment of their own community and, by extension, of all Indigenous peoples, since "The denial of Native womanhood is the reduction of the whole people to a subhuman level. Animals beget animals" (Maracle 17).

Nigel Hunt suggests that the men in the play suffer "the consequences of their own insecurity about women and their lack of trust for the traditional values which kept their societies strong for centuries" (60). In response to Big Joey's declaration that women took the power away from Indigenous men, Spooky responds, "They always had it" (120). We can understand Spooky's response if we consider the role of women in pre-colonial Indigenous societies as Paula Gunn Allen explains it: "During the five hundred years of Anglo-European colonization, the tribes have seen a progressive shift from gynocentric, egalitarian, ritual-based social systems to secularized structures closely imitative of the European patriarchal system" (195). Janice Acoose also identifies this change from a situation of balanced gender roles to an unbalanced hierarchical and patriarchal model: "Our once community – and consensually-based ways of governance, social organization, and economic practices were stripped of their legitimacy and authority by White Christian males, who imposed an ideologically contrasting hierarchical structure. Of specific importance... is the removal of women from all significant social, political, economic, and spiritual processes" (47). It is within the context of this colonial shift that Big Joey associates Indigenous women with colonial domination.

Big Joey's association of Indigenous women with colonial domination can be understood as a specifically gendered internalisation of the manichean degradation and dehumanisation of Indigenous peoples. In *The Sacred Hoop: Recovering the Feminine in American Indian Traditions*, Paula Gunn Allen writes "one wonders if the focus on male traditions and history that has characterized the whole field of American Indian literature and lore was not part of the plot to exterminate Native American tribal peoples and cultures... However he is viewed... the Indian is always he" (262). In a discussion of Lee Maracle's *I Am Woman*, Barbara Godard remarks upon "the centrality of this denial of womanhood to the imperialist project" and suggests that "In refusing a place for women and for love, the Native has played out the colonialist reduction of a people to a sub-human level" (209). The emphasis on male history that Gunn Allen identifies is reminiscent of Big Joey's preoccupation with Wounded Knee. Furthermore, since Joey seems to use the events at Wounded Knee as an excuse for his abuse of women, he is complicit in the colonial reduction identified by Godard. It is within the context of these complex operations of race and gender oppression that Big Joey's misogyny can be understood as an internalization of the White colonial manichean binary. Thus, while it is possible to trace the roots of Joey's misogyny, these roots do not excuse his behaviour and attitudes, and "During the rape scene, Big Joey is transformed from a harmless bully to a representative of weakness and evil in modern Native society" (Denis Johnston 261). The weakness and evil revealed are those of an Indigenous man whose misogyny makes him an active agent in the oppression of the women in the community.

The shift from cultures based upon balanced gender roles to patriarchal hierarchy can in part be ascribed to differences between the Indigenous languages in the play and the English language. Lucy Bashford observes, "the presence of the genderless Nanabush [although, in the play, Nanabush significantly appears only in female guises]... indicates the confusion the Cree/Ojibway speakers have with the gender differentiation of the English language. There is an underlying intimation, but not accusation, that much of the conflict between the sexes has been imported into the culture from outside" (109). Indeed, the play certainly supports Bashford's observation as indicated by the following exchange:

> Simon: ...Weesageechak! Come back! Rosie! Rosie Kakapetum, tell him to come back, not to run away, cuz we need him...
> Nanabush/Patsy: ... her...
> Simon: ...him...
> Nanabush/Patsy: ... her...
> Simon: ... *weetha* ("him/her" – no gender)... Christ! What is it? Him? Her? Stupid fucking language, fuck you, da Englesa Me no speakum no more da goodie Englesa, in Cree we say *weetha*, not "him" or "her" Nanabush, come back! (110-111)

What Highway and the play suggest is that at least part of the solution to the social problems that the play exposes lies in the men's returning to a healthy relationship with each other, with the women, and with Indigenous spiritual traditions which are governed by the internal logic of the non-gendered Indigenous languages, rather than gendered English. Simon Ortiz provides a useful context for these ideas when he states, "My formation with regards to language was the *dzehni niyah* of the Acoma people: 'the way they spoke'... The language I use in English. Nevertheless, my English language use is founded on the original and basic knowledge of myself as an Acoma person" (107). Highway does not simplistically advocate that Indigenous peoples abandon "da Englesa" (113); to do so would be to oversimplify grossly the situation and condition of Indigenous peoples in the late twentieth century. However, what the play does suggest is that Highway's Cree and Ojibway characters must progress to a situation which parallels what Jeannette Armstrong writes of: "the meanings of the English words I use arise out of my Okanagan understanding of the world" (75). For, as Armstrong states, "Words have a covering of meaning derived from unique relationships to things... Thousands of generations of relating to things in a given way give rise to cultural meaning attached to words" (76), and when these unique relationships and cultural meanings are lost or destroyed, the result is the kind of confusion and dislocation displayed by the men in *Dry Lips*.

Similarly, Maria Campbell, in "Strategies for Survival," states that, "For a long time I couldn't write anything, because I didn't know how to use English... [W]hen I was writing I always found that English *manipulated* me... then I was able to manipulate English, and once I was able to manipulate English, I felt that was personal liberation" (9-10). The use of language, then, becomes an issue of power, of resistance and liberation. Joy Asham Fedorick makes a statement similar to Campbell's when she writes, "I was trapped – trapped in English, in English structures, with English ideas of story content and formula, with English ideas of values" (49). Fedorick expands upon her theme when she observes that "understanding the structure of English and its noun-predominance freed me to begin to understand the materialistic influence... When one is immersed in a language that primarily gears our thoughts to *things*, we become trapped in a value system of materialism" (54). The play does not suggest that all, or even most speakers of English are necessarily more materialistic than are speakers of Cree or Ojibway. However, the men's ineptitude in the use of English suggests that they are highly susceptible to the materialistic bias that Fedorick points out. Further, it would seem that the men are also susceptible to the gender biases of the language. In other words, as with Campbell's experience, the men's ineptitude in their use of English means that they are manipulated by the language and its biases. The men are unable to manipulate the English language into a transformative decolonizing tool. Marc Maufort's comment, then, that dreams or goals which remain "purely materialistic [will] fail to re-establish connection with the spirit of [Nanabush]" (235), assumes a particular significance. Big Joey's and Zachary's dreams of an economic recovery based on a radio station or a bakery will not solve the spiritual crisis that plagues Wasaychigan hill. The spiritual bankruptcy that characterises the men in *Dry Lips* is reflected in their inability to harness the English language to their own need for decolonization. In turn, the aforementioned inability interferes with any attempt to reclaim a spiritual tradition that includes a balanced relationship between the genders.

While at the beginning of the play it seems as though the motivation for the action is going to be the rivalry between Joey and Zach, it is not long before the news of the women's hockey team becomes the true motivation. When Pierre initially arrives with news of the formation of the team, the men's reaction is one of disbelief and resistance. Big Joey's response is that "They never booked the ice" (30), but Pierre says "Booked it through Gazelle Nataways" (30), and it is clear that the male authority/power structure has been subverted. The women have even gone so far as to pick Pierre as their own referee because Big Joey's referee, as Pierre explains, is "too damn perschnickety. That drum-bangin' young whipperschnapper, Simon Starblanket, he's got all the rules mixed up [according to the women]. They kinda wanna play it their own way" (31). Interestingly enough, early in the play (16-17), it is clear that for the men, hockey is a domain of contest between White and Indigenous men. So the formation of a women's hockey team is understood by the men as a female invasion of one of the last bastions of male authority and power.

The most prolonged, extensive passages in Cree and Ojibway in the play are spoken by Big Joey during the hockey game sequences. It is quite natural for the play-by-play of a reserve hockey game to be delivered in the reserve's Indigenous language. However, since a return to the worldview embodied in these languages is part of the solution to the very misogyny that Big Joey represents, it is significant that he, the most violent misogynist, should deliver the lengthiest speeches in Cree/Ojibway. As Highway observes, Big Joey "talks in monosyllables" (Enright 24), but becomes most articulate when using Cree in his descriptions of the action on the ice. The significance of these connections lies in the fact that Big Joey's descriptions of the on-ice actions of the women represent an overcoming of the men's resistance to the perceived threat of the Wasy Wailerettes. For most of the play, the men perceive the women's forming of a hockey team as a challenge and a threat. The forming of the hockey team is characterized as a "revolution" (48), which is a term applied by those whose power is being threatened, and is called "Wounded Knee Three! Women's version!" (63), a reference that characterizes the women's efforts as violently confrontational. While it may be true that "the boys are exiled to the most powerless place, that of perpetual observer" (Baker 88), in providing commentary on the hockey games, Big Joey forgets, at least temporarily, his own feelings of powerlessness, and transcends his resistance to the women's initiative. He vicariously participates in the women's assertion of agency. Hence, Big Joey becomes articulate when he adopts his Indigenous language, blended with English, and in this way momentarily sets aside his fear and loathing of the women.

If the play makes it clear that the English language has significantly contributed to the men's inability to have a healthy relationship with the women in their lives, then it also makes clear that this language has perpetuated a similar disruption in the men's ability to understand Indigenous spiritual traditions. In an interview with Nancy Wigston, Highway states that when using the English language "you must always deal with the male-female-neuter *hierarchy*. God is male, irretrievable" (9). In an interview with William Morgan, Highway expands upon this theme: "The Cree and other native languages are structured in such a way that we look at the universe not according to that hierarchy... [I]n our mythology by virtue of the fact that the sexual hierarchy is completely absent[,]... our superhero figure is neither exclusively male nor exclusively female or is both, simultaneously interchangeable" (135). Further, Highway states his concern over what he calls "the Genesis to Revelations line: progress, progress, progress, from point A to point B, until the apocalypse comes. As a result, the circle [of Indigenous spirituality] was shattered, and got stretched open to a straight line. The impact, psychologically and spiritually, was devastating" (8). Thus, the English language is intimately involved with, and conditioned by, specific non-Indigenous spiritual traditions, which are founded upon the vertical male-female-neuter hierarchy and the straight line that extends from Genesis to Revelations. While such explanations cannot adequately account for the entire history and literature of the Christian religions, it must be remembered that Highway is, according to Enright, concerned with "a very specific type of experience with Roman Catholicism" (Enright 26). In the play, Spooky Lacroix is the representative of a specific type of Christianity, namely, a born-again, evangelistic Christianity. It is significant that the very first occurrence of Indigenous language in the play comes when Spooky says, "*Igwani eeweepoonaskeewuk* (The end of the world is at hand)" (36). Spooky, then, represents a very particular brand of Christianity that is presented in the play in a less than positive way. The antagonism between the Christianity that Spooky has adopted and the traditional Indigenous spirituality he has abandoned becomes clear when Spooky refers to Rosie Kakapetum, the reserve's only medicine woman and midwife, as a witch: "No way some witch is gonna come and put her witchy little fingers on my baby boy" (88). Spooky's use of his Indigenous language to express an idea that functions, within the context of the play, in an essentially foreign and destructive way emphasises the gulf that characterizes the men in their relationship, or lack thereof, with Indigenous spiritual traditions. Spooky's words seem to suggest that linear, hierarchical and misogynistic discourses have infiltrated his use of an Indigenous language. This flow of discourses is in the opposite direction to that documented by writers like Campbell and Fedorick.

The White colonial attempt to erase Indigenous languages and replace them with English was intimately related to the attempt to erase Indigenous spiritual traditions and replace them with Christian spirituality. In *A Tortured People*, Howard Adams argues that "the principles of Christianity were easily moulded into a racist ideology that matched the economic and political needs of expanding European colonialism... Western imperialism was a 'holy alliance' between European culture, Christianity and a colonial economy... The Christian church and its institutions was [sic] the arm of colonial destruction of indigenous culture and thought" (53). In *A Prison of Grass*, Adams argues that "The missionaries believed that God had commanded the clergy to save the souls of the heathen savages, so that conversion resulting in cultural genocide was regarded as Christian service" (31). The colonial destruction and cultural genocide Adams ascribes to the Christian churches were practised largely through these churches' role in *educating* Indigenous peoples. As Noel Elizabeth Currie points out, "the role of education and the Church – for a century indistinguishable forces in the lives of Native people – cannot be underestimated in any discussion of the imposition of European ideologies and traditions on Natives" (140). One of the primary effects of the Christian churches in the education of Indigenous peoples was the imposition of the English language and the attempt to erase Indigenous languages. The imposition of English was necessary to the imposition of European ideologies and traditions, including Christian spiritual traditions.

Central to the conflict between Spooky's brand of Christianity and a traditional Indigenous spirituality, represented by Simon Starblanket, is the mute figure of Dickie Bird Halked. Everyone seems to want Dickie Bird to speak – Spooky wants him to learn sign language so that Dickie can share the word of God with the people of the reserve (53); Pierre tries to get him to say 'daddy' (58); and Nanabush/Patsy tries to communicate with him just before he rapes her with the crucifix (98). If the rape functions as "a symbol that Christian civilisation has metaphorically destroyed Indian culture with the help of the Indians themselves" (Maufort 237), then it is also true that this complicity, symbolized by Dickie's rape of Nanabush, must be viewed in light of the disastrous confusion that Christianity has spawned in the minds of the characters. Just prior to the rape, Dickie holds the crucifix aloft and tries to chant like Simon, symbolizing Dickie's confused search for truth and the confused, precarious relationship between the two spiritual traditions. On three occasions in the play (68, 73, 78) Dickie appears on stage placed directly between Simon and Spooky to emphasise that he is "symbolically lost between the tradition of *Indian myths* and *Christian religion*" (Maufort 236, emphasis added). It must also be remembered that the rape is not only symbolic of a crime committed by Christianity against Indigenous culture, but that it is also a crime committed by a man against a woman. The rape is symbolic of the conflict between the irretrievably male Christian God and the female manifestation of Nanabush, which is a reflection of the rift between the Indigenous men and women.

If Spooky represents a clear abandonment of Indigenous spirituality to embrace White spirituality and Dickie Bird represents the confusion of being trapped between two historically antagonistic traditions, then it is Simon Starblanket who represents the hope of a return to a traditional spirituality. The obvious question that arises, then, is why is Simon allowed to die if Highway is interested in subverting the manichean binary that degrades and dehumanises Indigenous peoples? Why does Simon's quest fail? Again, a consideration of the languages Simon uses, when and where he uses an Indigenous language, for example, reveals some interesting possibilities. In the passage quoted earlier, Simon banters with Nanabush/Patsy, until the structure of his use of the English language begins to reflect his confused state. Simon concludes by saying "Me no speakum no more da goodie Englesa" (111). However, immediately after resolving to abandon English, because of the gender differentiation that hinders his attempts to contact Nanabush, Simon immediately reverts to English:

> Simon: ...Dey shove dis...whach-you-ma-call-it...da crucifix up your holy cunt ouch, eh? Ouch, eh? Nah... yessssss...noooo...oh, noooo! Crucifix! Fucking goddam crucifix yesssss..God! You're a man. You're a woman. You're a man? You're a woman? You see, *nineethoowan poogoo neetha* ("I speak only Cree"). (112)

For a second time, Simon rejects English and resolves to speak only Cree, but Simon immediately reverts to English. Simon then asks, "If God, you are a woman/man in Cree but only a man in da Englesa, then how come you still got a cun...," and Nanabush/Patsy corrects his derogatory term with, "womb" (113), symbolic of female generative/creative power. In these exchanges, it is clear that Simon has been unable to overcome the gender confusion that the English language has caused and that this gender confusion is largely responsible for his inability to realise his quest. At one point in the play, Simon sings "... and me I don't wanna go to the moon, I'm gonna leave that moon alone, I just wanna dance with the Rosebud Sioux this summer..." (113). Of course, the reference to the Rosebud Sioux recalls Wounded Knee. The Rosebud Sioux reservation in South Dakota was one of the centres of activity that led to the Wounded Knee conflict in 1973. If we understand the moon to be a symbol of female power, then Simon's words seem to indicate that he has in a sense forgotten the source of his teachings: Rosie and Patsy. He expresses a desire to return to the site of the male phallocentric conflict associated with Big Joey and his misogyny. Robert Imboden suggests that "Instead of being a source of transcendence, Wounded Knee casts a long shadow of devastating drunkenness, brutal rape, razor-edged misogyny and accidental death over the reservation [sic]" (117). However, Imboden further observes that "Big Joey and Simon had lived with the illusion that travelling to Wounded Knee would free them from the grinding poverty and misery of the reservation" (119). Simon's dying words are in Cree and after he has died *"we see Simon, wearing his powwow bustle"* (120) for the first time; throughout the play Simon had been carrying the bustle as if unsure what to do with it. The final image of Simon is of him *"dancing in the moon"* (120), the very place he said he did not want to go, symbolizing his reconciliation with female spiritual power.

Following Simon's death, Zachary engages in a monologue that is the dramatic climax to the play: "God of the Indian! God of the Whiteman! God-A-fucking-mighty! Whatever the fuck your name is. Why are you doing this to us?... Are you up there at all? Come down! *Astum oota!* ("Come down here!") Why don't you come down? I dare you to come down... and show us you got the guts to stop this... stupid way of living. It's got to stop" (116). Marc Maufort has interpreted Zachary's rant to indicate that "This monologue... unites the two traditions, Christian religion and Indian mythology... Departing from the depiction of the plight of Indians, Highway elevates this ethnic standpoint to universalise his vision and... manages to transcend the particular to formulate a compelling statement about mankind lost in a universe dominated by an indifferent God" (239-240). Maufort betrays his own biases in his use of the terms *religion* and *mythology*, and he seems to have entirely missed the irony of Zachary's monologue and the irony of the image of Nanabush "... sitting on a toilet having a good shit. He/she is dressed in an old man's White beard and wig, but also wearing sexy, elegant women's high-heeled pumps. Surrounded by White puffy clouds, he/she sits with her legs crossed, nonchalantly filing his/her fingernails" (117).

The irony in this image and in Zachary's monologue lies in the fact that Nanabush is not "up there in [the] stupid fucking clouds" and never has been. Scott Momaday has stated that, "before a man could write, he could draw; but writing is drawing, and so the image and the word cannot be divided" (96). The statement that image and word cannot be divided highlights the confusion the men in *Dry Lips* encounter when trying to approach traditional Indigenous spirituality through a vision of reality which is governed largely by the gender biases of the English language. When Indigenous peoples lose the vision of the world embodied in their first language they "lose not only the ability to express the simplest of daily sentiments and needs but they can no longer understand the ideas, concepts, insights, attitudes, rituals, ceremonies, institutions brought into being by their ancestors" (Basil Johnson 99-100). In his attempt to shout Nanabush from the sky, Zachary engages in the same hierarchical/linear thinking which plagues the quest for a return to a traditional spirituality.

While it may be true that "the essential characteristics of Highway's craft resides in the fusion of various types of influences" (Maufort 230), Tomson Highway is no advocate of easy answers, or the simplistic resolution of competing or divergent influences. Maufort's observation about the realism of language betrays an extremely limited understanding of the central importance that issues of language occupy in Highway's drama: "The use of realism is evident in the speech which the characters use, meant to reproduce as closely as possible the way *real Indians* speak. Passages in Cree and Ojibway are included, which augment this sense of realism" (235). Highway is well aware that language is the true embodiment of diversity and difference and that "it's a frightening prospect to be faced with, a world where nobody speaks any language but English" (Lutz 91). As has already been stated, and in keeping with his aversion to simple solutions, Highway never suggests a simple abandonment of one language in favour of any other. However, "For Highway, the road to recovery for the Native culture begins with the rediscovery of traditional spirituality" (Lewis 40), and this rediscovery is hampered by the gender biases of the English language. The play clearly shows that issues of language and spirituality are intimately interrelated to gender issues, which, in turn, have been complicated by patriarchal colonial competition.

The image of Marilyn Monroe represents Whiteness as desirable, while the conflict at Wounded Knee reveals Whiteness as a source of fear, death, loss and disempowerment. Both are gendered, since the latter was largely a conflict between White and Indigenous men. Big Joey is central here because the poster of Marilyn Monroe belongs to him and he is also the one to narrate the story of the defeat at Wounded Knee. It seems then that the female body is a site of contest for male domination. Big Joey views the defeat at Wounded Knee as a castration/emasculation. And, in a sense, he is doubly castrated/emasculated in that he cannot possess the ideal of feminine sexuality. It is after all an ideal and not a reality: "The Marilyn Monroe poster, with no powwow bustle draped over it at the beginning of the play, can be interpreted as a symbol of illusion. Norma Jean, the original name of Marilyn Monroe, was a signifier of the real, but the face of the woman named Marilyn on the poster is an image of illusion that led to drug abuse and suicide" (Imboden 119). The discourses of pop culture, Christian mythology, and the English language all seem to converge. Pop culture suggests that the female body is primarily an object of male desire, a construction of male fantasy, and an object of male domination. Christian mythology seems to offer little room for a female expression of divinity, and the language, with its gendered pronouns, offers no place for the female except in subjugation to the male.

And where are Indigenous women left in all of this? Well, they cannot live up to the idealized image of female sexuality, either in terms of gender or race. They cannot meet the ideal of female sexuality Monroe represents, nor can they meet the Whiteness of that ideal. They are left seemingly without value, worth or desirability. Hence, Indigenous women are left to bear the brunt of the frustration of men like Big Joey, who is frustrated on all fronts. It is these very women, however, who evade the conjunction of disempowering discourses and invade what the men understand to be an exclusively male realm of practice, namely hockey. In their invasion of this phallocentric male sphere, the women seize the initiative and assert their own agency, thereby holding a mirror up to the failure of the men's agency. At the end of the play, as Imboden observes, "Hera speaks Cree to Zachary, and a powwow bustle hangs over the poster of Marilyn Monroe on the wall... The bustle hanging over the photograph appears to imply that the richest roots of Native society can become more powerful than some of the more superficial, glossy Hollywood aspects of western society" (119). Furthermore, in the last scene of the play, Hera is clothed, while her husband Zachary is portrayed as vulnerably naked. Rather than being a misogynistic drama, Sheila Rabillard suggest that the languages and images of the play

> counteract any sense that women should be seen as victimisers and impress upon the audience, rather, a pervasive wounding in which the mutual enmity of male and female seems most closely allied with the self-inflicted wounds of alcohol, a species of self-division induced by a state of pain and oppression. In short, the drama seems to invite the audience to see the opposition between the genders as a hurtful condition analogous to – if not the product of – the sufferings brought about by White colonization. (15)

While Highway acknowledges that "the whole gender issue, the male/female dichotomy, the sexual hierarchy, knows no racial boundaries" (*Border Crossings* 24), it is equally true that "Through his work, the once sacred relationships of land, women, men and children are revealed as disconnection and distortion through subjugation to a patriarchal colonial society" (Loucks 11).

Dry Lips Oughta Move to Kapuskasing works toward disrupting the White colonial manichean binary that constructs Whiteness as desirable and Indigenous identity as degraded and undesirable. Idealisations of Whiteness are shown to be a disruptive force in the community, particularly in relations between the men and women of the community. Male desire for White female sexuality is shown to be a destructive idealization that interferes with the men's ability to value properly the Indigenous women in the community. Christian spirituality is revealed as supportive of patriarchal attitudes among the men, which contributes to the men's undervaluing of Indigenous women. The English language, with its gendered pronouns, is shown to contribute to the men's patriarchal biases, while interfering with any attempt to re-establish Indigenous spirituality and gender balance. Such White colonial invasions are given a more concrete expression in the Wounded Knee conflict, which further reveals Whiteness as a source of fear and oppression. The play directly levels responsibility for colonization and its effects at the White colonizer, but does not excuse the violent misogyny of the men. While the roots of the men's attitudes and behaviour are located in the violence of colonization, responsibility is assigned to Indigenous peoples to discover these roots and grow out of the violence and self-hatred we direct at ourselves and others within our communities.

For too many of our people, despair and self-destructive behaviours are undeniable daily realities, and, as Barbara Godard writes, "to hide the rage and madness created by the colonial process is to collaborate in maintaining an equally powerful mythology of the Native as untouched by imperialism" (213). While we must acknowledge rather than ignore or deny the impact the colonial process has upon our identities as Indigenous peoples, this does not mean that our cultural productions need represent us in destructively stereotypical ways, nor does it mean those productions need portray us as wallowing in victimisation. As Eduardo and Bonnie Duran argue, "intervention, albeit a theoretical one... starts from an intolerable present situation and then invents a genealogy of that situation that serves as a means for transforming the present" (110). If an Indigenous writer produces a play that depicts an intolerable situation, then one could argue that the writer is addressing the impact of the colonial process. Critics must then attend to the question of whether the play supports stereotypes held by the dominant culture or whether the play invents a genealogy of the situation, thereby offering a means for transforming the intolerable situation.

Highway's representations of Whiteness as domination in *Dry Lips Oughta Move to Kapuskasing* provide a context in which to understand the statement that "before the healing can take place, the poison must first be exposed" (6). A direct and active analysis of the representations of Whiteness in the play reveals colonial domination as the cause of intolerable social conditions and self-destructive behaviours. The play documents what Jeannette Armstrong in her essay "Racism" identifies as "psychological oppression and an internalized spiritual disintegration" (80). It is these oppressions and disintegrations, the effects of White domination, that provide the context for the despair and violence the play represents. It is these effects of White domination that make understandable the despair and violence and the complicity of the male characters in the intolerable conditions that largely dominate the reserve.

In a comment that might be applied directly to Highway's drama, Sharene Razack argues that "Understanding their [men's] violence begins with understanding the factors that minimise a sense of self, family, and community. In the Aboriginal context, this story has to begin with the violence of colonization" (65). Razack continues her argument by asserting that "continuing colonization and the devastating impact of past domination are the contexts in which Aboriginal family violence must be examined" (65). Razack's line of argumentation is one that is supported by Eduardo and Bonnie Duran when they write that "The objectification of Native American family violence deprives it of its material history and hence of a crucial aspect of its truth... The history of native/white relations since colonization... presents the context... of family violence" (26-27). In its representation of Whiteness as domination, Tomson Highway's *Dry Lips Oughta Move to Kapuskasing* returns the violence it depicts to its proper context, namely the violence of colonial genocide.

Works Cited

Acoose, Janice. (1995) *Iskwewak Kah'KiYaw Ni Wahkomakanak/Neither Indian Princesses Nor Easy Squaws.* Toronto: Women's Press.

Adams, Howard. (1995) *A Tortured People: The Politics of Colonization.* Penticton: Theytus Books

— . (1989) *Prison of Grass: Canada from a Native Point of View.* 1975. Saskatoon: Fifth House Publishers.

Allen, Paula Gunn. (1986) *The Sacred Hoop: Recovering the Feminine in American Indian Traditions.* Boston: Beacon Press.

Armstrong, Jeannette. (1992) "Racism." in Kelley. 141-146.

Baker, Marie Annharte. (1991) "Carte Blanche: Angry Enough To Spit But With *Dry Lips* It Hurts More Than You Know." *Canadian Theatre Review.* 68: 88-89.

Bashford, Lucy. (1990) "Review of *Dry Lips Oughta Move to Kapuskasing.*" *Malahat Review.* 91: 109-110.

Campbell, Maria. (1992) "Strategies for Survival." in Kelley. 6-14.

Coltelli, Laura, ed. (1990) *Winged Words: American Indian Writers Speak.* Lincoln and London: U of Nebraska Press.

Currie, Noel Elizabeth. (1991) "Jeannette Armstrong and the Colonial Legacy." in New. 139-152.

Duran, Eduardo, and Bonnie Duran. (1995) *Native American Postcolonial Psychology.* Albany: State U of New York Press.

Dyer, Richard. (1993) "White." *The Matter of Images: Essays on Representation.* London: Routledge. 141-163.

Fedorick, Joy Asham. (1992) "Decolonising Language," in Kelley. 47-60.

Filewood, Allan. (1992) "Averting the Colonial Gaze: Notes on Watching Native Theatre." *Aboriginal Voices.* Ed. Per Brask and William Morgan. Baltimore: John Hopkins Press. 17-28.

Fraser, Marion Botsford. (17 April 1991) Letter to the Editor. *The Globe and Mail.* C7.

Godard, Barbara. (1991) "The Politics of Representation: Some Native Canadian Women Writers." in New. 183-225.

Highway, Tomson. (1992) "Let us Now Combine Mythologies: The Theatrical Art of Tomson Highway." Interview, Robert Enright. *Border Crossings.* 11(4): 22-27.

— . (1990) Interview, Ann Wilson. *Other Solitudes: Canadian Multicultural Fictions.* Ed. Linda Hutcheon and Marion Richmond. Toronto: Oxford. 350-355.

— . (1989) *Dry Lips Oughta Move to Kapuskasing.* Saskatoon: Fifth House.

— . (1988) *The Rez Sisters.* Saskatoon: Fifth House.

hooks, bell. (1990) *Yearning, Race, Gender, and Cultural Politics.* Toronto: between the lines.

Hunt, Nigel. (1989) "Tracking the Trickster." *Brick.* 37: 58-60.

Imboden, Robert. (1995) "On the Highway with Tomson Highway's Blues Harmonica in *Dry Lips Oughta Move to Kapuskasing.*" *Canadian Literature*. 144: 113-124.

Johnston, Basil. (1992) "One Generation from Extinction." *An Anthology of Native Canadian Literature in English*. Ed. Daniel David Moses and Terry Goldie. Toronto: Oxford. 99-104.

Johnston, Denis W. (1991) "Lines and Circles: The 'Rez' Plays of Tomson Highway." in New. 254-264.

Kelley, Caffyn, ed. (1992) *Give Back: First Nations Perspectives on Cultural Practices*. Vancouver: Gallerie.

Loucks, Bryan. (1991) "Another Glimpse: Excerpts from a Conversation with Tomson Highway." *Canadian Theatre Review*. 68: 9-11.

Maracle, Lee. (1996) *I Am Woman: A Native Perspective on Sociology and Feminism*. Vancouver: Press Gang Publishers.

Maufort, Marc. (1993) "Recognising Difference in Canadian Drama: Tomson Highway's Poetic Realism." *British Journal of Canadian Studies*. 8(2): 230-240.

Momaday, N. Scott. (1990) "Interview." in Coltelli. 89-100.

New, W.H., ed. (1991) *Native Writers and Canadian Writing: Canadian Literature, Special Issue*. 1990. Vancouver: UBC Press.

Ortiz, Simon. (1990) "Interview." in Coltelli. 103-119.

Preston, Jennifer. (1992) "Weesageechak Begins to Dance: Native Earth Performing Arts Inc." *The Drama Review*. 36(1): 135-159.

Rabillard, Sheila. (1993) "Absorption, Elimination, and the Hybrid: Some Impure Questions of Gender and Culture in the Trickster Drama of Tomson Highway." *Essays in Theatre*. 12(1): 3-27.

Razack, Sherene H. (1998) *Looking White People in the Eye: Gender, Race, and Class in Courtrooms and Classrooms*. Toronto: U of Toronto Press.

Tuharsky, Anita. (April 1991) "An Aboriginal Women's Review of *Dry Lips Oughta Move to Kapuskasing*." Letter to the Editor. *New Breed*. 5 & 13.

Wigston, Nancy. (March 1989) "Nanabush in the City." *Books in Canada*. 7-9.

(Ad)dressing Our Words

Exploring Voice and Silence in the Poetry of Beth Cuthand, Louise Halfe and Marlene Nourbese Philip

Laura Ann Cranmer

The silencing of colonized people, either by brutal subjugation or by subtle erasure, does not mean their voices have vanished. Those voices live within the collective memory and the collective unconscious of colonized peoples and historically suppressed cultures. The task of making sense of colonialist history for those born in the midst of social and cultural upheaval is a difficult, but not impossible task. In re/visioning, re/claiming and re/voicing history there are a number of Aboriginal and minority poets who address the silences of the past in their poetry. In doing so, they provide the reader with clues as to how to proceed in a de-colonizing process. As we pick ourselves up to shake off the dust of years of oppression, the voices of Beth Cuthand, Bernice Louise Halfe, and Marlene Nourbese Philip emerge as cool, healing water. The English language blankets Indigenous history resulting in the illusory overlay of "l'anguish," a deadweight that sinks into the collective psyche of the colonized (Nourbese Philip, 1989:52).[1] The silence addressed by Nourbese Philip may be used as a guide to discuss that form of silence experienced by First Nations people in Canada, particularly through the images found in Cuthand's poem "Horse Dance to Emerald Mountain" (40) and Halfe's "Crying For Voice" (6).

What is de-colonization but the reversal of the colonized mindset that views the world through the prison bars of the language of the oppressor? What is being colonized but to be completely absorbed into the "body politic" (Titley 50)? One's personhood and language, the root and branch of culture, is subsumed by the language of the colonizer. Nourbese Philip's book *Looking for Livingstone* traces the speaker's quest in search of that history of silence signified by the dehumanizing treatment suffered at the hands of the so-called "white master." As part of an overall strategy, the colonists prohibited communication between slaves to prevent rebellion, and tribal members were therefore separated. This strategy was also applied in the enforced separation of Aboriginal children from their families during the residential school years and the attendant punitive treatment of those students who spoke their mother tongue in school. Nourbese Philip comments on the effect of growing up in the language of the oppressor in her essay "Managing the Unmanageable," in which she asserts that the colonizer uses language as a means to control the colonized, the "unmanageable." She states,

> The challenge for me was to use that language, albeit the language of my oppression, but the only one I had, to subvert the inner and hidden discourse – the discourse of my non-being. (Nourbese Philip, 1991:296)

As a product of my own colonial history, where the blood of the oppressor runs together with the blood of the oppressed in my veins, I embody the nature of the oppressor and the oppressed and by extension, the silence of the oppressed and the ability of the oppressor to speak. It is difficult to reconcile these internal oppositional forces. It is equally difficult to move through the obstacles of false perception and ultimately false consciousness and explode out of imposed definitions into a place that was always there.

That place is one of self-acceptance and trust in one's voice. If anything, it is a discovery of a place of courage out of which to express the cur/rage long silenced by years of oppression. As Halfe states in the afterword of her book *Bear Bones & Feathers*,

> I often suffered the rash of shame bursting through thin layers of skin. Yet my spirit demanded the spring of clear blood. I saw no need to run. The land, the Spirit doesn't betray you. I was learning to cry with the Spirit. I was safe to tear, to lick, to strip the stories from my bones and to offer them to the universe. (126)

To obey the call, the spirit directs us in a powerful healing act to confront what we carry in our bones and our blood. The "rash of shame bursting through the thin layers of skin" (ibid) calls for powerful medicine to help open the throat, through which one's authentic voice travels. Owing to its unconscious nature, the internalized voice of the critic (or in other cases the oppressor) spoken in "l'anguish" silences any initial attempts of the authentic voice to emerge.

Halfe has a recipe for voice which calls for many strong ingredients. Owing to the depth and breadth of wounds sustained in colonization, the struggle to subvert the internalized voice of the oppressor is great. The recipe found in Halfe's "Crying for Voice" requires the throat be cleared of obstructions. The speaker has to remove a "frog" in the first stanza described as firmly attached to the throat, "its webbed feet/from the snails in my throat" (Halfe 6). That the "frog" has to be "pryed" off implies a painful but necessary act. Halfe's recipe for voice is similar to Norbese Philip's poem "Mother's Recipes on How to Make a Language Yours or How Not to Get Raped," although she likens the obstruction in the throat to a phallus, "Love it, but if the word gags, does not nourish, bite it off – at its source – " (1989: 67).

Halfe's poem deals, as does Nourbese Philip's, with an invasion of the body and spirit by an oppressive force in the form of "l'anguish." In the preparation of these "recipes" one makes a fully conscious decision and deliberately acts to oust the unwelcome guest which resides in the body and the unconscious. The unconscious message of supremist ideology generates an epic internal struggle of both the mind and body to come to terms with the effects of the "discourse of my non-being" (Nourbese Philip, 1990: 296).

By adopting a deliberate stance with which to confront internalized demons, as the speaker does in *Looking for Livingstone* (Nourbese Philip, 1991), there is space made for deeper consciousness resulting in a new ability to respond to situations which have previously been met with silence. In quest/ioning her own history of silence, the speaker encounters the CLEENIS tribe. During her stay with the CLEENIS, the speaker is required to go through a cleansing ceremony in their Sweatlodge. The purpose of the ceremony is to cleanse herself of the "l'anguish" brought into her life. There is one step the speaker must take in order to prepare for the Sweatlodge. She is required to take only three words into the sweat lodge. After much deliberation she states, "Wordless except for my three words which refused to leave: 'Birth.' 'Death.' And 'Silence'" (ibid: 43). These words will see her through a test of spiritual endurance in which she releases the words of "l'anguish" from every pore and orifice, their "harsh, jagged edges ripping and tearing their way through my soft, secret folds – I hadn't conceived them so how could I birth them?" (ibid: 43). The speaker recognizes that she did not conceive the language that contributes to the "discourse of [her] non-being" (Nourbese Philip, 1990: 296). Owing to the power of "inner and hidden" or the unconscious, the healing act of making the internal external must be as equally conscious and powerful. As demonstrated by the massage given to the speaker by the CLEENIS women, it is imperative that the assistance of trusted friends be called on: "they bathed me in scented water filled with fragrant oils. When that was done they rubbed me with fragrant oils... every cell within me released its ancient and collective wisdom" (Nourbese Philip, 1991: 42). A massage acts to release not only tension but also toxins stored in the body. The toxins released from the speaker take the form of words, "and what a rout it was" (ibid: 44). The word "rout" is a military term indicating a violent internal struggle and necessitates the willingness to do battle, albeit an internal battle of one's oppositional voices. The speaker has cleansed herself of the toxins built up of life-denying "l'anguish" which makes space for her own language comprised of an "ancient and collective wisdom." The experience of the speaker bears testimony to the internal struggle that must be undertaken by Indigenous writers who attempt to subvert an internalized silence in order for an authentic voice to emerge.

The speaker in Halfe's poem "Crying for Voice" also demonstrates a deliberate confrontation with lessons learned in the "l'anguish" of the oppressor. The occasion requires nothing less than ceremony and ritual to honour the act of expulsion. With hands folded, the speaker kneels and invites "weasel to untangle/ my braids" (Halfe 6). Owing to the enormity of the task, the speaker in "Crying for Voice," as with the speaker in *Looking for Livingstone*, calls upon the assistance of trusted friends. In Halfe's poem, the friend is in the form of the weasel which is "known for its ability to 'weasel' out of difficult situations or tangles" and as such, is the right animal for the job (McGilvery, 1996). The ceremonial manner in which the recipe is prepared acknowledges the connection between the concrete body that resides in the world and the spirit in the unseen world. Here the speaker obeys the dictates of her heart through her body and consciousness to honour the directive of her spirit.

Beth Cuthand, another Canadian First Nations poet, also addresses silence and voice in her poetry. Ritual and ceremony constitute and inform to a high degree the structure of her poem "Horse Dance to Emerald Mountain," from her collection *Voices in the Waterfall*. Basically, the poem concerns itself with a spiritual ceremony that was historically outlawed by the Canadian government, but was integral to the Cree culture. The poem, as with Nourbese Philip's *Looking for Livingstone,* traces a physical journey on a metaphysical level. Structurally, it is divided into seven sections with each section describing various emotional states and voices, a journey of transformation and metamorphosis for the "self" in the poem. What is the "Emerald Mountain?" It is the essential self, which is "selfless/unfettered/free" (Cuthand 54). In Cree culture, the "... Horse Dance was traditionally a prelude to the Sun Dance, an important ceremony for the Cree in which the community gathered as a collective to pray for the well-being of the world" (Cuthand 1996).

In his yet unpublished book (at the time of writing) Geary Hobson, an English professor at the University of Oklahoma, surveys First Nations poets in both Canada and the U.S. and includes Cuthand's poem "Horse Dance to Emerald Mountain" in his survey. He interprets the various voices in Cuthand's poem to be "unclear and even contradictory" owing to the different personae that the "I" adopts in the poem (Hobson 6). However, I suggest that because it is a poem about transformation there are different and difficult stages with which the speaker has to negotiate in order to get to "Emerald Mountain." Hobson says that because the speaker takes on various guises, such as "an ancient grey stone," "a raw green stone," or "bear stone woman," the poem is lacking in "necessary concreteness" and that "one should read it expecting to find concretion and down-to-earthness" (Hobson 4). This is a puzzling interpretation in that there can be nothing more concrete than elements of "Mother Earth" found in the poem (Cuthand 45). According to *Webster,* concretion is "... drawing together so as to form one mass. Clearly, the mass or solid matter formed by drawing together" (Thatcher 173). In this regard, we only have to consider how the various voices and personae coalesce at the end of the poem to form "Emerald Mountain" (Cuthand 54).

In section I, the speaker begins in the first stanza as "an ancient grey stone" then transforms into "a prayer/a song/a raw green stone" (Cuthand 40). The speaker's silence is voiced through the stones in various stages of age whether "ancient" or "green." The speaker is seeking a way into the world. She is a spirit living within the stone. She is a living/stone struggling to voice her silence while Nourbese Philip's "Livingstone" is a dead stone which has silenced countless voices. The stones symbolize an essential element of silence, but for some cultures, such as the Cree culture, the stones have resident spirits. The struggle for the speaker is to locate the essential "I" she is journeying to find, and by extension, the authentic voice which rightfully belongs to the self that is "selfless/unfettered" (Cuthand 44).

The importance of the actual "Horse Dance" in the poem is

underscored by the line lengths. The lengths vary in a way that re-inforce the differing rhythms of horse riding, from long strides which throw the lines almost to the end of the page, "galloping gal-loping galloping galloping," to the short canter in these lines, "The horse/the horse/the horse and I/are one" (Cuthand 41). The vowels in the longer lines open up and slow down the line, while the shorter lines speed up, conveying a rapid rhythm missing in the longer lines. The sheer energy of the rhythm brilliantly reflects the spiritual determination of the speaker to find "Emerald Moun-tain" (Cuthand 46).

After travelling for some distance the speaker spies her "Emerald Mountain" and is compelled to travel on despite the hardship that she has to endure. She is drawn forward regardless of deprivation and fear. That it takes the speaker six sections for her to claim the mountain as her own indicates the difficulty of recog-nizing that which is inherently hers and the difficulty of moving through imposed and self-imposed obstacles in order to get through to that place of "never here/but always coming here" (Cuthand 51). According to Hobson, the various voices attest to the changing responses of the speaker to her experience, which under duress, may indeed seem "unclear and contradictory." The multiplicity of voices is representative of the speaker's singular experience of questing for vision. They finally coalesce in the last stanza.

The journey in "Horse Dance to Emerald Mountain" parallels the themes found in Nourbese Philip's *Looking for Livingstone*. A spiritual test is endured by both speakers initiated by the physical trials they choose. As the speaker in "Horse Dance to Emerald Mountain" says in section VI, "I am numb with fear and hunger/ chilled, thirsty/tired" (Cuthand 52). Cuthand's poem manifests the same internal journey found in *Looking for Livingstone*. The speaker declares, "to Livingstone and my Silence – I will open a way to the interior or – perish!" (Nourbese Philip, 1991:38). Here, the interior is the self, to confront demons which comprise a false consciousness and self-perception.

Any spiritual journey demands a kind of death of an old way of being in the world owing to the transformational process and change in perspective. The aim is to see with new eyes and to speak with an authentic voice that comes from being in touch with the spirit. While on her way to "Emerald Mountain" the speaker refers to her grandmother's death as well as her own, "My death/a different death/of a way of life" (Cuthand 48). The speaker's death then is not only her own, but also that of the life her grandmother experienced, now closed to subsequent generations because her culture was declared invalid until absorbed into the 'body politic.'

Writing from the position of the colonized calls for varied imaginative approaches and perspectives that undermine Western hegemony. To address the experience of the colonized in the "l'anguish" of the oppressor in a "logical, linear way" is to attempt the impossible and results in "a second violence," as Nourbese Philip says in her essay "The Habit of: Poetry, Rats and Cats" (1994: 212). In it, she addresses the unspoken assumption of universality in the rules of Western hegemonic discourse and outlines the problem that this has for colonized cultures: "This assumes the existence of certain universal values that would or could prompt the reader to share with the writer his emotions... so-called universal values were really a cover for imperialistic modes of thought and ways of acting upon the world" (ibid, 212). Her project is to de-universalize poetry and make it more particular.

It is that particular experience in Cuthand's "Horse Dance to Emerald Mountain" which alludes to Cree cultural practices that I as a *Kwakwaka'wakw* would have trouble understanding. Apart from reading the poem with attention to detail, rhythm, tone, and image, I can formulate an interpretation based on what I know of poetic convention as well as bringing my own history and experience to the text. But how can I know that the "Horse Dance" is a prelude to the all-important ceremony of the Sun Dance apart from interviewing the author? Cuthand says the poem is "very much like going on a fast to achieve a vision" (Cuthand, 1996). Thus a Cree poet and *Kwakwaka'wakw* critic reveal Norbese Philip's theory of cultural specificity that undercuts the notion of universality in traditional Western poetry. One fasts in order to arrive at some kind of personal truth, to achieve a sense of connection with self and by extension with one's own community.

In as much as Cuthand's poem traces the process of a vision quest, Halfe's poem "Crying for Voice" traces the process of a quest for voice which is essentially one and the same thing; for how can one be achieved without the other? The ingredients required for Halfe's recipe include "guts," "brains," "eyes" and "tongue" of various animals. These animals are spirit helpers evoked to help infuse one's being with senses from unseen sources and unheard voices in combination with "bible and tripe"(Halfe 6). "Bible and tripe" symbolize the ideological foundation upon which our historical oppression is based. To "rout" the ideology of the colonizer, one must take those symbols and "boil" them down to render an antidote, much like the venom of a poisonous snake is used to create an immunity to the bite.

The effectiveness of Halfe's recipe for voice is found in the abrupt shift in tone that occurs between the last and previous stanzas. The tone in the first five stanzas conveys complete absorption in the task at hand. The sixth stanza describes the actions and sensations of the speaker as she ingests the infusion, "Suck marrow from tiny bones/fill the place/where frog left slime/and salted snails/fell" (Halfe 6). Where the "salted snails" fall, the spirit and voice rise with the "tobacco" in the last stanza. Here, the shift in tone pivots away from all previous concerns and leads the reader in a surprising and unexpected direction. There is a palpable feeling of being unburdened, indicating the success of the antidote, "I'm fluttering wind/tobacco floating/against my face/mosquitoes up my nostrils/swatting memories/inside marrow" (Halfe 6). The speaker in Halfe's poem pulls memory out of marrow, stripping the stories from her bones (126).

The poetry of Cuthand and Halfe addresses silence in a way that points to the importance of journeying within to re/vision a collective past through the internal process of healing and becoming whole. Perhaps the point is not to become whole but striving to arrive at a place where Cuthand's speaker says, "never here/but always coming here"; a place that approximates wholeness given the depth of fractures and fissures created by our colonial history (Cuthand 51). By offering poems containing images and voices that express new ways of seeing and articulating, the work of Cuthand, Halfe and Norbese Philip establishes signposts with which to navigate, albeit in a metaphysical way, the difficult landscape of de-colonization. The achievement of their work is found in the connection between the metaphysical and physical – between the sacred and the profane, between the text of the page and the text of my body. The achievement of their work is also found in the way one reads one's history, the way one reads the messages from the body and spirit – both areas of the human experience not ordinarily given voice – when undertaking a process of transformation. One starts with silence, with the body, and with remembrance. The poetry of Cuthand, Halfe and Nourbese Philip acts as a cool balm for a spirit inflamed by my own unvoiced silences.

Notes

1. Throughout this discussion Nourbese Philip's "l'anguish" is used in conjunction with language owing to the experience of anguish absorbed from growing up in the language of the colonizer (1989:56).

Works Cited

Cuthand, Beth. (1992) *Voices in the Waterfall.* 2nd ed. Penticton, BC: Theytus Books.

— . Phone interview, April 12, 1996.

Halfe, Louise. (1994) *Bear Bones & Feathers.* Regina, Sk: Coteau Books.

Hobson, Geary. (1996) *Indian Country: American Indian and Canadian Native Writing and Publishing 1968-1990.* A work in progress, with permission from the author. (Oklahoma: University of Oklahoma).

McGilvery, Denise. Phone interview, April 13, 1996.

Nourbese Philip, Marlene. (1994) "The Habit of: Poetry, Rats and Cats." *Poetics of Criticism.* Ed. Juliana Spahr. Buffalo: Leave. 209-213.

— . (1991) *Looking for Livingstone: An Odyssey of Silence.* Stratford, Ont: Mercury Press.

— . (1990) "Managing the Unmanageable." *Caribbean Women Writers: Essays from the First International Conference.* Ed. R. Cudjoe-Selwyn. Wellesley: Calalaowx. 295-300.

— . (1989) *She Tries Her Tongue: her silence softly breaks.* Charlottetown, PEI: Ragweed Press.

Thatcher, Virginia, ed. (1971) *The New Webster Encyclopaedic Dictionary of the English Language.* Chicago: Consolidated Book Publishers.

(Ad)dressing Our Words

A Really Good Brown Girl:
Marilyn Dumont's Poems of
Grief and Celebration

Brenda Payne

As a Metis woman, mother, daughter, lover and literature student, Marilyn Dumont's poems give voice to many of my feelings and experiences of sorrow, frustration, discovery and determination. The power of Dumont's writing reinforces my belief in the significance of story and the ability to heal and be healed through creative expression and respectful acknowledgement.

Identity, politics and the politics of identity are themes that thread together the poems of Marilyn Dumont's *A Really Good Brown Girl*. Several other themes also surface repeatedly throughout the collection; specifically, many of Dumont's poems are reflections of her experiences of loss and grief. Her grief stems from multiple sources, some of which are universal experiences, such as the death of her father, while others arise from her experience as a Metis woman living in a White patriarchal society. Dumont not only shares her personal experiences of pain, she also laments the suffering of First Nations people, particularly Native women, today and throughout history. Although angry, Dumont is not bitter, cynical or hardened. Through her poetry, she reveals a willingness to face, mourn and, eventually, recover from her losses; that is, Dumont comes to revel in her identity as a Metis woman and find comfort and peace in the knowledge of her place in the natural, spiritual realm.

Dumont's grief stems from several sources, the most conspicuous of which is her experience of helplessly watching her father as he slowly lingers in the fissure between life and death, as exemplified in "let the ponies out" (23), "the pay wickets" (24) and "yellow sun days of leaving" (74). Dumont also presents images of her father as the vibrant, vital man of her childhood. In "The White Judges" (11) her father restructures the schoolhouse into a living space for his family and brings home a moose carcass that her mother honours and prepares. In "The Halfbreed Parade" (16) the schoolhouse appears once again as "the floating prairie structure" that her father "skids" into town with "a team of horses and a parade of snotty-nosed, home-haircut, patched halfbreeds." Dumont also provides glimpses of her father, the man she came to know as an adult, in such poems as "old fool and a five-year moon," (22) where her father is presented as "an old man/whose unschooled life/to you made more sense/than my learned life/would ever make to me," and "The Devil's Language," (54) in which she says "my father doesn't read or write/the King's English says he's/dumb but he speaks Cree." The images of Dumont's father in these poems provide a vivid contrast to the poignancy of the poems of mourning.

"old fool and a five-year moon" (22) precedes "let the ponies out" (23); the two poems are on facing pages, which allow the affectionate images of the first poem to complement the wistful tone of the second. "let the ponies out" (23) depicts the situation that every child fears most: the death of a parent. As Dumont demonstrates, debilitating illness can exacerbate and prolong an already unbearable experience because it forces the child to become a helpless witness to her/his parent's suffering. Dumont finds herself wishing for her father's death, to see him rise above his pitiful, painful existence and become part of the natural world: "oh papa, to have you drift up, some part of you drift up through water through/fresh water into the teal plate of sky." She shares her sense of helplessness and her desire to end her father's suffering: "I would open that gate if I could find it, if there was one/to let you go."

Dumont wants her father to escape not only his physical pain and the hospital environment, but also the emotional pain of being a Native man living within the confines of a White world: "to have your breath leave, escape you,... rising, escaping the white, the white/sheets" (23). She implores her father to allow his breath to be "taken in a gust of wind and unbridled ponies [and to] let the ponies/out... out, out/of this experiment into the dome of all breath and wind and/reappear" and to, therefore, rise beyond this White world and join the realm of nature. Dumont creates a sense of freedom, space and movement ("expanding, wafting, wings/of a bird over fields") and a kaleidoscope of natural images to reassure her father that his spirit will continue to be a part of her life. The final seven lines of the poem repeat the phrase "in the" to introduce the many sensations that will stimulate memories and evoke the essence of Dumont's father; she declares that she will sense his presence "in the": "prairie grass," "face of crocuses," "the smell of cedar dust... thick leather," "the whistling sounds of the trees," "sound of a chainsaw... chopping wood," "smooth curve of a felt hat" and, finally, in "unbridled ponies."

"let the ponies out" (23) consists of twenty-one lines that read as a continuous string of associated ideas within a single sentence; however, there is neither terminating punctuation, nor punctuation other than commas throughout the poem. In several lines, at the beginning of the poem in particular, commas appear in clusters of two, three, four and even five, but are conspicuously absent towards the end of the poem. The comma clusters slow the stride and force the reader to linger, like the subject, in the suffocating atmosphere of illness; this deliberate pace forces the reader to see that her father's spirit is now confined to a physical structure that is no longer functional or comfortable: "weight of bone, muscle and organ, escape you, to rise up, to loft." Dumont also uses a comma cluster to rhythmically and powerfully entice her father with the possible experiences that await him: "your eyes expanding, wafting, wings/of a bird over fields, fat ponies, spruce, birch and poplar."

This poem does not adhere to conventional metre or rhyme schemes, but employs alliteration, assonance and consonance to achieve a melodic effect. A proliferation of w's ("water," "white," "weight," "wind," "wafting," "wings," "wider," "whiteness") saturates the poem with a softening and seductive quality. As well, "s" sounds permeate the poem ("sky soaking," "face of crocuses," "smell of cedar dust off a saw," "whistling sounds of trees") and elicit a lulling, soothing sensation, echoing the tone one uses when speaking in a hospital environment. Repetition is also employed effectively; "Escape," "escape you," "escaping" and "breath," "breathe," "breathing" recur throughout the poem, as do, to a lesser extent, the terms "drift" and "white"/"Whiteness," conveying Dumont's desire to have her father escape this existence as peacefully, rhythmically and naturally as breath drifts from our bodies. "Ponies," as suggested by the title of the poem, is the most powerful image that Dumont evokes and repeats, the symbol of absolute freedom, the freedom of "unbridled ponies."

"the pay wickets" (24) follows "let the ponies out" (23) and continues the theme of a child maintaining a vigil at the hospital bedside of her dying father; the two poems reveal alternative strategies that Dumont employs to cope with the agony of her situation. In "let the ponies out" (ibid), Dumont uses her concepts of the afterlife to propel her father forward into images of nature. Conversely, "the pay wickets" (24) shows Dumont nostalgically projecting her father back into the man he once was. Again, her "dear papa" is hospitalized, but now Dumont reveals a little more of his condition, that he lies "buried/in a codeine sleep." Dumont speculates, "I know/you'd rather be betting #3 and #7/in the Quinella," a remark that becomes the catalyst for the recreation of his image from her memories, an image that succinctly captures both his personality and the depth of her affection for him and his foibles. "[P]apa" is a man who associates style with attitude and dresses with thought, care and panache: "dressing in leather/belt and boots, tailored,... hat and bolo tie/the one you braided and cut antler bone to finish." In addition, "papa" is a dreamer, who makes "a big-hearted bet, more than your hands could hold." Dumont further emphasizes the incongruity between the father she remembers and the man lying in the "sanitized gown" with the declaration that the former would be "testing the odds... just one more time before/ the wickets close." The papa she remembers was passionate and sanguine and bears no resemblance to the man who lies dormant, trapped in the space between life and death. Again, Dumont avoids conventional metres, rhyme schemes and structure; "the pay/ wickets" reads like a single, unending escape into the comfort of memories.

"yellow sun days of leaving" (74) is one of the last poems of this collection and seems to be Dumont's final, explicit comment on her reaction to her father's dying and, ultimately, his death. There is ambiguity about the actual moment of his death; that is, it is not quite clear if "papa" has died or if Dumont is now beginning to comprehend that "papa" will not be recovering from this illness: "your death, your going... you're gone papa you're gone... now that you are so long in the leaving." She reveals the denial that surfaces during the moments when the finality of death becomes overwhelming. She writes, "I can't believe your leaving," expressing the confusion that results from grief. Dumont's anguish intensifies as she recalls her previous experiences with death and abandonment and realizes that, once more, she will have to go through the various painful stages of the grieving process: "your death... reminds me of/all the leavings I've ever felt." In addition, Dumont must mourn the loss of her dreams ("I miss you and all the love I wanted to come near") and accept that she will never have the relationship with her father that she longed for.

In "yellow sun days of leaving" (74) Dumont is unable to fulfill the promises she made in "let the ponies out"; she is unable to sense her father's presence in nature. Dumont, however, still finds comfort in nature and immerses herself into the natural world and finds a release for her sorrow: "I want to climb/into leaves and molt... crawl into the dry death of leaves,... leaves/let go my grieving." Unlike "let the ponies out" (23), in which the pace is established with commas, extended spaces break the lines of "yellow sun days of leaving" into jagged sections. Theses broken sections convey the staggering effect of grief and highlights Dumont's use of extensive sensory images ("yellowyellow sun, yellow sky/your death, your going/on in my head like spruce falling in the bush or sun streaming through it/treestrees sun yellow heat.../other buried thoughts/let them drip saplike from my body...) to communicate the way in which grief is all-consuming. The poem's title emphasizes Dumont's bittersweet perception of nature. Here, yellow represents both the glorious, energizing "sun streaming" and also the final, vibrant colour of the leaves before their "dry death"; hence, Dumont struggles to accept her father's death through the images of death in nature. These images, however, also reveal nature's cyclical characteristics, which give her hope that her grief will abate in the Creator's time.

Another source of Dumont's grief arises from her experience of growing up as a Metis woman in a White, patriarchal society. Many of the poems in this collection lament the grievous experiences of Native women, including "Helen Betty Osborne" (20). Clearly these poems function as a commentary on the ways in which society propagates stereotypes of Native women and the devastating repercussions; she mourns for the "grandmothers,/ beasts of burden in the fur trade... left behind for 'British Standards of Womanhood,'" and blasts the "townsfolk who 'believed native girls were easy'/and 'less likely to complain if a sexual proposition led to violence'." In "Squaw Poems" (18), Dumont chronicles the experience of living under the shadows of the stereotypes that White society perpetually imposes upon Native women. The poem begins with the shout of "'hey squaw!',," a term that Dumont describes as the introduction to "the other words/like fists that would follow." Dumont does not capitalize "squaw" throughout the poem as she does in the title, a tactic that asserts that in its "real-life" application, "squaw" is derogatory and insulting and is not, as some profess, a term that simply means "Native woman." In this regard, Dumont employs the simile "her spirit drained like water from a basin" to describe the impact the term "squaw" has on Native women.

"Squaw Poems" (18) exposes the restricted choices open to

Native women in that Dumont reveals how White society tries to
force Native women into categories that lie in binary opposition to
each other. Native woman are categorized as either 'squaws' or
'Indian maidens/princesses,' depending on their sexual conduct.
Dumont clarifies the relationship between these terms and defines
the White concept behind their application: "squaw is to whore/as/
Indian maiden is to virgin... as/Indian princess is to lady." In order
to avoid the "squaw" label, Native women must deny their sexuality: "I could react naturally, spontaneously to/my puberty, my
newly discovered sexuality or I could be mindful/of the squaw
whose presence hounded my every choice." Dumont identifies the
rules that she adhered to as teenager in order to avert the "squaw"
label: "I should never be seen drunk in public," "I avoided red lip-
stick, never wore my skirts too/short or too tight, never chose
shoes that looked the least/'hooker-like.'" Dumont opts to
"become the Indian princess," although she has no information on
what such a life might entail; she simply reasons that a princess'
must be better than that of a squaw, whose existence consists of
"dragging/her soul after laundry, meals, needy kids and abusive
husbands."

"Squaw Poems" (18) is divided into six stanzas by numbers
written in Cree; the first, second, third and fifth are written in
prose, while the fourth and sixth consists of the use of comparisons
to define terms, such as "squaw" and "squawman." Interestingly,
"niyanan," like many Cree words, has a double meaning; that is, in
addition to being the Cree word for five, *"niyanan"* means "we/us/
our, but not you." In the fifth stanza, the narrator's decision to
"become the Indian princess" is the result of her rejection of the
term "squaw"; however, this decision also stands as an acceptance
of such categorization. Dumont uses *"niyanan"* to emphasize the
way in which such categorization divides the Native community;
as well, verse two illustrates how the term "squaw" has penetrated
the language of Native people to become a weapon of anger ("I
first heard it from my mother, who used it in anger against/another
Indian woman") and stands as the antithesis of who a woman
should aspire to be: "I held the image of that woman in my mind
and she became/the measure of what I should never be." Her
mother's insult, "'That black squaw,'" is also a sad reflection of
the way White society's notions of beauty infiltrate and impose
hierarchical divisions in the Native community – light skin colour
becomes a reflection of one's beauty and worth. In addition, this
observation combines with Dumont's definitions of "squawman"

to echo the history of the fur trade alluded to in "Helen Betty Osborne," the fact that in the first years of contact the fur trading companies forbade marriages to Native women and ridiculed those men that formed such alliances, and in later years, encouraged these men to abandon their Native wives for European "ladies."

The death of Dumont's father seems to be a relatively recent event; conversely, Dumont has experienced the treatment and history of Native women throughout her life. As such, many of her poems reflect a movement through various stages of the grieving process and into a celebration of her identity as a Native woman. "a bowl of smooth brown wood" (42) is a lyrical recognition of the unique and powerful characteristics of the female body and pays homage to its power of fertility. It consists of three verses that, similar to "let the ponies out" (23), contain no other punctuation but commas, which imbue a flowing, free association feeling into the poem. The first stanza consists of twelve lines, the final of which consists of the single, emancipating phrase "hips free of scrutiny" and begins with "a chant, a chant of movement, a movement chant" (42). This chant continues into the second stanza ("a chant, a movement chant, chain of movements linked to breath") and the last of the seven lines of this stanza consist of a single word: "positive." The repetition of the chanting phrases in combination with terms such as, "holding light/and letting go," "thrust out and back and around," "letting go, pulling back," "pulling back to pulling round" has a very rhythmic effect and evokes images of specific breathing patterns used by women during childbirth. Additionally, Dumont weaves a variety of verbs throughout the stanzas, such as "gathering," "garnering," "sweeping," "holding," "cradling," "passing," "opening," "changing," and "recomposing," which intensify the sense of movement in the poem.

Furthermore, Dumont employs flower imagery and wordplay that enhances the childbirth allusion and expands it to include the process of fertilization. There is a gathering, sweeping, and cradling of flowers "into the cave of the belly," which are passed into "our/tender dangerous opening, woman's space," (Dumont plays upon the use of "opening" as a noun and a verb.) to become "the stamen/stamina to fill out space" (42). In doing so, she rebels against the external forces that try to govern a woman's body and identifies the womb as the "woman's space, space free of rule or sin,/free to move… without censor." Dumont praises the "curl of your belly bow… a bowl of smooth brown/wood," praise that defies societal definitions of beauty that require white skin and angular bodies. In addition, Dumont honours the women of previous generations whose presence can be felt in the body, which is "older than the/memory of itself."

Intermingled with and central to Dumont's grief is her quest for and discovery of a spiritual belief that she can incorporate into her life as a source of comfort. Dumont ends this collection with "we are made of water" (77), which summarizes her evolution and reaffirms her ability to find comfort in the recognition of her connection to nature. Consequently, she discovers compassion for all of the Creator's children, Native, White or Metis, man or woman, and finds forgiveness in the realization that we are all made of water. We all experience pain and loss, and, most importantly, we are all equal in the eyes of the Creator.

Although she resists and confronts the oppressors, Dumont continues to experience the pain of living in the margins of a patriarchal society and pledges to "go for water every so often..." In other words, she pledges to remember the pain of her ancestors and those who are still suffering. Thus, she promises to continue to "go to that well and drink from it," to not turn away from or pretend that pain does not exist. In the end, Dumont recognizes that sometimes the greatest gift you can give to another is to acknowledge their pain and to share with them your own experiences, strength and hope, as she does with this collection of poetry.

Work Cited

Dumont, Marilyn. (1996) *A Really Good Brown Girl*. London, Ontario: Brick Books.

Erotica, Indigenous Style

Kateri Akiwenzie-Damm

"Many artists recognize that stories of the erotic have long been the source of inspiration and renewal in their communities."[1]

Sex in the First Person

About five years ago, I started thinking about sex. Seriously. I started thinking seriously about sex and sexuality and the utter lack of it in Indigenous writing. Or so it seemed to me. I've since realized that, of course, there was some erotic writing by Indigenous writers around – it just took some searching. A lot of searching. Too much searching. A person could reach puberty, live her entire adult life, go through menopause and still not have stumbled across a single erotic poem or story by a First Nations writer. Or, to make it even more depressing, I realized one could live and die as an Indigenous person and not come across a single erotic poem or story by an Indigenous writer from Canada, the US, Australia, Aotearoa (aka New Zealand)... I know, I looked. And although I didn't quite reach menopause before I found some, in a sense I cheated – I asked Indigenous writers to send erotica to me and I started writing it myself.

What is Indigenous erotica?

Indigenous erotica is political. More than that it's stimulating, inspiring, beautiful, sometimes explicit. It's written by Indigenous writers, painted by Indigenous painters, filmed by Indigenous filmmakers, photographed by Indigenous photographers, sung by Indigenous singers. But, for better or worse, because of the societies surrounding us, it is, like everything else we do, political. When one asks 'what is Indigenous literature?' it's a political question and the answer is political regardless of one's personal politics. Until now, it wouldn't have occurred to most people that Indigenous literature could encompass not only 'protest' literature, legends, myths, transcribed oratory, various forms and styles of storytelling, creative non-fiction, biography, autobiography, poetry, drama, and fiction but erotica as well. Somehow it was separated out from the perception of what Indigenous literature is or could be and excluded to the point that for the most part, we didn't even think of it. Yet, we know that our teachings and our perspectives as Indigenous peoples are inclusive and holistic. We know that "First Nations languages contain numerous words, stories and jokes depicting sexuality and the erotic as an important, and frequently humorous, aspect of life, love and spirituality."[2] All the more strange, therefore, that this aspect of our creative cultural and personal expression should be so absent.

Jo-Anne Grace, a Maori friend in Aotearoa who is a weaver and student in an arts program at a Maori university, tells me that many of the old *waiata* and chants were beautifully "erotic" and that the erotic was so much integrated into life and arts and song that these *waiata* or songs were not considered at all shocking or even different, despite their explicitness. This, as I understand it, is similar to the attitudes and traditions of the Anishnaabe and other First Nations and Inuit in North America. Old time stories included all aspects of life – sexuality was certainly not excluded. It was an accepted aspect of life.

Another friend, Haunani-Kay Trask, a Native Hawaiian poet and leader in the Hawaiian sovereignty movement, once told me that for Native Hawaiians, the world is eroticized: often food, the land, and all elements of the natural world are eroticized in Native Hawaiian song and poetry. Certainly this is evident in Haunani's poetry. In one of her poems, titled *"Ulu"* Haunani describes the breadfruit tree according to a traditional Hawaiian perspective in which *ulu* is, as she explains in a note, a male symbol and embodiment of male *mana* or power:

> testicles full
> with seed   sweet milk
> bubbling at the tip[3]

In many Indigenous societies, like that of the Anishnaabe, the earth and all who dwell within it contain a *'manitou,'* a vibrant energy that is creative and procreative and thus, I would argue, sexual.

So what happened?

In my estimation, the answer is simple: colonization and genocide. When the colonizers arrived, who we are as Indigenous peoples was disrupted and controlled. No longer was it a natural result living as we always had in our own homelands. On the one hand, we were defined and categorized by the colonizers. Set on small parcels of land called reserves, marae and missions, we were renamed and then those names were defined and legislated so as to separate us from the colonizers and settlers. On the other, we were beset by missionaries bent on offering us 'salvation' for our sinful ways, and in the view of many of them sex is a sin, unless for procreation.

Neither the colonizing governments with their missions of genocide and assimilation nor the missionaries with their sexually repressive dogma of 'good' and 'evil' cared to accept our attitudes to sexuality and certainly not any open expressions of it, cultural, artistic, creative or not! Certainly they didn't want us procreating. That wasn't the solution to "The Indian Problem" – we were supposed to vanish, to die, to assimilate into oblivion, not procreate for God's sake! Although miscegenation was not acceptable, it was tolerated because at least it fit in with the Master Plan of wiping us out. After a few generations of mixing our recessive genes with their dominant ones, we'd be as good as White, no problem. Besides, we were simple creatures who needed to be taught proper civilized behaviour. To this end, a good many of our ceremonies were banned and of course we were taught that those 'erotic' songs and stories which were so much a part of our cultures were unacceptable in a civilized society.

Why?

As Joy Harjo has said "To be 'in the erotic,' so to speak, is to be alive. Yes, eroticism presents political problems, cultural difficulties, religious problems because the dominant culture can't function with a society of alive people."[4] To deny the erotic, to create an absence of erotica, is another weapon in the oppressor's genocidal arsenal. When this part of us is dead, our future survival is in jeopardy.

So what happened?

Many of the songs were 'translated' into English in a way that changed them into something more acceptable. Stories were repressed and hidden away like some dirty secret. Or they were collected and retold by people like Herbert Schwartz in *Tales from the Smokehouse*, in such a way as to be more acceptable (though still titillatingly risqué and scandalous) for a non-Native audience. As Lee-Ann Martin says, "The legacy of colonialism contributed to the collision between the worldviews of Aboriginal and Euro-Canadian communities. Eventually, many Aboriginal stories became silenced and the images invisible."[5] No longer told or written by us or for us, the stories seemingly were only acceptable within academic contexts, for the gaze and study of anthropologists and such Others. *Fascinating.*

Unfortunately, it seems we got the subtle and not-so-subtle messages about the acceptability of Indigenous sexuality. By the late 1980s and early 1990s, when I was working on an AIDS awareness campaign for First Nations communities in Canada, I realized that, in terms of sexuality, many of our communities were at least as repressive (and hypocritical?) as the colonizing cultures that surround us. Though I didn't know it at the time, this was when my own awareness of the sexual repression of Indigenous peoples really began. Imagine trying to inform vulnerable First Nations communities of the potential onset of a health disaster like AIDS and being told that in some First Nations communities, it wasn't acceptable to discuss sex in public. How do you inform people of the risks of AIDS so they can protect themselves if you can't make any reference to sex? In retrospect, as a result, we did a lousy job of it. Today AIDS is rampant in some First Nations communities, just as was predicted.

So is it political? Damn right it is.

Erotic Without Reservation

Since I became consciously aware of all of this, I have spent more than five years collecting and editing an anthology of erotica by Indigenous writers. From the outset, the intention of the project was to advance an alterNative to some of the stereotypes and misconceptions about Indigenous peoples, particularly with regards to relationships and sexuality. Like many others, I was tired of images of Indigenous men as violent, monosyllabic studs, abusers of Indigenous women and ravishers of White women or as noble savage type shamans, warriors and chiefs. I was sickened by stereotypes of Indigenous women as promiscuous, drunken whores or sexless Mother Earth types. All of those stereotypes and images that make us less than the whole, complex, loving, sexual, spiritual beings we are.

I began to realize that there were few positive, affirming portrayals of relationships, especially romantic and sexual relationships, **between Indigenous peoples** in the arts or mass media (even by our own artists and communicators). Like Janice Acoose, who, in one of her essays in *Iskwewak – Kah' Ki Yaw Ni Wahkomakanak, Neither Indian Princess Nor Easy Squaws* asks "how stereotypical images like the Indian princess or easy squaw affect our values, beliefs, and attitudes,"[6] I began to wonder how the stereotypes, combined with the lack of realistic images, was affecting our self-image, especially in the minds of our young peoples, many of whom have dealt either directly or indirectly (through intergenerational impacts) with violence, abuse, cultural deprivations, and the forced imposition of foreign values.

It seems to me that the repression of erotic art is symptomatic of our oppression and signifies a deep psychological and spiritual break between a healthy and holistic tradition and an oppressed, repressed, shamed and imposed sense of reality. If erotic art is "a vital aspect of the human condition – of being human,"[7] then our very humanity is attacked and skewed when our erotic arts are repressed. Writing particularly about Native women, Acoose says,

> Stereotypic images of Indian princesses, squaw drudges, suffering helpless victims, tawny temptresses, or loose squaws falsify our realities and suggest in a subliminal way that those stereotypic images are us. As a consequence, those images foster cultural attitudes that encourage sexual, physical, verbal, or psychological violence against Indian women.[8]

Not only do these images affect us and our communities, they are absorbed by the societies around us and provide a sort of self-fulfilling justification of their genocidal actions on both political and social levels. Racism, violence, and disrespect are so much easier when the targets of it have been dehumanized.

Eroticism is uniquely human. To deny it in any culture or individual denies a basic aspect of the individual or group's humanity. "Erotic art determines the boundaries of sexuality that are permissible within historical and cultural categories of the aesthetic."[9] The silencing of our erotic expression says our sexuality is not 'permissible,' that its expression is unacceptable, that we must remain unseen and ignored, that we must accept the dehumanizing impacts of being oppressed and colonized.

I, like others, absolutely refuse! The erotic must be reclaimed, expressed, and celebrated, as an aspect of our humanity. When I became conscious of the importance of being alive and whole in the erotic, I decided to put together an anthology of Indigenous erotica and to begin discussing 'erotica' with other Indigenous writers.

One intent of this decision was to break down some of the barriers within our communities and within ourselves. How can we be healthy in a holistic way if we are deprived of this view of ourselves or if we only see ourselves portrayed as damaged and unhealthy? I don't believe we can. Overcoming this requires that we rid ourselves of the poison of those stereotypes and lies. To heal, I believe that our own stories, poems and songs that celebrate our erotic natures must be part of the antidote. As Linda Hogan says in *Listening to the Land*:

> [W]ords have a great potential for healing, in all respects. And we have a need to learn them, to find a way to speak first the problem, the truth, against destruction, then to find a way to use language to put things back together, to live respectfully, to praise and celebrate earth, to love.[10]

We need to see images of ourselves as healthy, whole people. People who love each other and who love ourselves. People who fall in love and out of love, who have lovers, who make love, who have sex. We need to create a healthy legacy for our peoples.

I have spoken to quite a few Indigenous writers, many in person, about erotica over the past five years. A few years ago, when I first started this, erotica was not as mainstream as it has become in the past few years. More to the point, it was not AT ALL so in the Indigenous community. There was virtually no talk about erotica within the Indigenous community and very little in the Indigenous arts community. I was determined to change this but I was a little nervous initially that I would be laughed at or shunned. I imagined whispered conversations at Native lit gatherings filled with speculations about the *real* reasons I was asking people to send me erotica **nudge nudge wink wink**.

Thankfully, these small fears were unfounded. There was no laughing, well, actually there was a great deal of laughing and joking around, but none aimed AT me. No shunning. And, to the best of my knowledge, no speculating. Like the serious artists we are, we discussed it seriously. Because it is serious. There is something seriously wrong when sexuality and erotic expression are repressed. In an individual person, it might raise a few eyebrows. Amongst a whole people, it raises a red flag. Amongst Indigenous peoples from various parts of the world, it raises enormously serious concerns with huge implications about our futures.

What is interesting (though not surprising) is that the underlying political aspect of Indigenous erotica was a reality that virtually every Indigenous writer and artist I spoke with seemed to recognize immediately. Although I was prepared to explain the deeper significance of my undertaking, it was unnecessary. As in so many cases when Indigenous peoples speak with each other, there is an unspoken understanding of our situation that does not require explanations. Consequently, I did have some wonderful discussions and conversations with other Indigenous artists and writers, including Lee-Ann Martin, Jo-Anne Grace, Haunani-Kay Trask, Joy Harjo, Sherman Alexie, Richard Van Camp, Morgan Wood, Geary Hobson, Melissa Lucashenko, Armand Garnet Ruffo, Briar Grace-Smith, Beth Cuthand, Joseph Bruchac, Kenny Laughton, Susan Heavens, Gregory Scofield, and many others. Engaging in these discussions has been one of the most inspiring, gratifying, worthwhile and fun aspects of this quest.

Defining the Ineffable

So what is Indigenous erotica? From the outset, I have resisted defining 'erotica.' I prefer to allow Indigenous artists and writers and the work they produce to define this on their terms and using their own perspectives, aesthetics and cultural perspectives. This is also what I have chosen to do in my own work. To re-discover the erotic voice. To give voice to the erotic, the loving, the sexual, the repressed, the oppressed, the 'dirty,' outrageous, intimacies of womanhood and sexuality that had only been hinted at in my earlier work. What I have been interested in is providing the opportunity, or at least the catalyst, for other writers and artists to consider the erotic and what it means for us, as writers from specific cultures and homelands with our own artistic, cultural and literary traditions.

To me, this sort of diversity is important. By defining, limits are set and barriers created. I have chosen to let this notion of what Indigenous erotica is emerge in a more organic way. By leaving it open so that we can create a canon together, for ourselves, is to allow our erotica to be free of those imposed boundaries. I call it erotica "without reservation."

What I can say, based on my work in this area, is that in a broad sense Indigenous erotica speaks about the healing nature of love, about love that celebrates us as whole people, about love that is openly sexual, sensual, emotional, and spiritual. Love, and the expression of it, is a medicine to heal the pain of oppression, hatred, lovelessness, and colonization. It is a way for Indigenous writers and other artists to freely express themselves and their ideas about love and sexuality, without being constrained by imposed moral codes or definitions. Like the artwork in *Exposed*, Indigenous erotica serves to "reject the colonial history that has hidden Aboriginal erotic images for too long... [and] reaffirm the important place of the erotic in human existence."[11]

Over the past few years a real breakthrough has occurred. Gregory Scofield's collection of poems *Love Medicine and One Song* was released in 1997 and contains some of the most beautiful erotic poetry I've read. Reading it for the first time affirmed to me the importance of rediscovering and celebrating the Indigenous erotic voice and provided encouragement to me in the early stages of this work. Then throughout 1998 I spoke to Morgan Wood and Lee-Ann Martin about the exhibition of First Nations Indigenous visual art they were co-curating. The controversial and incredible exhibition *Exposed: Aesthetics of Aboriginal Art* opened at the MacKenzie Art Gallery in late 1999, along with an exhibition catalogue that included erotic poetry by Aboriginal writers. *Exposed* subsequently toured to the Ottawa Art Gallery, where I was able to see the exhibit and read selections of erotic literature from my own work and from the work I had been collecting from Indigenous writers internationally. During the exhibit I was interviewed about erotica for an Aboriginal Peoples Television Network (APTN) show and performed a reading of an erotic poem for another APTN programme. The *Exposed* exhibit, which includes work by Norval Morriseau, Thirza Cuthand, Rosalie Favell, G. Ray McCallum, Robert Markle, Ahasiw Maskegon-Iskwew, Daphne Odjig, Lawrence Paul Yuxweluptun and Patricia Deadman has continued to tour. Finally, I hear through the moccasin telegraph that Drew Hayden Taylor is conducting research for the National Film Board on Indigenous erotica.

Beyond these more 'high profile' advancements, I frequently hear from artists and writers about various erotic works they are contemplating or completing. This is perhaps the most positive step forward – that individual artists and writers are accepting and portraying the erotic in their everyday work. To me it signals an important shift. I predict that over the next few years the erotic will regain its rightful and natural place in our arts. Although it may become an increasingly 'hot' topic or fad for the next while, I believe that eventually it will settle into a more normal and intrinsic aspect of Indigenous arts.

In my own work, I believe I am finally breaking through most barriers and can write freely, without obliviously dragging along the hang ups that I acquired as an Anishnaabe woman who was raised under the *Indian Act*, as a Roman Catholic, without having seen an erotic story or poem by an Indigenous writer until I was in my late 20s. I can be, and have been, undaunted in giving readings where the mention that I might read some love poetry or erotic poetry produces initial shock and surprise from the audience. No worries. I enjoy it. I enjoy writing it, reading it, presenting it, talking about it. In a way, it's like sex, once you do it, it becomes a part of who you are. Just one more aspect of life, one more element of what you do.

To be so much a part of the movement to look at erotica and, consequently, the huge and vast array of issues that surround it, is a gratifying and passionate pursuit. I see very clearly that this is a huge political statement. To reclaim and express our sexuality is part of the larger path to de-colonization and freedom. And so the work continues because I believe passionately that when Indigenous people de-colonize ourselves we'll not only free our minds, we'll free our bodies, our spirits, our whole selves. We'll live without reservation.

Without reservation. *Mashkow-aendun*!

Notes

1. Lee-Ann Martin, (1999) "Reclaiming Desire," *Exposed: Aesthetics of Aboriginal Erotic Art,* (Regina: The MacKenzie Art Gallery) 44.

2. ibid, 36.

3. Haunani-Kay Trask, (1994) "Ulu," *Light in the Crevice Never Seen*, (Corvallis: Calyx Books) 82.

4. Joy Harjo, (1996) "The Spectrum of Other Languages: Interview with Bill Aull, James McGowan, Bruce Morgan, Fay Rouseff-Baker, and Cai Fitzgerald," from *The Spiral of Memory: Interviews*, Laura Coltelli, ed., (Ann Arbour: The University of Michigan Press) 108.

5. Martin, 36.

6. Janice Acoose, (1995) *Iskwewak: Kah' Ki Yaw Ni Wahkomakanak, Neither Indian Princess Nor Easy Squaws*, (Toronto: Women's Press) 49.

7. Kate Davis, (1999) "Foreword," in Martin, 7.

8. Acoose, 55.

9. Martin, 36-37.

10. Derrick Jensen, (1995) "Linda Hogan," *Listening to the Land: Conversations About Nature, Culture, and Eros*, (San Francisco: Sierra Club Books) 122.

11. Martin, 44.

(Ad)dressing Our Words

A Syphilitic Western:
Making "The... Medicine Shows"

Daniel David Moses

1. Where is this coming from?

That's the question I had started asking myself, kept on asking myself, even though I had neither the time then nor, I admit now, the
nerve to try for an answer.

Where's this coming from?

There I was, in the process of writing the first draft of a one act
play, a little drama that had begun with the title "The Moon and
Dead Indians,"[1] a mix of the poetic and the morbid that was from
the start, without question, the right title. I was writing the play in
its dramatic and chronological order, scene by scene, but I was doing the writing of each scene by hand, then having to pause to take
my turn to type it up on the IBM Selectric I was sharing with the
other writers in the common room.

Where's this coming from?

By the time I started asking myself this question I had already
completed the first two scenes of the play and was almost done the
third. Those scenes had introduced me to the main elements of the
piece: the simple setting, the porch and yard of a cabin perched
high on barely arable land in the foothills of the mountains of New
Mexico in the year 1878; the not unexpected characters, the inhabi-
tants of the cabin, the anxious widow of a settler and her son, and
their one visitor, a young cowboy. Each new scene appeared first
in almost illegible inky scratches on the yellow pages of the news-
print quality pad I had been supplied with. Then each scene re-
appeared clearly in courier font on the white eight and a half by
eleven sheets that inched out of the Selectric.

And I had been surprised and intrigued by the way a complex
of dark emotions rose up through the play, and then surprised and
appalled as those emotions got steadily darker. But could anyone
have foreseen this piece that began with the widow, the mother,
Ma, appearing like an insomniac ghost in the night in her bed-
clothes on the porch, a rifle in her hands and the name of her son

and a lullaby on her lips? I only knew it was right for the play that she called for Jonny and then for Jesus, that she sang one of the few hymns I still had in my head from my own childhood going to an Anglican mission church. And then when she coughed and fell into silence, into sleep there in the night, I knew it wasn't just a cold. I knew it was not only T. B., tuberculosis, the disease that had forced my own mother to spend the early years of her young married life away from my father in a sanatorium, and I knew – or rather momentarily suspected, because in the process of writing you don't take time for deep acknowledgment – that Ma's cough was both a symptom of that historical disease 'consumption,' and a thread of what was just starting to go on in the play.

And it was that focus on the disease, the "dis-ease" of the scene, that kept me in contact with that little drama despite its darkness, the feelings of isolation, the fear and hopelessness that first scene embodied, the mystery of what it all might mean that kept me in contact long enough to meet the characters in the following scenes. The son, Jon, coming home with the dawn, efficiently starts to take care of his mother's physical needs like he's clearly done many times before. And because she seems to think his brusqueness is evidence of his shame at failing to bring her home a cure or comfort – he's been down to the town overnight in hopes of getting medicine from a travelling doctor's show – she tries to return his caring by speaking to his emotional needs. But why does he respond almost not at all to her comfort, her small talk, her teasing? And then why does he refuse to even listen to her fears?

Her fears. My metaphorical ears perk up, perversely or ironically, when I hear that what she fears are "sneaky" Indians. It's partly because it's nice to be mentioned, 'Indian' that I am, partly because it's even better to have power, even if it's only the power to be fictionally frightful. And finally it's partly because this might be an opportunity to figure out just what this fictional fear that beats in the chest of every western I've ever seen is really about.

But then the widow's fear is echoed by the sound of a gun shot, and the play shifts to its next scene and in walks not an Indian, not "the sound of death" Jon's widowed mother feared, but the young cowboy, the usual hero of the western. And cowboy Billy looks and acts that part, with his "pretty" hands and his "How do you do on this beautiful blue morning?" manners. His presence, a "gun in the house," lightens the widow's mood, makes her feel young again, but it does nothing for her son. Jonny's mood darkens when cowboy Billy starts waving his 'beaut' of a gun around, talking about 'hunting' and 'fresh meat.' Billy also talks about the widow behind her back as "*la vieja*" and "*un loco*" who "will die soon enough."

In Jon's rejection of Billy's repeated suggestions, there's a secret, one that I, even as I write, am beginning to remember is in part erotic. But as the scenes play out, I am also forced to admit that that secret also seems to be largely made up of a meanness, a cruelty, even an anger, which I, as I read it, do not want to take any credit or blame for, which I have no sure memory or knowledge of. No, this sick, ugly mix of emotions, it can't be coming out of me.

2. Where is this coming from?

There in Whitehorse, Yukon Territory, the last week of March 1991, a guest of the Nakai Theatre Ensemble, a facilitator for their Writers Festival, I remember now a part of the answer. In the last week, I had given a poetry reading, a workshop, and advice on and critiques of poetry. I had been staying up late, drinking and talking in a smoke filled cafe, and had slept in a sleeping bag on someone's hard, albeit carpeted, floor. At the end of the exhausting week, along with the other writer/facilitators, I was fulfilling my contract by taking part in the final event of Nakai's Festival, a twenty-four hour playwriting competition. I had arrived intending to use the ordeal to work on one particular project I had in mind. But after the van picked me up to bring me over to the community college, when it turned to drive from my mountainside billet down into and through the town, I saw the last quarter of the moon fading into the early blue morning above the snow covered mountains, and remembered another project I had long had in a line of projects as one worthy of investigation. It was a single scene in which a young cowboy, on the run after committing his first murder, stops to pass the time of day with the widow of a settler and her son. It's in the mountains in New Mexico, the place and the time of the frontier. And the two young men talk in what seem deliberate banalities, as if it's the only way to ignore the craziness and the questions the woman keeps asking about the dangerous proximity of Indians. The moon over those Yukon mountains had brought back that strange little scene, full of slightly warped clichés of the west. And of course that last quarter moon was what had so immediately given me the play's title.

Where is this coming from?

I knew where that particular scene had come from. From a play I'd written about Billy the Kid – was it called "Billy the Kid Shoots for the Stars"? – a play I'd written for a workshop one year when I was enrolled at York University back in the early seventies, a play I'd written with some intent of writing a history play and had afterward almost forgotten about, except for that one odd scene.

An arts journalist once asked me with apparent naiveté about "The Indian Medicine Shows. "Why would I want or choose to write about cowboys? "Isn't the western a dead genre?" My reply had something to do with the idea that even a dead genre leaves telltale marks on reality. Or why else does history not tell the truth as I knew it growing up Indian? The myth of the frontier is a story of exploration and conquest. The way my folks remember it, however, it's a story of strange visitors who overstay their welcome and take over the house. 'Indian' that I am in this country, culturally, legally, and sometimes professionally, I had and still do have a strategic, if not perpetual interest, thanks to what passes for North American history, American mythology, and even the imagery of children's games, in knowing something more about the reality of cowboy life. I'm imagining that journalist might next have asked, "But then why Billy, Billy the Kid?" And now I can only wonder if maybe, back there at York in the early seventies, I had dared – undergraduate, working class (I grew up on a farm) Indian – to feel that the upper class, educated shadow of Michael Ondaatje's already celebrated romance of Billy[2] hid more than it revealed.

Or maybe I had already discovered my own alternate entrée into the story. As a student working for the Education Branch of the Department of Indian Affairs in Ottawa, I was writing short book reviews, annotations for a bibliography of materials about Indians, a great job for an Indian intent on becoming a writer. So one of those summers in that library, flipping through encyclopaedias, maybe already researching that history play, I discovered what to me seemed a tasty tidbit. According to one source – certainly not one of interest to Ondaatje – Billy the Kid had probably died as the result of a quarrel with his lover, the Sheriff Pat Garrett. "Whoa," as we rarely say nowadays. Fancy that. I did more research, and although I found no other evidence in the historical documents about the Kid's sexuality specifically, I did find further support in the situation for the possibility of this sort of story. The historical West, at the edge of the civilized world of the time, was

literally almost lawless, without established customs, elder states-
men or available women. And when you consider the demograph-
ics, all the drinking, the violence, their class and their youth, it becomes hard to imagine how the heroes of our western story would
or could include among their manly virtues that of chastity. If you
also subtract a great part of our century's taboo against homosexu-
ality, suddenly every cowboy who cared more about his sidekick
than his horse looks more like a kindred spirit than previously
imagined.

And so I went on to write an oddly tragic piece, odd partly because this history play, this western, also turns out to be a clown
play. That first Billy I wrote is a white-faced clown innocent, first
an orphan and then a juvenile delinquent, searching for a replacement for the family the journey west destroys with disease, alcohol, violence, poverty, an innocent caught up in and finally destroyed by the New Mexico Territory's cattle wars. My odd little
scene where he meets the widow and her son fits in here, where
Billy sees in that pair a family, a refuge, and not the widow's fear-
fulness. That first play is also odd because the sexuality in it is
ironically or perversely chaste, a comic accident of a kiss, the one
action that Billy builds all his hopes on. For his friend Sheriff Pat,
however, that kiss is a threat to his transformation from a wild and
crazy gun for hire to a pillar of the community. Garrett sacrifices
his relationship with Billy to consolidate his position. Finally, this
odd little play lands well inside the typology of the western, which
may explain why it won an honourable mention in a playwriting
competition at Queen's University. Or maybe it was mentioned
because it's written in a concise and narratively forceful free verse,
or maybe because I imagined it taking place in a blank-page-white
playing space where stage blood can be spilled as the tragic action
progresses, a notion no stage manager concerned with running
costs, I know now, would thank me for. But in clown plays you're
allowed to make messes. When I heard the news about the honour
of the mention, I was in Ottawa again, reviewing more books. I
was surprised because I had forgotten that I had entered the contest. But the honour made me take a second happy look over the
play and it seemed to me that, though I had managed to present a
distillation of the historical facts adequately, theatrically, it was
only that one scene we're concerned with here that held any continuing human interest. Something about that woman and her craziness and fear of Indians intrigued me. It was a mystery I felt I
could learn from, so I promised myself I would return to it some-

day.

But not quite twenty years later, in Whitehorse, Yukon Territory, in keeping that promise to myself, I was again face to face with the craziness, the cruelty in the piece, and I still didn't feel like I was learning anything. I had thought I knew these characters, archetypes of the myth of the American west, the widow, the good son, the handsome stranger, thought I knew them well enough to be comfortable with them, but I had never before really experienced this darkness. Maybe I had never before had to take the western seriously, never quite believed it, always identifying with the Indians. My friend and director Colin Taylor would one day typify "The Moon and Dead Indians" with justice and succinctness as "a syphilitic western," but for the time being the only way to distance myself enough from its darkness to keep writing was to answer my own persistent questioning with an occasional mock insouciant reply.

Must be because it's my first play with White characters.

I was feeling, needed to feel, that the play didn't have much to do with me. I knew when I started on the piece that it was a western, which meant that, by the conventions of the genre, there would be no fully realized 'Indians' in the foreground of the story. But wasn't that part of the challenge for me, an Indian, to write about Cowboys, perhaps surprisingly or with a bit of irony or even some political pleasure, claiming or reclaiming or just re-telling a frontier story from my own 'Other' point of view? And wasn't I also puzzled, wanting to figure out what those settlers thought they were doing out there in the middle of what for them was nowhere? Just what were those characters running towards? Why was the new life they saw ahead so much better than the old one left behind? And just what did they think about the mess they had gotten themselves into, Indians and all?

Yes, I knew from the get-go that the play was a foreground-free-of-Indians western but had also realized that that wouldn't stop me from trying to see my own reflection in the background. And of course the central character of the play, the mother, Ma Jones – an actual name I found at some point in my research – does see that reflection. The woman's haunted by an idea of Indians as the cause of all her troubles – Where have we heard that one before? – Indians who lurk just beyond her line of sight, which is pretty much the line of the frontier. But of course I couldn't let the character Ma know it was really just the author, keeping his distance just over the horizon or most likely just offstage like the ghosts the play's title suggests. All in all it was a rich and strange position I found myself exploring.

And I had known when I started the play that as a western, it would have to do with guns and violence and alcohol – I had done, as I said, my research. I suppose I had told myself I needed to see how that social complex – guns etc. – fit into the heroic myth of civilizing the frontier, particularly now that I realized that that myth didn't quite fit the complexity I knew of sexuality. Maybe I should simply say that I had wanted to get at the reality of the settling of the West.

Where is this coming from?

I knew I was in trouble when the Winchester rifle, introduced in the first scene, the western genre's promise of a conflict's climax, went off like a practical joke – the characters even laugh about it: "We were just fooling around" – before the play was even halfway done. Things could only get worse from there on in. Worse? Just what was bothering me? This was dramatic pay dirt. I knew it was silly to be having second thoughts, but the high level of conflict in the piece was bothering me. The combination of the unrelenting aggression under the charm and chat of the character Billy, without which I admit the play wouldn't go anywhere, with the almost equal resistance in the character Jon together created the sort of emotional ugliness that being civilized is supposed to mediate.

Must be because it's my first play with White characters.

I know conflict in plays is, supposedly, a good thing. In school I had heard it like a litany that conflict is essential for drama. "There's not enough conflict in this scene" would be a classroom critical refrain. At first, I didn't fully understand. Maybe it was because, as an Indian, even one who's mostly westernized – my family has been Christian since at least my great grandfather's generation on my father's side. Although English is my "native language," I was still finding that there were traditional values, if not customs, that gave me direction through life, and those values, I was beginning to suspect, were the source of my confusion. For example, I had been brought up to not give in to, or give value to, conflict. Yes, maybe it was because I'm the oldest child, maybe because I've always been big for my age and had nothing to prove, maybe because I'm just a 'wuss' – or maybe it's because I'm Delaware and we were looked to as mediators.

I still perceive engagement in conflict as a symptom of a lack of imagination, compassion, if not humanity. The reason I persist in writing for the theatre, I occasionally think, is because every night it gathers an audience which embodies a valued harmonious community.

Imagine the discomfort I felt – I still remember it more than a quarter of a century later – as a student wanting to become a playwright and hearing this stuff about conflict being of the essence. I felt like I was being told that I had to give up my values as a human being to become an artist, which just didn't feel healthy to me. Of course, I didn't understand at the time that this particular "conflict" they were talking so blithely about in class – everybody else seemed to understand it without a doubt (I was the only Indian there) – was an aesthetic quality, one present if you look for it in any art. This conflict could very well be embodied, as it was in so many of those student plays, in a representation of the unhealthy relationships between psychologically realistic characters. What I didn't understand then was that that quality described as "conflict" could also be embodied in other parts of the play, in the ideas presented, in the storyline, or even in form and style.

Before I could continue writing, trying to be a writer, I needed to come up with my own idea about what that quality was, and I ended up somehow identifying it with what my undergraduate photography professor had called "contrast." Once I decided that what I was interested in was tension, a dramatic texture created by contrast, I got along quite nicely for years without that dreaded character to character conflict I found so unhealthy, so culturally incorrect, discomforting and distasteful. All was well until that moment in Whitehorse when I was caught up in the writing of "The Moon and Dead Indians."

Must be because this is my first play with White characters.

Over the next fourteen or so hours, those first three scenes were joined by five more, telling a story so strange to me in so many ways. By the time I typed "The End" on the last white sheet and handed the manuscript over, I had a first draft that was half the length of the final version and didn't yet contain all the historical details or the transitions necessary to make it playable. But it did contain all the necessary plot details, characters and emotions. It even included the waltz "The Blue Danube," because it was a piece of music I had chosen to learn during the years of my childhood when I was required to take piano lessons, as well as an abbreviated rendition of the ballad "Danny Boy" because, well, it's nice to be mentioned. I chose to describe that first draft as "the emotional skeleton of the play," perhaps because of the crime it uncovers, a solution to the play's conflict that both shocked and satisfied me. Even now I hesitate to talk about the concrete details of the murder of the effeminate Indian boy and the suicide of the mother. Even now I prefer to speak more abstractly.

Years later, when the final version of "The Moon and Dead Indians" did win a prize in a contest sponsored by what was then the New Play Centre in Vancouver, the director of the public reading told me that, even silently reading the play, he had felt the unconscious working through it. By then, thanks to the prize, and just being wiser about its several origins, I was able to accept his remark as praise and not start talking about how afraid I'd been writing the piece. I had written plays before, had experienced the welling up of a story without me having to worry too much about it. I had always prepared the way, done the research and thinking, sometimes for years, before the story was ready to be told, ready to unfold. And always before I had found I liked, even loved, the characters in my plays. What scared me about this experience was not only that I didn't believe I'd prepared for it, that it did seem to me to be arriving from out of nowhere, but also that these characters were as appalling to me as they were thrilling. It was as if I were afraid to take responsibility for the wounded, monstrous human beings the play presented. I couldn't have made them, could I? How could they come out of me, be part of me? It scared me so that when I got back home to Toronto, I put my little skeleton play away in a drawer with all the other unfinished projects and tried to forget about it.

3. Where is this coming from?

A couple years later, my director phoned to forcefully remind me that Cahoots Theatre Projects was about to embark on a new script/play development program. Although I didn't think I had a project ready for public development, I agreed to submit something, and in my drawer I found, just waiting for such an opportunity, that skeleton of a play. Resurrection followed quickly over a period of months. "The Moon and Dead Indians" was accepted into the Cahoots program, and I found myself, despite hesitations, now being encouraged, supported through revising it, researching, owning up to it. This process included clarifying my version of western speech patterns, a lyrical mix of manners and vulgarity, and deciding just where the phrases of Spanish would come into the dialogue. I also decided that performing the whole of "Danny Boy" would not do the drama of the play any harm. I found a definition of "psychopath" and became more understanding of, if not more comfortable with, the Billy character. This understanding included the idea that, as a dramatic creation, he's someone a playwright has to love. There was a new book out about Billy the Kid and I used it for concrete details, although I hesitated to connect my Billy directly to the historical one. As the actor who played him pointed out, my Billy was much better looking.

Beyond all the encouragement and the piece's now obvious strengths as a piece of theatre, what also helped me deal with "the horror, the horror," what helped me talk about it more abstractly and make sense of it, at least for my own purposes, were two related set of ideas I came across, probably months after the workshop itself. These ideas seemed comforting to me, vaguely familiar.

The first set are ideas in books by Walter L. Williams and Will Roscoe, anthropological studies entitled, respectively, *The Spirit and the Flesh*[3] and *The Zuni Man-Woman*[4]. These books detail the places in a variety of Native American traditional cultures of individuals who our western culture would have called names like "homosexual." In these Native traditions, which value individual spirits and their gathering to make a community, gays are seen as individuals who are gifted with both male and female spirits, "two-spirited." These "two spirits" could be seen as the resolution of the divide of the sexes and therefore representative of the value of the harmony these societies sought for their own balance and well-being. Because of this, these individuals could take on roles as medicine people, artists, caretakers of children and the elderly, and mediators. The book *The Zuni Man Woman* is a biography of one two-spirit who served as ambassador from his/her Nation to the American government. This set of ideas lets me see the play's murder victim, the effeminate Indian boy, as representative of yet another set of Native American traditions that have been repressed and almost destroyed. This allowed me to be sure that the "sickness" in "The Moon and Dead Indians" is not limited to consumption.

I add to this certainty a second set of ideas from an essay by the Native scholar Paula Gunn Allen in her book *The Sacred Hoop*.[5] Gunn Allen sees the meaning of the story of the settling of the west in an Aboriginal and spiritual context, sees it as the detailing of the near lethal unbalancing of Native America through the destruction of its female principle. This allowed me to think of "The Moon and Dead Indians," which tells of a murder of an effeminate boy and shows the suicide of a mother, as making sense, meaning something more to me than a dark horror show thrill. In the context of these sets of ideas, the play becomes an illustration of Manifest Destiny, showing the tragedy of North America's history in miniature, and as such, is something I should have been able to take pride in. That should have been enough.

But still, I was hesitant to put the play out there as it was another tragic vision of the west, even if in this case, "my first play with White characters," it was the White characters and not the Indians who were suffering. The tragic west is a story I, as an Indian, feel have heard too many times before. Telling it again, even with this particular slant just didn't quite feel like a healthy thing to do. On the other hand, spending all this time with a play just to put it back into the drawer also did not seem an option.

So where was this, this hesitation, coming from?

For a long time, I've had an ongoing argument with the idea of the tragedy, probably ever since I read a book about the Greek plays that suggested they were a conservative form, politically as well as aesthetically. As I remember it, the book argued that the tragic emotion these plays evoke functions to immobilize the audience, to get them to accept life as it is, things as they are, to present problems as mysterious and immutable, at the whim of the gods. Tragedy asks questions of such apparent complexity, it expects no answers. From the initial stunned silence with which "The Moon and Dead Indians" was usually greeted – it took a couple of breaths before the audience could find their applause – it felt to me that my play was meeting this set of artistic/political definitions.

But I have always felt that this set of artistic/political definitions is something that I need to get around. And I've done that getting around in other works, for instance in the play "Almighty Voice and His Wife,"[6] where I found the conventions of the minstrel show were an aesthetic way out of the bind I had got into retelling a historical incident that ended badly. This getting around things is both an artistic and a cultural strategy. It's a way to express non-conservative values like transformation and growth, even though I, like so many of us, have a penchant for the ruined beauty of the tragic. It's also a way, certainly as illustrated by

"Almighty Voice and His Wife," of bringing into a conservative theatrical tradition that seems to value the tragic most highly, my own personal and/or traditional culture's valuing of the healing and the comic.

The audience not immobilized always asks the proverbial narrative question: But what happens next? I knew the character Billy, from the histories that had inspired him, was going off to his death at the guns of Pat Garrett. But what about Jon? Could he go on? How did he go on? Where did he go? I was slowly realizing that what I needed to do was write a play that would be a companion, a reply, and a sequel to the sad and solitary questions that "The Moon and Dead Indians" had asked. I needed to write a comedy to balance out the tragedy before I could feel like I had written a complete work.

I'm sure my first explanation of what I thought the "Angel of the Medicine Show"[7] was about included phrases like "the return of the repressed" and "a comedy of western manners." I'm sure that I had realized that in addition to the character Jon, I would need to present the essences of the victims in the previous play, the two-spirited Indian and the mother, if I were to find a story that would be healing. And I knew that the action would take place in 1890, a dozen years after the first play, the year the American government had declared the frontier, that wound, officially closed. And as the history of the medicine show itself allowed, the two-spirited Indian could be someone I felt more familiar with than the off stage Apaches that had haunted "The Moon and Dead Indians." "Angel of the Medicine Show" featured a Mohawk from Caughnawaga. And of course the mention of 'Angie' in "The Moon and Dead Indians" really made me want to know just who that girl, now clearly a mother, was. She would also, of course, be my title, my central character, just as the mother had been in Part One. And then of course, from my previous experience with the Almighty Voice play, I knew that to mount part of *The Medicine Shows*,[8] the songs and repartee that stay far off stage in Part One, would have to have centre stage in Part Two.

My memory of the making Part Two has no clear narrative. The process of creating it was the process of ideas first, emotion and actions second, making the actual writing difficult. Where Part One had resulted from, as my Vancouver director had suggested, "the unconscious working through the piece," Part Two required my conscious mind, weighed with ideas and new research, to sink into the depths of the anguish of the characters. This unpleasant submersion is much easier done when you have a story pulling you along. You can just blink in surprise and ask yourself "Where is this coming from?" In the making of Part Two, I knew intellectually where I should be going but had to find ways of knowing and imagining the physical experience of my characters. I think I wrote the first scene of the play a dozen times before I could get deep enough to believe that my character had just escaped a lynching. The slapstick moments became a bit of a refuge as I felt myself finally begin to experience the drama. And of course the ambivalence of the ending of the play, the creation of what is clearly not a stable couple, thanks mostly to the unexpected pregnancy (not exactly a new story), was as close as I could get in this work to healing, at least under that weight of ideas and history.

My explanation of *The Indian Medicine Shows* project eventually came to include the following text, composed, I believe, for a grant application the theatre needed me to fill out.

"The Moon and Dead Indians" was a theatrically conservative but poetic exploration of the downside of the frontier. That downside was revealed as having much to do with the interwoven anguishes of alcohol, violence, sex and racism, only made bearable by the play's conventional presentation. The play was described both as wonderfully reminiscent of [Eugene] O'Neill and as honestly unsettling.

"Angel of the Medicine Show" starts with the given of the tragic emotion and activates it by focussing on the body. It is an intensely physical play, a challenge for both the actors and the audience in its presentation of literal blood, sweat and tears as the living and traumatic result of conflicts, in this specific narrative, those defined by both the metaphorical and literal frontier.

The play blends conservative narrative theatrical conventions with the vibrant, vulgar shtick of the medicine show to create an almost surreal narrative that allows for both aesthetic and narrative outs and real but unsteady reconciliations. It is in that sense a comedy.

The process that got me to the point where I could describe "Angel of the Medicine Show" that way took at least another year. Then I got myself and my director into a workshop for the script at the 1995 Page to Stage Festival at the Atelier of the National Arts Centre in Ottawa. We had our workshop time with the actors at the start of the festival, after which I retired to my hotel room to write. I completed an entirely new draft of the piece, a draft that I felt completed the work, and satisfied my impulse, which finally answered my question completely. I was finally sure where it had all come from.

4. Where is this coming from?

I found myself at my computer that fall, at the end of a long day doing a polish of the text, preparing it for publication even before the play went into production. I was tired, losing my focus, so I shut the machine down, turned the television on; a documentary about Carl Jung was in progress. They were explaining how Jung would interpret dreams and myths. Suddenly I remembered exactly where the emotional knot that formed into "The Moon and Dead Indians" originated. In adolescence, one day in about 1963, the boy I thought of as my best friend, a White boy named Billy, started a fight with me. How could I know then, what I suppose now, that he was trying to prove his new and fragile masculinity? I was puzzled and hurt and wouldn't fight back and would only protect myself, which frustrated him. He wanted a fight. He left me flat on my back on the ground and walked away, muttering what exactly I don't remember. But let's admit to the process of fiction that memory is enough to imagine the words were "stupid fairy" which would not be anachronistic and would be right for this story.

In that moment of remembering, in the context of that example of Jungian dream analysis, I suddenly saw that moment of adolescent anguish as the seed of the crime that was the morbid heart of "The Moon and Dead Indians." I suddenly saw that both the murderous character Jon and the effeminate Indian boy he victimizes at the behest of the Billy the Kid character were aspects of myself. "The Moon and Dead Indians" is, most simply, an early lesson about what I, in this post-feminist world, blithely try to refer to as "the hell of masculinity." But this is not a simple problem or one, I suspect, that concerns me alone. My "Angel of the Medicine Show" is a first attempt at contradicting that lesson. I'm still talking about it six years later. Clearly it's a lesson I haven't managed to forget, a wound so radical I haven't yet found a scar to cover it.

What this probably means in practical terms is that one day I will write plays about what happens next to the Indian character David Smoke and the baby Angie will have, both of them, I'm sure, aspects of myself. I will also write about what it means to try to be a balanced, healthy man or sissy or Indian in the new world that was created as a wound on the back of Turtle Island.

Excerpted from a talk given at Dalhousie University, Halifax, Nova Scotia, February 2001 as part of the MacKay Lecture Series "Healing in Human Contexts: Cultural Dimensions of Health" organized by the Faculty of Arts and Social Sciences.

Notes

1. Daniel David Moses, (1995) "The Moon and Dead Indians," in *The Indian Medicine Shows,* 9-70.

2. Michael Ondaatje, (1970) *The Collected Works of Billy the Kid,* (Toronto: House of Anansi Press).

3. Walter L. Williams, (1986) *The Spirit and the Flesh: Sexual Diversity in American Indian Culture,* (Boston: Beacon Press).

4. Will Roscoe, (1991) *The Zuni Man-Woman,* (Albuquerque: University of New Mexico).

5. Paula Gunn Allen, (1986) *The Sacred Hoop: Recovering the Feminine in American Indian Traditions,* (Boston: Beacon Press).

6. Daniel David Moses, (1992) *Almighty Voice and His Wife,* (Stratford: Williams-Wallace Publisher).

7. Daniel David Moses, (1995) "Angel of the Medicine Show," in *The Indian Medicine Shows,* 73-138.

8. Daniel David Moses, (1995) *The Indian Medicine Shows, Two One-act Plays,* (Toronto: Exile Editions).

The Beginning of
Cree Performance Culture

Geraldine Manossa

I decided to begin this article with a Cree story because I wanted a
Cree worldview to be the basis for my writing. The article explores
Native Performance Culture by examining the contemporary sociological significance between the viewer, writer and performer. The
sharing of cultural knowledge through storytelling is something
that occurred prior to contact and perseveres today and continues
to shape the realm of Native Performance Culture.

I have listened to many Cree interpretations of the *Wasakay-*
chak creation story, and each time the storyteller has insisted on
including his or her own twists and experiences into the adventures
of *Wasakaychak.* Each time, as well, the storyteller announced before the telling of the story that "this is how it really happened."
One of the most memorable occasions I recall was when I was
eighteen. I graduated from high school and was admitted into a
Native Communications/Journalism course at a local college. Before classes started in the fall each admitted student was required
to participate in a cultural camp, held during the summer, near the
Rocky Mountains. I was the youngest student among my peers and
listened for the next seven days to a lifetime of knowledge from
the Elders who taught there. Ten students attended the camp, the
head of the Native Communication/Journalism Program, and two
spiritual advisors. Eddie Bellrose, one of the spiritual advisors, had
done a lot of counselling and work in northern communities. So,
there we were, thirteen of us, all of us strangers to each other.

On the first night we gather into a sitting room. Eddie sits
down in a brown leather recliner. He weaves his fingers through
the holes on the worn armrest. A few of us congregate around the
doorway; his eyes give off a soft radiance, welcoming us with a
content grin. Eddie's skinny braids rest below the front of his
shoulders. He motions us with his shaky hand to come in and sit.
"My girl," he says, pointing with his lips, "Sit there." I sit next to
him. His gesture of calling me "my girl" brings me home to my
family. Relatives older in age and family friends, when visiting our
home, would talk to us kids in this comforting manner. Feeling
more at ease, I nestle into my chair and scan the room. Two other

students, Tom and Harley, continue a quiet conversation with the occasional outbursts of laughter. The rest of us watch Eddie as he quietly rolls a cigarette and then proceeds to roll a couple of extras. I think to myself, "Yep, this is going to be a long night." Eddie looks up as he finishes licking the last of his rolled cigarettes and begins, "Okay, tonight I'm going to tell you about *Wasakaychak*."

Eddie is wearing a plaid shirt neatly tucked into brown pants. He appears at ease with everything he does. He slowly brushes off the leftover tobacco that has fallen onto his shirt and pants while rolling his cigarettes. Eddie focuses his attention on lighting his cigarette; he takes a puff and smiles, "Yes, he was quite the character, that one." I look around the room and everyone has a smile that seems to confirm Eddie's interpretation of *Wasakaychak*. Tom chuckles and elbows an already smiling Harley. Since we arrived at the camp, Tom is either smiling or laughing. Harley, more composed, nods his head a few times in response to Tom's elbowing. I laugh at Harley and Tom and soon the entire group is laughing. I look toward Judy, and she is shaking her head while laughing at the same time. I can tell by the quizzical look on her face that she really has no idea why she is laughing. Then Eddie begins, "This is how it really happened, a very long time ago."

"Okay, this one day, *Wasakaychak* and his brother were floating on a raft. They were not alone and had many of their animal relatives floating with them down this river." Eddie pauses and takes a deep breath and heavily exhales. He hesitates and again takes another deep breath, as if it pains him to go on. "Okay, the earth is flooded because of *Wasakaychak*. He took revenge against the water creatures that had earlier killed his brother." Eddie's eyes solemnly search the room. He tilts his head to the side and shares his pain with us by cupping his chest with both hands. "Even though *Wasakaychak* brought his brother back to life, he still went ahead and killed those creatures." Bewildered, Eddie shakes his head. "Maybe the water spirits took revenge too...cause I just don't know...I..." He stops talking, as if lost in the spiteful actions of *Wasakaychak*. There is a look of puzzlement on everyone's face in the room except Tom's. Tom cannot contain his grin any more and quietly laughs to himself. I want to laugh too because of Tom's flightiness. I also wonder why *Wasakaychak*, even though his brother was brought back to life, decided to kill these creatures. I remember asking my brother, Basil, the reasoning behind *Wasakaychak*'s actions. He didn't really know either, but he did inform me that *Wasakaychak* was warned by a medicine man that a flood would occur if these creatures were killed. It was based on this warning that Wasakaychak built a raft; he knew the consequences of his actions.

Eddie's voice lowers and he looks around the room. "Shhhh..." he continues. The room is quiet and still. He captures our attention further by waving his hands toward himself. "Closer," he says. Everyone except Harley leans forward. He sits back, in a reclined position, with his arms folded over his chest and nods his head. The rest of us wait anxiously for Eddie to speak. "You know the one thing he forgot to do?" Eddie asks. Eddie drops his head into his hands and shakes his head in disbelief. "That *Wasakaychak* forgot to do something very important. What was it?" He asks again. Tom confidently blurts, "He forgot to grab a piece of the earth." Cheryl meticulously picks the lint off her cardigan. Yawning, she says, "That's *Wasakaychak* for you."

Not everyone at the cultural camp is Cree, so the entire group may not be familiar with the *Wasakaychak* creation story. I did get the feeling though that the entire group could identify with the excitement, energy, and multi-dimensional personality of *Wasakaychak*'s character. Within all Indigenous communities there exist numerous mythological figures. In general, a trickster character is overly confident, boastful, arrogant and conceited; he seems to ridicule with his shortcomings. Even though *Wasakaychak* is capable of transforming into various beings, his powers are limited, and in the end he is held accountable for his wrong doings. For Cree people he is responsible for the creation of many land formations that exist today. We are part of *Wasakaychak*'s journey and have been since time memorial; we see ourselves in him. This is why Tom found the events leading up to Eddie's announcement of *Wasakaychak*'s misfortune so entertaining; he was familiar and could relate to *Wasakaychak*'s fate.

In all of the adventures of *Wasakaychak* it appears that *Wasakaychak* may succeed in tricking an unsuspecting creature or being; however, an unforeseen event occurs, catching *Wasakaychak* off-guard. Eddie's voice is calm, and once again he is ready to continue. "That's right," he says, "*Wasakaychak* is always ahead of himself...you know...always trying to trick the animals and not thinking clearly. That's why he gets into so much trouble...he tries to do too much at a time." Eddie sits back in his chair and lights another cigarette and comfortably rests his hands on his round stomach. Like Tom, I have laughed or held my breath, anticipating the consequences *Wasakaychak* will face, due to his hasty and careless actions. I laugh because *Wasakaychak's* character always assumes and believes that everything is going to end up the way he envisioned. However, just when you think this character is going to succeed in tricking or conning someone, his scheme falls apart leaving *Wasakaychak* scrambling for order. Eddie's voice interrupts my thoughts. "So for many days and nights, *Wasakaychak*, his brother and the animals floated on the raft, in search of land or even the tiniest speck of dirt."

Eddie shakes his head and butts out his cigarette. "It doesn't look too good for them. They have no food and the animals are getting tired." Eddie sighs. "So do you know what he does?" He calls Beaver over because *Wasakaychak* knows he is a good swimmer," Eddie bolts upright and takes in a deep breath. He unbuttons the cuffs on his shirt and quickly rolls up his sleeves. Still holding his breath, Eddie sticks out his chest. I see the powerful and confident *Wasakaychak* emerge from Eddie's body. With his hands on his hips, he stands unyielding. Eddie's voice deepens. He says, "my brother, Beaver, I need you to dive deep into the water until you reach the earth." Eddie makes out like he is diving, pushing the water to his sides, blowing air out of his lungs. He continues this diving motion like a wave flowing up and down. Still swimming, Eddie turns to Judy and says, "Beaver you are my brother, and I know you can do this." Judy smiles calmly and accepts *Wasakaychak's* request. Eddie takes another deep breath and continues the diving motion. His arms curve downward and then arc up; the rest of his body follows curving like a snake. Eddie makes his way toward Colleen who is sitting next to Judy. Attempting to discourage Eddie's advance, Colleen curls up her body, hugging her legs toward her chest. She tucks her head into her arms. Tom chuckles loudly, which seems to cheer on Eddie. Even Harley is doubled over laughing. Eddie continues to dive, plunge, rise and swim around Colleen, but now each movement is greatly exaggerated. He sways his hips from side to side, adding some new choreography to the story. By this time, the whole room echoes laughter. Tom is hysterical, holding his stomach; he laughs uncontrollably, falling off his chair. In a loud, drawn out voice, Eddie instructs Colleen. "You need to grab a speck of dirt and bring it up to me, and then I can make the land appear again." Peeking up at him, she nods shyly, giggles and drops her head into her lap, hiding her face. Pleased with her response, Eddie relaxes and *Wasakaychak* disappears.

Eddie sinks into his chair and grabs a handkerchief from his pant pocket and gently blots his forehead. By now, he is out of breath but still continues. "The Beaver dived into the water," he announces. Eddie's hand shakes as he carries out the downward diving motion, this time like Beaver's paws dog paddling. He adds, "You know...those animals waited and waited for that Beaver to come up from the water, but it was a long time, and still he didn't show. They gave up, and thought that their brother, the Beaver, had drowned." Eddie's hands and arm movements flow gracefully from side to side, like waves washing upon shore. His upper body follows the wavy trail that his hands and arms are tracing out. His movements remind me of the waves back home in Calling Lake, gently washing against the sand. The sudden sound of Eddie's voice brings me back to the Rocky Mountains. He shouts, "From these waves came Beaver, gasping for air. It was *Wasakaychak* who pulled him from the water." Eddie's voice slows. " He didn't make it to the bottom. He has no dirt." Again, Eddie's body transforms into *Wasakaychak*. Sitting grand, he inhales, and his entire chest protrudes. Carefully, his eyes scan the room, until he finds another capable assistant. "You," Eddie's voice calls. His eyes focus intently on Harley. "It's up to you, my brother, Otter. You must dive deep into the water until you reach the earth. We need just a small speck of dirt, even the tiniest particle will do. It's up to you, my brother." Harley sits up, honoured that *Wasakaychak* calls on him to help in the recovery of the earth. After announcing the dilemma to Otter, Eddie settles back into his chair. It is as if he is waiting for a response. We all wait. The room is quiet. Harley looks toward us with admiration, as if we are the other animals on the raft. He doesn't speak, but nods his head self-importantly, accepting Eddie's request. We anxiously wait for the change in tone and rhythm of Eddie's voice. His voice is the orchestra that dictates the movements of his body. This is how he brings to life all the beings of the story. I look at my fellow listeners and notice that everyone is captivated by Eddie's presence.

He lights a cigarette, takes a couple of long puffs and lets the smoke escape out of the sides of his mouth. He opens his mouth to talk but stops. He rubs his forehead and briskly shakes his head. He is now ready to speak as if whatever he was previously going to say has escaped him. "The Otter really had no choice. His animal brothers were starving. There really was no one else who could do this, who could dive deep into the water and clutch some dirt." Eddie's 'matter-of-fact' tone came about because he needed to emphasize how important Otter's actions were for the survival of the entire animal community. In other words, *Wasakaychak* singles out Otter to help shape the destiny of all the animals; therefore, this gesture is not a time for the individual (Harley/Otter) to bathe in his own spotlight. Eddie puffs on his cigarette; he adds. "So, the animals waited and waited for the Otter to return. Things didn't look good. The animals wait for their brother to resurface from the blackness of the water." Eddie shakes his head from side to side, butts out his cigarette and exhales a mouthful of smoke. "Otter's body rose to the top of the water. He, like the Beaver, was breathless. He didn't make it to the earth. He had no dirt for *Wasakaychak*." Eddie carefully scans his audience. He throws his hands up into the air, and asks us, "Now what?" We all sit quietly, waiting for Eddie's cue.

Harley sits in his usual reclined position, legs stretched out and arms folded over his chest. He focuses on the floor; his spotlight is dim. "All of a sudden, *Wasakaychak* and the other animals hear a tiny sound coming from the far corner of the raft." Eddie whispers. "It's coming from Muskrat. I will do it, Muskrat tells *Wasakaychak*. I will dive deep into the water and I will snatch some dirt for you." Eddie looks to us, posing another question. "Do you know what *Wasakaychak* said to Muskrat?" We remain silent. He answers. "Nothing! *Wasakaychak* brushed Muskrat off, by turning his back on his own brother." There is an urgent sound in Eddie's voice; his breath quickens. "And in that moment, a splash shakes the raft and Muskrat is gone. He disappeared into the water." I can hear the deep hollow sound that comes from Muskrat's plunge into the water. I can see the ripples of his dive, reaching the unsteady raft and still reaching outward beyond the deepest and blackest areas of the lake. Eddie quietly adds, "*Wasakaychak* dragged himself to the corner of the raft and sat there, slumped over. That *Wasakaychak* sure could pout...almost as well as he could gloat." Eddie slips in a smile, but then returns to his remorse. "*Wasakaychak* had given up, and some of the animals on the raft started to say their good-byes to one another. It was a very sad moment."

Eddie's exhausted body lazily reclines into the armchair. Again, we wait in silence; we wait for the return of Muskrat. Out of the stillness, Eddie reaches his cupped hand forward, barely having enough strength to steady it. His body holds that pose, and he stares beyond the walls in this room. In one motion, Eddie slowly lifts himself up from the chair, pulling and lifting something heavy toward his chest. It is Muskrat's body. Eddie's body shifts to a neutral stance, and he announces. "*Wasakaychak* was the first to spot Muskrat's body surfacing. He alone picked him up from the water. Eddie repeats the same slow sequence of the pulling and lifting of Muskrat's body. "*Wasakaychak* couldn't help but pity his brother. He laid his brother's lifeless body down on the raft and walked away." Eddie lowers his head, as if he were about to pray for Muskrat. He takes out his handkerchief and wipes along his forehead and around his eyes. As if not wanting to be part of the dialogue, Eddie says: "Now, the animals really began to worry because they had never seen *Wasakaychak* act so lost. He always had a plan or trick for every situation, and he always had a back up plan." Eddie clears his voice. He whispers and pronounces every word quietly as if it were his last. "The raft continued to float on the lake without a word or sound coming from *Wasakaychak* or the animals."

Eddie lights the last of his rolled cigarettes and again leans back into his chair. He lazily blows the smoke from his cigarette toward the ceiling, where his eyes remain focused. "You see," Eddie says, "one of the animals discovered that Muskrat did get some dirt under his claws. *Wasakaychak* didn't even bother to look. He had given up hope on his little brother and didn't even check his claws." Eddie's body remains reclined in the armchair. Still looking up toward the ceiling in a daze, he continues. "*Wasakaychak* came over to Muskrat and blew into his mouth, bringing him back to life. He took the tiny particle of dirt and began to roll it and as he rolled it, *Wasakaychak* blew into his own hand and the dirt grew and grew with each magical breath. Eddie leans toward his audience and manages to smile proudly at each of us, as if we were his own children. I beam back at him.

During the course of his storytelling, some of Eddie's hair slipped out from his braids. His gray hair hangs loose around his jaw, and he clumsily brushes it away, tucking it behind his ear. Eventually, his hair wins out and remains dangling around his face. His performance ends. No longer transformed into *Wasakaychak* or the water, he, like the rest of us, enjoys the decline of the story's events. "Yes, *Wasakaychak* recreated the earth as we know it today. With his breath he grew forests and lakes. *Wasakaychak* wanted to make sure that the earth was large enough for everyone to live on, so he sent his brother the Wolf on a journey to make sure it was. When Wolf didn't return after a long time, *Wasakaychak* knew the earth was large enough." Eddie grins. "You know something? *Wasakaychak* sure missed his brother, and he's been roaming the earth looking for him ever since...really...Good thing, eh?" he adds, "...'cause us Indians wouldn't have anything to talk about, eh?"

Eddie is referring to the many stories that exist today which continue to be recounted by the storytellers of the community. The *Wasakaychak* stories that we have today are a result of the encounters *Wasakaychak* had with his animal brothers and the land. There is actually a story about *Wasakaychak* misplacing his eyes balls, and about *Wasakaychak* whipping the birch tree, giving the birch its stripped markings. Eddie slaps his lap with one hand and wipes the tears from his eyes with another. Still laughing, he says, "Oh that *Wasakaychak* sure was something." A Cree person just has to mention the name *Wasakaychak* and people grin. How can we not smile when picturing *Wasakaychak* on the ground, clumsily looking for his eyeballs? I recall on many occasions, during a *Wasakaychak* story, thinking "oh no, not again," as *Wasakaychak* was about to trick yet another animal relative. A *Wasakaychak* story always captivates an audience. The listener never really knows how the storyteller will dramatize the story's events. I have seen one storyteller interpret *Wasakaychak* in a more "clown-like" fashion. Rather than portraying *Wasakaychak* the way Eddie does, where *Wasakaychak* appears physically powerful, forceful and strong, he made his physical attributes comical. This storyteller portrayed *Wasakaychak* slouched over with a protruding buttock and arms as limp as spaghetti.

The collective manner through which knowledge, images, symbols, actions and humour are shared from listener to listener and from storyteller to listener is where I believe the essence of Native performance arises. This is also the core of contemporary Native theatre. If someone asked me to imitate *Wasakaychak*, I could do so because he is so full of life, comedy, energy and magic. He comes from Cree land. Through our storytellers, we as listeners are exposed to and witness the movements, songs and dances of water, of trees and of various life beings. *Wasakaychak*'s breath is magic; he can breathe life into the dead. Through his breath he created the earth. For centuries Cree storytellers retained and passed on this knowledge to their community. Today, thanks to the storytellers of Native communities, I, as a performer, can approach my work and training based upon the history of my ancestors.

One story that I heard from my mother about my Great-granny has had a profound effect on how I view the ideas around sharing everything from food, to stories, to worldviews. My mother remembers eating a meal with her Granny outside of her tee-pee. My Great-granny refused to live inside a house after they had been built for the people, and she stationed herself in her tee-pee, outside of her daughter's home. My mother remembers, her Granny made this terrific stew full of vegetables. I say terrific because usually Granny's stews consisted only of potatoes, turnips and moose meat. However, this stew was different. Not only did it contain its usual blend, but also the stew was full of carrots, peas and beans. Both Granny and granddaughter slowly slurped and savoured each spoonful. A man, yelling and screaming outside of their tee-pee, interrupted them. My mother said that the louder he screamed the more his face seemed to glow red. Clutched in his hand was a piece of string that he kept waving about while he yelled. Based on the anger and anxiety of this man in the long black dress, my mom thought that he was going to take the string to her Granny's neck. He didn't.

Earlier, the priest discovered some carrots, peas and beans missing from his garden. The priest had used the string to measure the footprints he found near the missing vegetables. He stood there, clutching the string, an invaluable witness, ready to prove that Granny was the guilty culprit. This man pointed at her feet and continued to scream at her in an unfamiliar language. He wanted to measure her feet. Unmoved by the priest's emotional outpouring, Granny disappeared back into the tee-pee and returned with a pair of non-matching black rubbers. Granny wore the rubbers over her moccasins to protect them, when she journeyed away from home. Granny was infamous for collecting and wearing mis-matched rubbers on her feet. No two pairs of Granny's rubbers matched up. So when the priest began the meticulous procedure of measuring the string to the size of each rubber, his calculations didn't work out as expected. Not exactly your Cinderella story, eh? The man was furious; he knew something wasn't quite right but couldn't figure it out. He took one last look at Granny, pointed his finger at her accusingly, muttered something to himself and stomped off. I'm sure he vowed vengeance, as my mother remembers it, because the two of them continued to share these bowls of hearty stew, and the priest made regular appearances at her Granny's tee-pee with his piece of string.

Granny's relations still came to see her, reminding her that the priest's vegetable garden was his and his alone. They hoped that these visits would stop this stubborn old woman from helping herself to the priest's garden. Like *Wasakaychak*, the stories of Great-granny shared among my family have the listener shaking her head in disbelief. When Great-granny is talked about in a joking manner, she is called crazy and eccentric. I view her, however, as a woman whose life was shaped by her experiences with her surrounding landscapes. Throughout her whole life, the earth had nourished her and her children. So why was the priest's section of land (all of a sudden) any different from the rest of the territory that she knew so well? This story comes from Cree land and from the collective interactions of Cree community members with each other on Cree land. These are some of the origins of Native performance and contemporary Native drama.

Floyd Favel Starr is a Cree from Poundmaker, Saskatchewan; he is a playwright, director and actor. In his article "The Artificial Tree," he defines Native Performance Culture as the "developing practices of our ancestors" (83). Before her death, Great-granny, like *Wasakaychak*, continued to shape the land. Even when it meant defying a priest, a government imposed authority figure within her community. She allowed the land to nourish her because according to her Cree worldview, food is a gift from the creator. In return, Great-granny would be both respectful and thankful in prayer to the land because it provided food for her and her family.

When Eddie tells a story, he acknowledges his listeners; therefore, making them part of his performance. Both the listener and the teller are actively involved in the process of storytelling, an exchange occurs. Eddie feeds off the energy of the listener and something is shared, be it laughter or a new perspective. Sharing is vital to Cree performance because sharing is vital to Cree culture. Great-granny understood everything that comes from these lands has the potential to be shared. That is why she could never understand why the priest scolded her for taking from his garden. Storytelling is a time of sharing. Sharing knowledge, humour, tears, songs and dances. Storytelling is about sharing the history and knowledge of the land, by recounting how beings since the beginning of time have interacted with it. According to Highway, when Native theatre performance is shared on stage, the audience witnesses "treasures that have been there for thousands of years. It [is] like finding a treasure chest filled with diamonds and silver" (2). Native performers are taking "the gems out of those chests[,] ... showing them to a world that never realized what a richness of culture was hidden away just under the top soil" (Highway 2).

Starr Favel's article is based on his research of Native Performance Culture over a five-year period (1991-96). In an attempt to develop a working methodology for it, he discovered it was necessary to reduce Native songs and dances to their "bare essentials" and find the essence of what makes them Native (83). He feels this process, which he labels "reductionism," allows the Native performer to "isolate the basic building blocks of the song and dance, [where] these become the staring points for a creative and vital action" (83). These building blocks can then be developed, modified, revised or expanded. But since their Indigenous core has been carefully considered, they retain their Native cultural integrity in the face of artistic change. In order for Native artists to carry this out, we must know our own tribal songs and dances. It is up to us to conduct the necessary research. For the Native performer, the outcome, through the process of reductionism, is the starting point for Native Performance Culture. We need to listen and learn from Great-granny stories. As artists we should be able to be inspired by our land's powerful beings, like *Wasakaychak*, Coyote, Raven and *Nanaboozoo*. Salish writer/performer, Lee Maracle reminds us that prior to the colonization of North America, there existed a theatre tradition for Native people: "Anyone who has seen those story dance knows we have a theatrical tradition. Anyone who has watched Basil Johnston perform a story knows that the Ojibway have a theatrical tradition. We all have theatrical traditions. We all have theatrical tradition in our cultures [and] we haven't been schooled in that (Maracle 11).

Starr Favel also points out that the artist's "starting points for creative and vital action" do not "differ in principle from other performance traditions" (83). An important distinction to mention between Western and Native Performance Culture is that for the Native artist his or her "reference points are from Native culture [which] originate in this land. The artistic source is not transplanted and colonial" (83). To reiterate, the idea of working from an Indigenous source through songs, dances and stories reinforces the worldview of a Native performer whose creative starting points would then originate from the land of his or her ancestors.

Starr Favel disputes the idea that Native Performance Culture is a fusion/synthesis of the traditional and the contemporary. He states that Native artists need to continue to develop and maintain a "working practical knowledge of our language, songs, dances, stories and histories" (85). In doing so, as artists we will continue, like Great-granny, to be influenced by a great worldview, reflecting and representing on stage who we are as contemporary Native people.

Through Starr Favel's research into the methodology of Native Culture Performance, he locates where Native artists can find their story, song, dance, rhythm and their spirit, without "internal conflict, colonization or beggary" (85). Native Culture Performance is not about Native people on stage merely imitating Western theatre. As Starr Favel discovered, Native Performance is its own culture, rooted, upheld, suspended and dancing from the magical breath of *Wasakaychak* and from the determination and stubbornness of our Great-grannies.

A main distinction between contemporary Native performance and colonial Western theatre is that the roots of Native performance can be traced to the lands of this country. When a Cree storyteller, like Eddie, tells a story, his sounds, words and movements are inspired by the land that he has experienced. When he imitates the sounds of the waves, unfolding upon a shore, it is a body of water that he has visited and experienced. It is a shore where his grandfather or great-grandfather fished from and prayed to, offering thanks. It may also be a body of water that the old people have warned Eddie to stay away from because *Wintigo* (Cree/Ojibway cannibalistic creature) has been spotted there. Native performance theatre comes from a specific source and entails a particular language, which unfolds movements true to the story. These specifics reflect Native performance as distinct from western theatre based on where the creative process arises. That is why Native performers, writers and directors need to do the necessary ancestral research, so they can continually be inspired from these unambiguous and powerful sources.

Works Cited

D'Aponte, G.M., ed. (1999) *An Anthology of Native American Plays.* New York: Theatre Communications Group.

Highway, T. (June 1998) Opening Address. "What is the Purpose of Native Theatre." Croft Chapter House, University of Toronto. National Native Theatre Symposium, Native Earth Performing Arts, Inc., Toronto.

Maracle, L. (June 1998) "Training in all fields of theatre." Croft Chapter House, University of Toronto. National Native Theatre Symposium, Native Earth Performing Arts, Inc., Toronto.

Starr Favel, F. (1997) "The artificial tree: Native Performance Culture Research 1991-1996." *Canadian Theatre Review.* 90: 83-85.

"Time is a fish": The Spirit of Nanapush and the Power of Transformation in the Stories of Louise Erdrich

David T. McNab

Introduction

In Louise Erdrich's latest novel, *The Last Report on the Miracles at Little No Horse (2001)*, Nanapush, one of her major characters in this novel, says at the outset, in speaking to Father Damien Modeste, aka Agnes DeWitt, whom he heals and transforms, that "Time is a fish and all of us are living on the rib of its fin." Not comprehending Nanapush's ontological Anishinabe meaning, Father Damien asks "what kind of fish." Nanapush responds plainly, "A moving fish that never stops. Sometimes in swimming through the weeds one or another of us will be shaken off time's fin." "Into the Water?" asks Father Damien; the reply is "No into something called not time." Without providing any further explanation to the cross-dressing Catholic woman priest, Nanapush ends his story by saying, "Let's find something to eat" (Erdrich, 2001: 223) driving home the philosophical point about the place of people in the universe, the power of the natural and spirit worlds and the significance of time in Creation.

This notion of time is a central theme in the stories of Louise Erdrich. Throughout, Nanapush as storyteller is both a spirit and human possessing the power of the trickster. In *Last Report* he opens the book with the following statement about the framework of Creation: "*Nindinawemaganidok* There are four layers above the earth and four layers below. Sometimes in our dreams and creations we pass through the layers, which are also space and time. In saying the word *nindinawemaganidok*, or my relatives, we speak of everything that has existed in time, the known and the unknown, the unseen, the obvious, all that lived before or is living now in the worlds above and below" (Erdrich, 2001). And so time, according to Erdrich's understanding of Indigenous knowledge, is indeed a fish and we are on its fin, whether we are in the natural or the spirit worlds. Accordingly, without this Indigenous knowledge, one cannot fully understand Erdrich's storytelling (Jacobs, 2001).

It is said traditionally "storytelling like hunting is a holy [or spiritual] occupation" (Gish, 1999). Situating her work within Anishinabe storytelling tradition, Erdrich bases many of her stories on the spiritual figure of *Way-na-boo'-zhoo*, also known as Nanabush, or in her fiction, her protagonist, Nanapush, who in many instances has been seen as a Trickster figure. But although Nanapush does exhibit the ability to change into the form of a Trickster, this interpretation misses the larger significance of the spirit of Erdrich's literary creation. Edward Benton-Banai has described this person as "not really a man but... a spirit who had many adventures during the early years of the Earth. Some people say that *Waynaboozhoo* provided the link through which human form was gradually given to the spiritual beings of the Earth" (Benton-Banai 29-31) As a human, Nanapush made many errors along his journey but he was also able to learn from them. Thus, Nanapush could "accomplish many things and could become better at living in harmony with the Earth" (ibid). As a hero, he could act as a mirror into the soul of wo/man and help others through the telling of stories by others about himself and help all to better understand themselves and to grow in a balanced and a good way. Nanapush then is more than a trickster figure in a corporeal form; he is the "spirit of the Anishinabe or Original Man" (ibid). Nanapush thus appears in Erdrich's stories as a way of bringing about healing, balance, and the good life, and above all, peace.

This article is excerpted from a larger study of the power of transformation in the literary writings of Louise Erdrich. A central theme in the storytelling of her work is the power of transformation through the character of Nanapush. Utilizing a pre-colonial approach to understanding Erdrich's writing, this article focuses on the following work: *Tracks* (1988), *The Blue Jay's Dance* (1995), *Tales of Burning Love* (1996), *The Birchbark House* (1999) and *Last Report on the Miracle at Little No Horse* (2001).

"Just Like Tracks"

In his *A History of Reading* (1996), the writer Alberto Manguel has observed that "a society can exist – many do exist – without writing" (1996:1-2), but no society can exist without reading and that even "in societies that set down a record of their passing, reading precedes writing; the would-be writer must be able to recognize and decipher the social system of signs before setting them down on the page" (ibid). Similarly, it is necessary to learn how to 'read the signs' and come to some understanding of Aboriginal culture before one can understand the oral tradition(s) and comprehend ideas of history and concepts of time.

More recently, Manguel has written in his *Reading Pictures, A History of Love and Hate* that "we are all somehow reflected in the many and different images that surround us, since they are already part of who we are: images that we create and images that we frame; images that we assemble physically, by hand, and images that come together, unbidden, in the mind's eye; images of faces, trees, buildings, clouds, landscapes, instruments, water, fire, [and it may be added earth and air] and images of those images – painted, sculpted, acted out, photographed, printed, filmed. [Thus, we are] essentially creatures of images, of pictures" (ibid).[1] From this suggestion, Manguel argues that it is important to be able to "read pictures" and not just write or read the writing as pictures. Pictures are images – which also tell stories, if we care to listen to them. The images tell stories, which in turn tell us about ourselves. In this sense, we also read the images as part of the land and as part of ourselves; Indigenous knowledge tells us simply and profoundly where we are from, where we are now and where we are going.

Indeed, Erdrich herself expressed the relationship between image, meaning and place in one of her recent works *The Birchbark House* in the following way: Angeline, the sister of *Omakayas* (Little Frog), the hero of the story, goes to the mission school in the Spring to learn the White man's language. She comes home and shows her Nokomis the language "which looked like odd tracks." Angeline explains to her that the drawings are "letters… One follows the next. You look at them, just like tracks. You read them. They have a meaning and a sound." Her *Nokomis* responded "Howah! That's a good idea! Like our picture writing." *Omakayas* remembers "last winter, before the sickness began, she had seen Fishtail walking from the mission school. Had he learned to make the white man's tracks? Had he learned to write his name? Had he learned to read the words of the treaties so that his people could not be cheated of land?" (Erdrich, 1999:189-193) Referencing 'picture writing' in the context of the written word, Erdrich draws both similarities and differences between the two forms of communication. Writing has power, but images in the context of stories are also extremely significant, if not more powerful. Moreover, the written word can be manipulated to dis/place people, in other words, to cheat them from their land.

Within all of her writings, Erdrich employs images representing the four natural elements – earth, water, air and fire – as one of the main organizing principles for her themes (McNab, 1998). The four natural elements of the 'places' of Turtle Island are the sources of life and comprise the essence of our spiritual beings as original peoples. They are all around us and are sacred (Jacobs 12-13), and so are the names of these places. This idea has been well expressed by N. Scott Momaday, in *The Names*,

> I have no notion of time; the moment does not exist for me as time, but it exists only as pain or puzzlement, perhaps a sound, a word. What I shall come to know as time is now an imperceptible succession of colors, of dawns and dusks, mornings and afternoons, a concentration of days into one day, or is it simply the inside of eternity, the hollow of a great wing. (6)

Within the "hollow of a great wing," the spiritual world of our places, and our Names for them, is the way in which we see our land from a different angle as Earth, Water, Air and Fire.

There is a continuous collision internally and externally in Erdrich's literary works, especially concerning the ideas of history or in the conflicting worldviews presented in her various works.[2] Like a cultural intersection, they are symbolized, to provide but one example, in *The Antelope Wife*, by the words of Klaus Shawano, the Chippewa trader: "My stories have stories. My beadwork is made by relatives and friends whose tales branch off in an ever more complicated set of barriers" (Erdrich, 1998:27). It is important to listen carefully to, and to understand, these "complicated set of barriers." The Aboriginal symbol for family history is the bead. Gerald Hausman has poignantly described the purpose of the bead, which, "like the basket, is round; and, like the old tribal culture, a single part of many other parts. The string of beads, the blazon of beads told a story in which the single bead was a necessary link to all the others." It was also a metaphor for the "meaning of the tribe. Together there is strength, unity. The tribal man or woman was as strong as the tribe from which he/she came. And the tribe, naturally, got its strength from the single bead, the pearl, the individual man or woman" (8-9). The bead then is a representation of circles of time – family history – the one and many.

Circles of Time

In the literary works of Erdrich the idea of family history and the individual as part of that family (and community) are both circular and linear in form and substance as well as parallel in structure. In their concepts of time, they never meet; in the end they are circles.

They evoke Aboriginal voices and their persistence in the late twentieth century. The idea of circles of time is common to all Indigenous peoples, including the Anishinabe.[3] In the mid-nineteenth century, in his writings, *Kahgegagahbowh*, George Copway described the concept succinctly: "The Ojibwas, as well as many others, acknowledged that there was but one Great Spirit, who made the world; they gave him the name of good or benevolent; _kesha_ is benevolent, _monedoo_ is spirit; *Ke-sha-mon-e-doo*. They supposed he lived in the heavens; but the most of the time he was in the Sun. They said it was from him they received all that was good through life and that he seldom needs the offering of his Red children, for he was seldom angry" (Ruoff & Smith 81). The Sun, the sustainer of life, is also a metaphor for time.[4]

The continuing power and presence of the Aboriginal Oral Traditions, like Aboriginal spirituality, have often been either overlooked, ignored or dismissed as inconsequential. As a result, this history has been written and viewed through the lens of written history based on documents left by European visitors who wrote about what they believed they saw for a fleeting moment within the context of European imperial history. This approach frequently has left a highly distorted portrayal of Aboriginal people, epitomized by "pen and ink." For Aboriginal people, circles of time are part of the natural world and nature, of life and living. Every living thing has a relationship to every other and the events that occur in one's lifetime have an immediate impact on one's children and grandchildren. The Seventh Generation is immediate and close. In the spiritual and natural worlds, we are then situated within multi-dimensional circles of time.

The Blue Jay's Dance (1995)

Erdrich's fictional world is inhabited by unpredictable two leggeds who desperately, almost crazily, strive for balance and better relationships with one another, with the four leggeds, and with the places from which they have come and to which they always return home. Such is the 'place' created by Erdrich in all of her writings. As an Anishinabe storyteller, all of her writings are, in fact, based on her own and her family's history.[5] Knowledge of the clans and the clan system is therefore important, for without this Indigenous knowledge one cannot know who Erdrich's characters are – her literary animals – and where they are going, much less interpret them. The Bears are the policemen and the healers and they suffer a great deal in their life journey. But her characters are not one-dimensional. Each clan is like an extended spiritual family which cuts across First Nations. Not all of these Nations have the same clans. Each of the clans has different responsibilities – political, social, cultural, philosophical and spiritual – though these categories do not do justice to the character of the duties (Benton-Banai 74-78).[6]

Erdrich has two clans on her mother's side of her family, both of which are significant. On her Anishinabe side Erdrich is a *Be-nays*. *Be-nays* is a bird – likely of the Great Blue Heron Clan[7] – as indicated repeatedly in her autobiography of a birth year, *The Blue Jay's Dance* (36). In the Anishinabe clan system birds are spiritual leaders. Benton-Banai has described birds as "noted for their intuition and sense of knowledge of what the future would bring. They were said to have the characteristics of the eagle, the head of their clan, in that they pursued the higher elevations of the mind just as the eagle pursued the higher elevations of the sky" (76).[8] All of Erdrich's literary works are filled with these traditional characteristics; above all, her work exhibits the gift of *ah-mun'-ni-soo-win/* intuition, which includes *nee-goni-wa'bun-gi-gay-win'*, the ability to see into the future. On her mother's side of the family, she is also Cree of the Bear Clan (Erdrich, 1995:81-82). Spiritual messages through storytelling, warnings and healing are dominant themes in all of her work. This is made even more potent because she has the female spirit of the Bear within her – the gift of prophecies. The Birds are also the spirit protectors of the Bears. Her two clans are powerfully linked together.

Erdrich tells stories – indeed her life story is one of testing, trial and stress – to find her own sense of self, her place and her spirituality. *The Blue Jay's Dance* is Erdrich's autobiography of a birth year, a composite of her experiences from her diaries of the birth of her children in the early 1990's from her marriage with Michael Dorris (1945-1997). It is seasonal in structure, beginning in the winter and ending in the fall. Lyrical and haunting, it is a series of thematically connected stories about her family, the birth of her children, time and the natural world, as the following example "The Chickadee's Tongue" indicates:

> Today a chickadee hits the window with a small surprising thunk. I walk outside, pluck it off the warming earth. The bird is stunned, blinking, undamaged. I stand motionless with the bird in my hand, examining it carefully, but not a feather seems to have snapped or ruffled... I have always wanted to catch a chickadee and look at its tongue, but

now that I've got one, my hands seem as big and clumsy as paws. I don't dare try to open its beak. Regaining its wits, the bird seems to trust me... It looks up at me, alert and needle – sharp, but very calm, and I feel suddenly that I am an amazingly fortunate woman. (Erdrich, 1995:82-83)

Erdrich draws the connection between self and place as she situates herself as part of the natural world. Her hands are "big and clumsy as paws." As a bear, she cares for and heals the chickadee. Her place – Turtle Mountain – is powerful. It is a home of the eagles and the bears. It is border country between the Cree and the Anishinabe: "I've lived in many different places but feel most attached to the outdoor West and Great Plains, the sky, the mountains, the broad reaches" (Chavkin & Chavkin 227). This place infuses her writings.

Erdrich understands that her writing is spiritual, acknowledging in an interview: "Life is religious, I think, and that includes writing" (ibid 228). In this respect she goes on to explain the "common themes and preoccupations" in her work which include: "Abandonment and return. Pleasure and denial. Failure. Absurdity. The inability to get a sound night's sleep" (ibid 228). *The Blue Jay's Dance* begins with "Winter" which is the time for the telling stories – for spiritual renewal – among the Cree and Anishinabe. Erdrich explains the spiritual component of her writing: "The world tips away when we look into our children's faces. The days flood by. Time with children runs through our fingers like water as we lift our hands, try to hold, to capture, to fix moments in a lens, a magic circle of images and words. We snap photos, videotape, memorialize while we experience a fast-forward in which there is no replay of even a single instant" (Erdrich, 1995:4). The Aboriginal concept of history is both specific to a place and infinite – circular. This explains the difficulties that most readers have with Erdrich's lack of linear chronology in her narratives and with her characters. Her concept of time as a bird and a bear enable her to foretell events through intuition and prophecy (ibid 8).[9]

For Erdrich, time is also connected to the female body and it involves an understanding of narrative about oneself as events take place. She states in *The Blue Jay's Dance* that the "problem of narrative" is "more than just embarrassment about a physical process" (1955:44-5). It is the cycle of birth and rebirth: "We're taught to suppress its importance over time, to devalue and belittle an experience in which we are bound up in the circular drama of human fate, in a state of heightened awareness and receptivity, at a crux where we intuit connections and, for a moment, unlock time's hold like a brace, even step from our bodies." It is a narrative of a child, its birth and its own story. The act of giving birth "often becomes both paradigm and parable" (ibid). The process of birth and rebirth is connected to the water where time and fish swim and creation begins. The woman's body "becomes a touchstone, a predictor. A mother or a father, in describing their labor, relates the personality of the child to some piece of the event, makes the story into a frame, an introduction, a prelude to the child's life, molds the labor into the story that is no longer a woman's story or a man's story, but the story of a child" (ibid). It is abundantly clear that her concept of time is circular and not linear (ibid 82-4). From this perspective, she begins to understand that her home is also a spiritual place (ibid 86-8).

In "Finches and the Grand Sky," Erdrich observes that

> I picture the female goldfinch settling herself into a nest the color of her husband and suddenly I think – *that's what I've done, moving to this, my husband's farm.* All around me, kind trees and slabs of rocky land, violet and archaic gold shadows that Maxfield Parrish painted into his Saturday Evening Post covers. This is a beautiful place but it is not where I belong. Over and over, in anguish, in hope, we utter the same lines in a long established argument 'I'm homesick,' I keep saying. 'This is home,' he keeps answering. Each of us is absolutely right. (ibid 88-92)

It is from this realization that Erdrich went home to the 'Place of the Grand Sky' and found her own voice.

Most literary critics have commented on Erdrich's fiction as a place inhabited by dysfunctional and fragmented "Indians" – a view of "Indians" as a twentieth century vision of poor ignorant savages utterly incapable of dealing with the modern world. It is seen as a bleak view of twentieth century reservation life filled with violence and fear and danger. Joyce Carol Oates has also stated that her writings can be classified by the term "magic realism" (Chavkin & Chavkin 220). In an interview Louise Erdrich disclaimed both of these views, remarking that her fiction is about creating a spiritual world and that writing was a holy or spiritual occupation for her:

> Probably your word unpredictable is more accurate. It is certainly the reaction I'd like. The thing is, the events peo-

ple pick out as magical don't seem unreal to me. Unusual, yes, but I was raised believing in miracles and hearing of true events that may seem unbelievable. I think the term is one applied to writers from cultures more closely aligned to religious oddities and the natural and strange world. (ibid)[10]

In this sense, her stories embody the spirit of the Trickster in that they (re)imagine an Anishinabe worldview. She has stated that she loves the "names" of her characters (Erdrich, 1995:227-8). There is 'power' in a name, medicine power.[11] There is also 'power' in Erdrich's ability to dream, to know the future and understand the past and the present.[12] For it is both the natural as well as the spiritual worlds that operate through the world of dreams:

> Grand elk moving underneath the grand sky. Tyrant blue jays. Cats loping banner-like across the fields... The beating of a heart perhaps, moving in, moving out. My own voice – perhaps she dreams my own voice as I dream hers – starting out of sleep, awake, certain that she's cried out./For years now I have been dreaming the powerful anxiety dreams of all parents. Something is lost, something must be protected./Now, as I move into the pages of manuscripts, I fall asleep anxious but embark on no tiring searches through piles of bricks and train stations. The dream junk and dream treasure, the excess bliss and paranoia, goes into the pages of books. (Erdrich, 1995:219)

Thus, grounded in a particular place, Erdrich draws upon her traditions as a mixed blood Cree/Chippewa/German woman and carries her dreams into the world of storytelling.

Tracks (1988)

Tracks, Erdrich's third novel, speaks of the power of stories to transform and heal. Using Mother Earth as an organizing principle, the novel 'tracks' the life of Fleur Pillager. The novel begins in 1912 (and ends in 1924) with Nanapush rescuing her, the rest of her family having perished in the "spotted sickness." Acting as her guardian, Nanapush describes Fleur as having the power of healing, medicine power. In *Tracks,* Fleur leaves the Reservation and goes to Argus, the local non-Aboriginal town and finds work at a local butcher shop. She uses her powers to win at cards in a game that was only played by the local four White men who see her as an easy target. Fleur uses her knowledge and power to lure them into the game and then in the end when the stakes are high she wins. When the White men come after her and try to forcibly get their money back, Fleur uses her medicine power to call up a wind that hits and virtually wrecks the town and escapes.

Thereafter, when Fleur returns to the Reservation (with the large amount of cash which she had won at the card game), the Anishinabe, having heard what has happened at Argus, are afraid of her medicine power. As Pauline Puyat (later Sister Leopolda) explains: "Power travels in the bloodlines, handed out before birth. It comes down through the hands, which in the Pillagers are strong and knotted, big, spidery and rough, with sensitive fingertips good at dealing cards. It comes through the eyes, too, belligerent, darkest brown, the eyes of those in the Bear clan, impolite as they gaze directly at a person" (Erdrich, 1998:31). Later Fleur has a child named Lulu who also has the medicine power. When, at the end of the novel, the lumbermen come to cut the standing people – the trees, Fleur again uses her powers to wreak havoc and has to leave the Reservation. She then leaves for the city and marries the lumber baron, John Mauser, who was responsible for the devastation on the Reservations, and thereby captures him and saves her land. Lulu, in the interim, is left behind and sent to a boarding school which she hates, and when Fleur returns, failing to understand what Fleur has done and why she has done it, she blames her mother and refuses to be with her. Many years later, Fleur's grandson, Jack Mauser, also inherits her medicine power. This story is taken up in the *Tales of Burning Love*.

So we have three generations of the Bear clan using their medicine power to heal and, in the process, protect the land for the generations to come. Much of this story in *Tracks* is kept alive and told by Nanapush. It is he who understands the forces from the spirit world that have protected the Anishinabe through their darkest and most troubled times. The power then resides in the stories themselves – both in the remembrance and the telling – of medicine power to shape events in the natural world. This is the power of transformation and the significance of Nanapush (and Erdrich) as a storyteller. Thus, the power in the stories is the ability of storytelling to heal across the generations.

Tales of Burning Love (1996)

The framework of *Tales of Burning Love* is based on the organizing principle of Fire. It is filled with "literary animals" – to use Gerald Vizenor's term. Erdrich's characters are thus animals in the guise of the two legged. The stories in the *Tales* are framed by the character named Jack Mauser who is described as a German with an Ojibwa trapdoor in his soul. He is polygamous. Two of his wives are Anishinabe and three are not. The first and the fifth wives are Anishinabe – June Morrissey who freezes to death in an Easter blizzard in 1981 and Dot Adare Nanapush, who is already married to Gerry Nanapush, a son of Nanapush, and whom he fears and who is a distant relative. The others are non-Aboriginal – Marlis and Candice – the second and the fourth wife – much to Jack's consternation both reject Jack and then bond as lesbian lovers and partners. The third – Eleanor Schlick – is German-American. She continues to love him right to the end. Jack's family name – Mauser – comes from his father's side of the family, which in German is mouser, meaning wildcat. He is also a grandson of the timber baron John Mauser and Fleur Pillager, and therefore a Bear but until the end a fairly mixed-up Bear. On his mother's side, his Anishinabe name is Kashpaw.[13]

The narrative line of *Tales* draws on the motifs of the Anishinabe Oral Tradition. Animals take on human form (they shapeshift back and forth) and show their imperfections and failings with the purpose of moral and spiritual instructions to help to create a world that is in harmony and balance with the Creator or Great Mystery. Educated as an engineer in the White world, Jack shows his failings in his work as a construction owner. He treats his employees badly and goes bankrupt. He burns his model home down to escape his creditors. He betrays his Anishinabe spirituality by constructing overpasses and new sub-divisions on sacred land. His relationship to his five wives is entirely reprehensible, if not cruel and vicious – filled with lust, abandonment, jealousy, alcoholism and self-loathing. Yet, in a sense, he is an Anishinabe 'everyman,' a "Nanabush," and in a comic sense – likeable and fascinating to watch.

Tales culminates in a North Dakota blizzard outside of Fargo. The five wives get trapped in Jack's red Ford Explorer on the highway. To keep from dying from carbon monoxide poisoning, they keep awake by telling stories about how they each got to know Jack and what happened to their relationships. It turns out that they each know a different Jack. In this sense, Jack saves them from death. In reality though, Jack saves his only son from the blizzard; in the end, he finds peace, balance and harmony and returns to his Anishinabe spirituality and to his mother's reservation, accepting the fact that he is both German and Anishinabe.

The novel opens with a wonderful story of Jack the mouser and his stray cat. It illustrates the important role of literary animals in Erdrich's fiction. It is Easter Saturday in 1981 in Williston, North Dakota. Jack has a very bad toothache. While talking to the dental receptionist to get an appointment, Jack 'cuffs' a stray cat that has found its way into his room; the cat responses violently:

> the cat, determined, launched itself straight upward to climb Jack like a tree. It sank thick razor claws a half inch deep into Jack's thigh. Hung there.
> Jack screamed into the telephone. The claws clenched in panic, and Jack, whirling in an awful dance, ripped the cat from his legs and threw the creature with such force that it bounced off a wall, but twisted over and came up strolling. No loss of dignity.
> There was silence on the other end of the connection, and then the voice, less chipper.
> "Are you experiencing discomfort?"
> Jack whimpered...   (Erdrich, 1996:4)

Tales – the comic sexual pun on the title is not lost on the reader – is also a comedy in the classical sense of the term. One of the best examples occurs when Eleanor Schlick – described by Jack as a "two-bit intellectual" – gets fired from her teaching job for 'screwing' a young male student literally and academically. She ends up in a convent. Here she hopes to make her literary mark by such projects as "the spaces between words." She says to herself: "Who has investigated the spaces between words? Any link to the messenger chemicals, connections in the brain?" (ibid 42)

Eleanor then turns to interviewing and producing a biography of the first mixed-blood saint Sister Leopolda. This results in the death of the 108 years old candidate for sainthood in the convent's garden. Jack laughs when Sister Leopolda continues to make fun of Eleanor's attempts to quiz her about prayer and its results: "She turned her head to glare at Eleanor. 'My prayer is a tale of burning love, child, but you aren't ready to hear it'" (ibid 53). Eleanor replies that she is ready and the Sister's "voice shook with emotion, broke from her like strings ripping from a harp. 'End this torment,' the old nun whispered" (ibid). The black comedy of the scene is heightened as her prayer is granted:

> With a terrible effort, as if a tree tried to straighten its own crooked limb, the old nun cocked her head and rolled her eyes upward... to catch a glimpse of the blessed statue.

> What she saw transfixed her... [T]he Virgin leaned down off her pedestal, and ever so gently, as Leopolda stretched out her fingers, transferred the carved bundle she carried into the cradle of the nun's arms... Leopolda sank down breathing the fragrance of the limp, white petals with such strong and vigorous ecstasy that her heart cracked, she pitched straight over... (ibid 53)

After the good sister's demise, Jack follows Eleanor up to her garret room and fornicates twelve times in succession with his former wife who falls back into love with him. Meanwhile the storm continues unabated and lightning strikes Jack's hydraulic lift:

> Instead of grounding harmlessly, the spark had leaped, surged toward something in the garden path, probably Sister Leopolda's shiny walker, which was found later – twisted, blackened, and somehow shrunk no larger than a pair of bobby pins. Some of the sisters maintained that Leopolda herself lay next to it, reduced to a pile of ash in the shape of a cross. Kneeling at the empty base of the statue the next morning, Eleanor watched the dust of the holy nun carried off by bees. (ibid 63)

Disputing the term 'magical,' Erdrich again displays her penchant for what she calls "the unpredictable" in her writing. As the swarm of bees carry Sister Leopolda away, Eleanor concludes that "all of her bitterness [will be] turned into honey... (ibid 63). It is a fitting if ironic ending for her in that she attains a kind of grace through lightning and bees, both elements of the natural world.

Originally, Jack had bought the quarter section west of Fargo and leased it back to his uncle Chuck Mauser to grow sunflowers. Three years before in 1992, he had not renewed the lease and had turned the sunflowers into a new subdivision and had founded his construction company Mauser & Mauser. But Jack's whole project soon self-destructs before his very eyes. He is going bankrupt and he begins to think that he is being punished because he left June Morrissey freeze to death in 1981. He recalls that it was his hustling that brought in the White man's dollars while forsaking the land. He begins to question his very being: "*And here he was.* Jack faltered. *Here I am.* He was about to think *in Fargo,* but instead he thought *an Indian.*" (151) But Jack has not yet come to terms with the implications of the word spirituality in his own life: "That part of his background was like a secret joke he had on everyone. His crews. His banker. Asshole clients. Even his own wives. He'd thought, strangely sometimes, when walking through those bank lobbies, *the hell with all of you. Your doors would swing the other way if you knew who I am!* But who did? He was a mixed-blood with dark eyes and dark hair and a big white German grandfather and a crazy mother. He never thought of her. Or him, either. Both eaten up by time." (ibid 151) The joke is on him as he discovers through a vision that he receives later in a snowstorm. With profound consequences, the vision leaves him marked for life.

Jack finally gets the message the Creator has sent to him through his own spiritual journey. While attempting to rescue his son in the January 1995 North Dakota blizzard, he travels in the four sacred directions. First he drives due north to the northern gateway – to find home: "Jack was now beginning to see, just catching at the design of his life. Bits and pieces of understanding he had carefully collected and hidden from himself were magically assembling (ibid 380). He continues on with his search finding his Anishinabe mother in the land of the spirits to the west, and he thinks "of his mother's laugh, her eyes. He remembered her as a shadow, as a protective arm, her face again wild and fascinated. He saw her hand throwing down the cards and heard the roar of her blood. The beat of her heart sounded in his ears, and he missed her like a child" (ibid 384). At this point, he comes to terms with himself and his relationship to June whom he had abandoned and left to die:

> She was wearing a wedding dress, a real one this time, white net full and stiff with lace. Confidently, over the brilliant drifts, she stepped forward. His tracks were obscured, his trail drifted over, his path back to the living blown clean. He followed her meekly. She was bringing him home. (ibid 385)

Erdrich again illustrates the power of vision to effect real change in someone's life. Not simply restricted to the ephemeral world of sleep, Jack's vision moves him to 'transform' as nothing else can. The Elders tell us that some people are slower learners than others. This certainly pertains to Jack Mauser, who discovers the 'Anishinabe trap-door' in his soul only after inflicting much hardship on himself, his son, his five wives and those around him. In this often comic, sometimes considerably raunchy novel, Jack finally does discover the presence of the Anishinabe within himself and achieves balance, harmony and peace.

The Birchbark House (1999)

Erdrich's *The Birchbark House* is a continuation of her autobiography and family history begun in *The Blue Jay's Dance*. It is dedicated to her daughter "Persia, whose song heals." It is also illustrated with beautiful black and white drawings. The "Thanks and Acknowledgements" is given to her mother Rita Gourneau Erdrich and her sister Lise Erdrich who researched their family life and found "ancestors on both sides who lived on Madeline Island during the time on which this book is set. One of them was *Gatay Manomin*, or Old Wild Rice." Madeline Island is the seventh, and final, stopping place in Midewiwin history (Benton-Banai 101-2).

For the history of the Anishinabe people places are extremely significant. It is these places from whence comes their knowledge of themselves as a people, literally who they are and where they are going. This notion of history encompasses the past to be sure but also the present and the future in the form of prophecy. So, in this way, Spirit and Madeline Islands are central to their history and understanding of time. For example, according to Anishinabe Oral Traditions, Madeline Island has been described as follows: "One of the prophets of long ago had spoken of a turtle-shaped island that awaited them at the end of their journey. The people sought out this island and placed tobacco on its shore. The sacred shell rose up out of the water and told the people this was the place they had been searching for. Here, the Waterdrum made its seventh and final stop on the migration" (Benton-Banai 102). And it is in this place where Erdrich begins her exposition of Anishinabe history in *The Birchbark House*.

The story of *The Birchbark House* takes place in the year 1847 and its heroine is *Omakayas* or Little Frog in Anishinabe.[14] Again the structure of the narrative is seasonal but this time the story is historical. It initially begins in the winter of 1840 when Anishinabe voyageurs find young *Omakayas* alone on Spirit Island, a sacred spot and the sixth stopping place in Anishinabe history." (Benton-Banai 101) Being the last person left alive among her people after smallpox has devastated them, *Omakayas* is adopted by the Anishinabe. The story resumes seven years later in *Neebin* (Summer), which is followed by *Dagwaging* (Fall), *Biboon* (Winter), *Zeegwun* (Spring). As a Cree of the Bear clan, *Omakayas* is adopted by Old Tallow, an Anishinabe Medicine Woman. She becomes transformed into a healer (since she has had the smallpox as a baby she cannot get it again) and goes on to save the Anishinabe from the dreaded disease another seven years later on Madeline Island

(Erdrich, 1999:2). Thus, the circular events of *Omakayas's* life give the novel its themes of self-discovery and transformation.

Old Tallow is also a transformer in this story and in Erdrich's family history.[15] Like Fleur Pillager, she is an Anishinabe of the Bear clan as evidenced by "the bear claw that swung on a silver hoop from Old Tallow's ear lobe" as well as by Erdrich's illustration and description of her and of her dog and wolf companions (Erdrich, 1999:19-32). Her role is to assist *Omakayas* to discover who she is. It is Old Tallow who sends the female Bear spirit to *Omakayas* on her return to the Birchbark House. This first encounter clearly indicates the kinship between *Omakayas* and the Bear.

> For long moments, the bear tested her with every sense, staring down with her weak eyes, listening, and most of all smelling her... The bear smelled all... *Omakayas* couldn't help but smell her back. Bears eat anything and this one had just eaten something ancient and foul. Hiyn! *Omakayas* took shallow breaths. Perhaps it was to take her mind off the scent of dead things on the bear's breath that she accidentally closed the scissors shearing off a tiny clip of bear fur, and then to cover her horror at this mistake, started to talk... '*Nokomis*,' she said to the bear, calling her grandmother. 'Didn't mean any harm? I was only playing with your children. *Gaween onjidah*. Please forgive me.' (ibid 29-31)

It is at this point that the mother bear recognizes that *Omakayas* is also a bear, having the spirit of the bear. This event transforms *Omakayas*. She becomes a woman and a healer saving her adopted family in the winter and thereby transforming their family history making it a story of survival.

From this encounter with the female Bear in the narrative, *Omakayas* discovers more and more about herself. Her grandmother helps her to understand that the spirits of the plants and herbs can talk to her and tell her how they can heal the sick or those in pain. In turn, she helps to heal her family when the smallpox comes during a cruel winter to destroy them. The Bear spirit also comes to *Omakayas* in the Maple Sugar time when she is feeling very low and weak spirited and needs to be healed herself. She meets her bear brothers in the woods and offers tobacco to them as a gift. She asks them if they will give her their Bear medicine – not for herself but "strong medicines to save my family" (ibid 210). After the bears leave, she hears the voices of the spirits of the plants talking to her and telling her of their medicines, which enables her to discover that she is indeed a Bear and a healer. And *Omakayas* does become a Medicine Woman, and helps to heal her brother when he accidentally scalds himself during the maple sugaring time, providing to the Anishinabe the return of the Creator's gift – the sense of humor (ibid, 210-215) And so the story comes 'full circle' when *Omakayas* visits Old Tallow who tells *Omakayas* who she is and where she is going: "'You were sent here so you could save the others,' she said. 'Because you'd had the sickness, you were strong enough to nurse them through it. They did a good thing when they took you in, and you saved them for their good act. Now the circle that began when I found you is complete" (ibid 221-237). Thus, Erdrich once again uses the metaphor of the circle – the Medicine Wheel – to denote time and Aboriginal history.

And so it is the continuity provided by Aboriginal storytellers like Erdrich, through their stories, which enable Aboriginal people to continue on their spirit journeys and to survive as *Omakayas* does. In completing the circle of her story, Erdrich tells us that on a sunny spring morning *Omakayas* discovers her brother in the voices of the tiny sparrows: "She heard *Neewo*. She heard her little brother as though he still existed in the world. She heard him telling her to cheer up and live. *I'm all right,* his voice was saying, *I'm in a peaceful place. You can depend on me. I'm always here to help you, my sister. Omakayas* tucked her hands behind her head, lay back, closed her eyes, and smiled as the song of the white-throated sparrow sank again and again through the air like a shining needle, and sewed up her broken heart" (ibid 238-239). She has now been joined with her younger brother who is in the spirit world. Through this process she has been healed spiritually. There the story ends, and the seasonal circles of life are renewed.

Last Report on the Miracles at Little No Horse (2001)

Erdrich's latest novel begins in 1996 when Father Damien Modeste, who is a cross-dressing woman priest (who is not a priest at all), writes to the Pope reporting on the miracles at the Reservation, of the place called Little No Horse. In fact, there are no miracles at all in any sense of the word, Catholic or otherwise. The story take us back to the early twentieth century (1912), when *Tracks* begins, and opens with a creation story of a flood on the Red River which catapults Agnes DeWitt into the role of Father Damien Modeste who has drowned in the flood. Agnes assumes his identity and takes his money and proceeds to Little No Horse in his stead. It is here, after attempting suicide, that she meets up with Nanapush who transforms her through the use of the sweat lodge and vision quest from an pseudo Catholic priest (who Nanapush knows is not a priest) into someone with an understanding of Anishinabe spirituality.

In *Last Report* Nanapush not only uses his power of storytelling and healing but also his power of transformation. The spirit of Nanapush thus infuses and allows the characters, the so-called literary animals, to transcend their confused and harmful identities. Transforming Agnes from the inside out, Nanapush turns her into a better person, and, in the process, she exposes the absurd Catholic "miracles" of the deceased Pauline Puyat who has become Sister Leopolda, the first mixed blood saint. Utilizing Aboriginal spirituality and its powers, Agnes tells the truth of the matter to the Pope's emissary, that the so-called saint is a murderess, while holding up to scrutiny the Catholic Church for the damage it has done to Aboriginal people for hundreds of years. While Agnes becomes her own self and develops a better relationship with the people of Little No Horse, Father Jude Miller, the Pope's Emissary, discovers the truth about Sister Leopolda, and the Catholic Church (and all Christian churches by implication).

The last 'story' in the novel is in the "Epilogue" entitled "A Fax from the Beyond 1997" (Erdrich, 2001: 352-5). The first fax Father Jude Miller receives is from the Pope to the deceased Father Damien telling him to send copies of all his reports over the span of his lengthy career to the Vatican. It appears that the 'paper trail' has ended up by 'mistake' in the hands of a 'layperson' in the vicinity of Little No Horse. The Pope explains in his fax:

> My assistant is shocked to discover that a certain writer local to your region (but published even in languages and places as distant as our own) has included a quantity of first-person confessions in the body of her otherwise phantasmagoric and fictional works.
> Could this writer have possibly come by those letters?
> If so, we are most distressed, beg your apology, and have certain plans to take up the matter with the writer, Louise Erdrich (ibid 358*)*.

Louise Erdrich, aka Nanapush, knows the power of the spirit of Nanabush, the power that it has over the transitory character of the written word, which exist only in the natural world. Paper disappears with time but the stories, the Oral Tradition(s), remain. As

Erdrich observes in her commentary on the Pope's fax, the stories are powerful entities in their own right:

> The source of these early narratives is mysterious to me also. Voices spoke to me in dreams, while I drove long distances, nursed my babies, and so on. Sometimes in sleepwalking I would find I'd written book sections. There they would be the next morning, on my desk. I feel sure they originated in my own mind, those stories, however they appeared. Yet sometimes, as I scrutinize the hand-writing in those early drafts, I wonder. Who is the writer? Who is the voice? Sometimes the script is unfamiliar – the careful spidery flourish of a hand trained early in the last century. At other times – I am sure, I am positive – it is my own. (ibid 358)

And so, in the end, Erdrich asks, where do the stories come from? To answer this question, ironically, we must turn to the stories themselves. And yet, things are not always what they appear to be. Louise Erdrich has also written that "[t]he Ojibwa word for mirror, *wabimujichagwan*, means 'looking at your soul,' a concept that captures some of the mystery of image and substance." (1995:99) To connect to the stories then is ultimately to connect to yourself and your place. Thus, we must follow the Names and the land, as Erdrich reminds us at the end of *Last Report*. Nanapush tells Father Damien about the meaning and significance of Little No Horse: "We never had a name for the whole place, said Nanapush, except the word *ishkonigam*. The leftovers. Our words for the place are many and describe every corner and hole. We are called Little No Horse now because of a dead *Bwaan* and a drenched map. Think of it, *nindinawemaganidok*, my relatives" (Erdrich, 2001:3).

Indigenous knowledge comes from the land: "Do the rocks here know us, do the trees, do the waters of the lakes? Not unless they are addressed by the names they themselves told us to call them in our dreams. Every feature of the land around us spoke its name to an ancestor. Perhaps, in the end, that is all that we are. We Anishinaabeg are the keepers of the names of the earth" (ibid). Through her stories, through the spirit of Nanabush, Erdrich provides us with a cosmic and comic vision of a path to a spiritual life through the fusion of the past, present and the future – in short – through the power of transformation.

Acknowledgement

I would especially like to thank Professor Bernie Harder of the University of Windsor who shared with me his extensive knowledge of Native American literature and commented upon this paper. I would also like to thank Professors Ute Lischke, Wilfrid Laurier University, and the editor of this volume for their comments. An earlier draft of this chapter entitled "'A Trapdoor in his Soul': Tracking the Idea of Time and History in the Literary Work of Louise Erdrich," was read at the Tenth Annual Conference on "Origins, Identity and Ethnicity," Binghamton University, on March 6, 1999, which I could attend thanks to the assistance from the Trent University Professional Development Fund.

Notes

1. Alberto Manguel, (2000) *Reading Pictures, A History of Love and Hate*, 6. See also his (1996) *A History of Reading*.

2. Her other writings include, among others, *Love Medicine* (1984, 1993), *The Beet Queen* (1986), *Tracks* (1988), *The Crown of Columbus* (with Michael Dorris) (1991), *The Bingo Palace* (1994), and *The Antelope Wife* (1998), *The Last Report on the Miracles at Little No Horse* (2001).

3. This idea of history as a circle of time can be seen in the star maps of the Cree and the legends or myths of the Algonquian peoples. What connects them is that they are all dreams of *Kinh* within a circle of time. See, for an Ojibwa perspective, Basil Johnston, (1995).

4. For a recent Cree view see Andrew Bainbridge, (1992).

5. Colours in Erdrich's work are important signifiers of time and history highlighting persons and their connections with events. The colours also correspond to the Clans of the characters. The Bear clan's colours are red and the Bird clan is blue, for example. The combination of red and blue is extremely powerful in terms of time such as in the case of Blue Prairie Woman in *The Antelope Wife*.

6. For example, the Anishinabe cranes are the political leaders and the fish, including turtles, are the philosophers or intellectuals and the deer are the gentle people – the poets and artists. The clans tell us who Erdrich is in circles of time. Some Aboriginal people, if they are adopted, have two clans.

7. Author's trip to Manitoulin Island, this event took place on Monday, September 6, 1999.

8. Edward Benton-Banai, (July 1988) "The Clan System," 74-78.

9. In *The Blue Jay's Dance*, there is the foretelling of the suicide of Michael Dorris, then her husband. She writes, "There was also, in this house's short life, a suicide. I don't know much about him except that he was young, lived alone, rode a motorcycle to work. I don't know where in the house he was when he shot himself. I do not want to know, except I

do know. There is only one place. It is here, where I sit, before the window, looking out into the dark shapes of trees. Perhaps it is odd to contemplate a subject as grim as suicide while anticipating a child so new she'll wear a navel tassel and smell of nothing but her purest self, but beginnings suggest endings and I can't help thinking about the continuum, the span, the afters, and the befores."

10. Chavkin and Chavkin. "An Interview with Louise Erdrich," 220-253. "This interview was conducted by mail from September 1992 through April 1993," 220. She stated that she was a religious writer – yes – "Life is religious, I think, and that includes writing."

11. Erdrich, *The Blue Jay's Dance.* 193-196.

The hawk sweeps over, light shining through her rust red tail. She makes an immaculate cross in flight, her shadow running along the ground behind her as I'm walking below. Our shadows join, momentarily, and then separate, both to our appointed rounds. Always, she hunts flying into the east of the sun, making a pass east to west. Once inside, I settle baby, resettle baby, settle and resettle my hands to proofread a page when a blur outside my vision causes me to look up.

The hawk drops headfirst out of a cloud. She folds her wings hard against her and plunges into the low branches of the apple tree, moving at such dazzling speed I can barely follow. She strikes at one of the seven blue jays who make up the raucous gang, and it tumbles before her, head over feet, end over end. She plunges after it from the branches, flops in the sun. They both light on the ground and square off, about a foot apart in the snow.

The struck jay thrusts out its head, screams, raises its wings, and dances toward the gray hawk. The plain of snow must seem endless, an arena without shelter, and the bird gets no help from the other six jays except loud encouragement at a safe distance. I hardly breathe. The hawk, on the ground, its wings clattering against the packed crust, is so much larger than its shadow, which has long brushed in and out of mine. It screams back, eyes filled with yellow light. Its hooked beak opens and it feints with its neck. Yet the jay, ridiculous, continues to dance, hopping forward, hornpiping up and down with tiny leaps, all of its feathers on end to increase its size, Its crest is sharp, its beak open in a continual shriek, its eye-mask fierce. It pedals its feet in the air. The hawk steps backward. She seems confused, cocks her head, and does not snap the blue jay's neck. She watches. Although I know nothing of the hawk and cannot imagine what moves her, it does seem to me that she is fascinated, that she puzzles at the absurd display before she raises her wings and lifts off.

Past the gray moralizing and the fierce Roman Catholic embrace of suffering and fate that so often clouds the subject of suicide, there is the blue jay's dance. Beyond the impossible corners, stark cliffs, dark wells of trapped longing, there is that manic, successful jig-cocky, exuberant, entirely a bluff, a joke. That dance makes me clench down hard on life. But it is also a dance that in no other circumstances might lead me, you anyone, to choose a voluntary death. I see in that small bird's crazy courage some of what it took for my grandparents to live out the tough times. I peer around me, stroke my own skin, look into this baby's eyes that register me as a blurred self-extension, as a function of her will. I have made a pact with life: if I were to die now it would be a form of suicide for her. Since the two of us are still in the process of differentiating, since my acts are hers and I do not even think, yet, where I stop for her or where her needs, exactly begin, I must dance for her. I must be the one to dip and twirl [page 196] in the cold glare and I must teach her, as she grows, the unlikely steps.

12. Erdrich, *The Blue Jay's Dance.* 196-201. "Outwalking Death." On the death of her German grand-mother she wrote:

Mary Erdrich Korll had lost her mother young and was raised by her father, a rough man. She adopted my father and his three brothers just before the Second World War, and she never developed a maternal voice around children, but treated them as equals and fixed upon us a fascinated eye. She had supported herself by writing newspaper jokes, wrapping butter, working as a telephone operator and in a travelling circus show. Running a butcher shop, ordering around grown men, taking care of several children at once, might have daunted anyone, but she seemed fearless to me and I felt in her a bracing lack of sweetness and a stringent honesty that lasted between us into adulthood. She was everybody's worthy adversary. Combative, sensual, aroused to protective furies, she was attentive to me as a person. She was my witness.

Now, looking down at the flowerless crowns of Eastern white pines, I remember the only old-growth trees I ever saw as a child, a grove in Little Falls, Minnesota, where I was born. The last time I visited my grandmother there, we went looking at those pines again, those sad giant remnants. Pens for wolves had been constructed among them. The sight [page 201] of the caged wolves, one black, three gray, stopped my tongue. In the distance a train wailed and the wolves answered, tossing high their muzzles in speech that froze meaning.

My grandmother reached toward the wolves muttering as she would to a dog. Her eyes were cat-yellow. The implications of the moment were lost to her because she saw the wolves as simply there, existing, not tragic or more beautiful or interesting than anything else. She put her hands through the wires to pet them and when they didn't move close, just stood in their own power and evaded her stare, she shrugged, drew her hand back. She had in her pockets a couple of pounds of homemade dog biscuits. Tossing them over the fence she called out, resignedly, to the whole pack, 'All right, be that way!'

13. Benton-Banai. *The Mishomis Book.* Chapter 10, "The Clan System," 74-78. Erdrich, *The Blue Jay's Dance*, 28. 'You're from that line, the old strain, the ones...' She does not finish. 'Kashpaws,' she changes direction, are my branch of course. We're probably related.'

14. The name *Omakayas*, Erdrich notes, is on a Turtle Mountain census – and you bring honour to the name when you speak it out loud: "This book and those that will follow are an attempt to retrace my own family's history." (1999: Acknowledgements).

15. See tallow-definition – "any of the various greases or greasy substances obtained from plants, minerals, etc.". – Oxford Dictionary 3212. See also McNab (2001b).

Works Cited

Bainbridge, Andrew. (1992) "The Rise of the Loving Son [Sun]." *Co-existence? Studies in Ontario-First Nation Relations.* Peterborough: Frost Centre for Canadian Heritage and Development Studies, Trent University. 6-10.

Benton-Banai, Edward. (1993) *The Mishomis Book, The Voice of the Ojibway.* Minneapolis: Red School House.

Brown, Lesley, ed. (1988) *The New Shorter Oxford English Dictionary on Historical Principles.* Vol. 2. Oxford: Clarendon Press.

Chavkin, Allan and Nancy Feyl Chavkin, eds. (1994) *Conversations with Louise Erdrich & Michael Dorris.* Literary Conversations Series. Jackson: University Press of Mississippi.

Erdrich, Louise. (2001) *The Last Report on the Miracles at Little No Horse.* New York: HarperCollins Publishers.

— . (1999) *The Birchbark House.* New York: Hyperion Books for Children.

— . (1998) *The Antelope Wife.* New York: Harper Flamingo.

— . (1996) *Tales of Burning Love.* New York: HarperCollins Publishers.

— . (1995) *The Blue Jay's Dance, A Birth Year.* New York: HarperCollins Publishers.

— . (1989) *Tracks.* New York: Harper & Row Publishers.

— . (1986) *The Beet Queen.* New York: HarperCollins Publishers.

Erdrich, Louise, Michael Dorris. (1991). *The Crown of Columbus.* New York: HarperCollins Publishers.

Gish, Robert F. (1999) "Life into Death, Death into Life." *The Chippewa Landscape of Louise Erdrich.* Ed. Allan Chavkin. Tuscaloosa and London: The University of Alabama Press. 67-83.

Hausman, Gerald. (1992) *Turtle Island Alphabet, A Lexicon of Native American Symbols and Culture.* New York: St. Martin's Press.

Jacobs, Connie. (2001) *The Novels of Louise Erdrich, Stories of Her People.* New York: Greenwood Press.

Jacobs, Dean, M. (1998) "Bkejwanong – 'The Place Where the Waters Divide': A Perspective on Earth, Water, Air and Fire." In McNab. (1998).

Johnston, Basil. (1995) *The Manitous, The Spiritual World of the Ojibway.* Toronto: Key Porter Books.

Manguel, Alberto. (2000) *Reading Pictures, A History of Love and Hate.* Toronto: Alfred A. Knopf Canada.

— . (1996) *A History of Reading.* Toronto: Alfred A. Knopf Canada.

McNab, David T. (2001a) "Of Beads and a Crystal Vase, Michael Dorris's *The Broken Cord and Cloud Chamber.*" *West Virginia University, Philological Papers,* Vol. 47, 109-119.

— (2001b) "The Perfect Disguise: Frank Speck's Pilgrimage to Ktaqamkuk-the Place of Fog-in 1914." *The American Review of Canadian Studies.* Spring-Summer. 85-104.

— . (1999) *Circles of Time: Aboriginal Land Rights and Resistance in Ontario.* Waterloo: Wilfrid Laurier University Press.

— . (Editor for Nin.Da.Waab.Jig). (1998) *Earth, Water, Air and Fire: Studies in Canadian Ethnohistory.* Wilfrid Laurier University Press.

— . (Fall 2000) "Indigenous Voices, Indigenous Histories Part IV - Gathering Gum from the Silver Pine: A Cree Woman's Dream and the Battle of Belly River Crossing of October, 1870." *Saskatchewan History.* 52(2): 15-27.

McNab, David. T., Bruce Hodgins, S. Dale Standen. (2001.) "Black with Canoes": Aboriginal Resistance and the Canoe: Diplomacy, Trade and Warfare in the Meeting Grounds of Northeastern North America, 1600-1800." *Technology, Disease and Colonial Conquests, Sixteenth to Eighteenth Centuries. Essays Reappraising the Guns and Germs Theories.* Ed. George Raudzens. Amsterdam: Brill International. 237-292.

Momaday, N. Scott. (1976) *The Names, A memoir, Sun Tracks, an American Indian Literary Series.* Tuscon and London: University of Arizona Press.

Ruoff, A. LaVonne Brown, and Donald B. Smith, eds. (1997) *Life, Letters and Speeches: George Copway (Kahgegagahbowh).* (1850). Lincoln: University of Nebraska Press.

Aboriginal Identity and Its Effects on Writing

Anita Heiss

Defining Aboriginality

Historically, the need to define Aboriginality never came from within Aboriginal communities. We have never been advocates of, or accepted titles like half-caste, quarter-caste, quadroon and so on, like our Native American sisters and brothers who also were categorised by governments according to blood quantum to measure Indigeneity.[1]

Definitions of Aboriginality based on blood were designed by White governments to "water-down" Aborigines and to assist assimilation of Black people into White society. Being defined as "half-caste" or "part-Aboriginal" not only detracted from someone's Aboriginality, forcing even Aboriginal people to question their identity, but also supported the policy of assimilation designed in 1951 and amended in 1965 at the Native Welfare Conference, which stated:

> The policy of assimilation seeks that all persons of Aboriginal descent will choose to attain a similar manner of living to that of other Australians and live as members of a single community – enjoying the same rights and privileges, accepting the same responsibilities and influenced by the same hopes and loyalties as other Australians.[2]

Tony Birch believes that the intervention of the government in the lives of Aboriginal people has both erased and reconstructed categories of "Aborigines" to suit whatever the contemporary policies may be. He says,

> Attempts to gain full understanding of the identities of Aboriginal people are not possible, as our communities, which frame our identities, are multi-layered and diverse. Aboriginal people realise this in a positive way. Non-Aboriginal representations of our cultures have failed to recognise this, often deliberately so. This has resulted from attempts to re-imagine us, and re-present us as objects suitable for, and benefiting non-Aboriginal society. These

negative categories and imagery serve one end: to deny self-identity and therefore self-determination by capturing and controlling definitions of "the other" in the colonial imagination.[3]

And so it has become necessary for Aboriginal people to define ourselves, for the purpose of broader community acceptance, for the purpose of census counts and employment/education opportunities, and to satisfy the needs of such a complex society as Australia that is struggling for its own identity – an identity, it seems, that can only be determined once Aboriginality has been defined and recognised.

The problem and practice of classifying Indigeneity has been something "given to" and "expected of" Aboriginal people, something we seem to have accepted and run with, as our own organisations have taken it upon themselves to require certificates or confirmations of Aboriginality. They do so for other reasons however. In the case of publishing for example, a Proof of Aboriginality form is used as protection from exploitation by White frauds in light of the 1997 outing of Leon Carmen as "Wanda Koolmatrie."

Marcia Langton points out that even with the imposed need to categorise, the difficulty Aboriginal people face when trying to define Aboriginality themselves is compounded by past government policies of taking children and the fact the Australian Government still has a role:

> The label "Aboriginal" has become one of the most disputed terms in the Australian language. Legal scholar, John McCorquordale, has noted sixty-seven definitions of Aboriginal people, mostly relating to their status as wards of the State and to criteria for incarceration in institutional reserves...[4]

In contrast to the legal and other "external" definitions of Aboriginality offered, artist and writer Nellie Green from the Badimia people of Western Australia believes that for Aboriginal people

> [t]he notion of Aboriginality is inseparable from that of identity and identifying with the land we come from. This concept is intrinsically linked to the sense of belonging or the homelands of Indigenous people.[5] Aboriginality is not something that can be or should be classified or measured. Rather, it is an inherent identifying quality that cannot be dismissed or denied.[6]

For the purposes of Commonwealth Government requirements a "working definition" of Aboriginality was accepted in 1978 in the administration of its programs which says that "An Aboriginal or Torres Strait Islander is a person of Aboriginal or Torres Strait Islander descent who identifies as an Aboriginal or Torres Strait Islander and is accepted as such by the community in which s/he is associated."[7] This definition is supported and endorsed by other organisations "outside" of Aboriginal communities like the Australia Council for the Arts.

Sonja Kurtzer reinforces the point that "Aboriginality" is something that has been introduced to Aboriginal people from the White society. While she admits that the actual concept of Aboriginality didn't even exist before colonisation, she sees the impact of this in the way the Indigenous community restrains the Indigenous author by expecting to have Aboriginality "authentically" represented to the hegemonic culture.[8] Kurtzer points out that historically Aboriginal Australians referred to themselves and each other according to kinship groups, skin groups, or on the basis of their relationship to totems, the Dreaming or particular areas of land.[9]

In terms of Aboriginal literature and those who create it, it's important to see how Aboriginal writers define themselves and their peers. Jackie Huggins pointed out at the Brisbane Writers' Festival in 1997 that Aboriginality is largely based on the experience of community life. Reinforcing her earlier writings in relation to Sally Morgan, Huggins adds, "Solely swallowing the genetic cocktail mixture does not constitute 'being' Aboriginal as so many Johnny-come-latelies would have whites believe."[10] Using Morgan as an example, Huggins argues that it is simply not sufficient to have Aboriginal bloodlines without the lived Aboriginal experience. Genetically, Morgan may be Aboriginal, but there was nothing in her writing that suggested to Huggins that the author had identified or lived as an Aboriginal person.

Yet even with the diversity of Aboriginal cultures, and without resorting to pan-Aboriginality, it must be recognised that there is a shared sense of Aboriginality nationally (and internationally with other Indigenous peoples), regardless of the geographical location or socio-economic experience of the individual. And so while writers may write of their own individual experience as an Aboriginal person living in a remote, rural or urban setting, they can also express through their writing a unified sense of belonging to a larger Aboriginal community.

So what makes an Aboriginal writer?

With the question of Aboriginality comes the question of what makes an Aboriginal writer. Is it someone who is genetically Aboriginal and who writes, or can it be someone who is White but who writes on Aboriginal issues? Although I will not attempt to give a final definition of Aboriginality, I will attempt to give some idea of how Aboriginal writers define themselves and their peers. Numerous interviews with Aboriginal writers suggest a variety of views, all of which relate to the notion of one community but many experiences.

In line with Huggins' views, Jeanie Bell, Murri author of *Talking About Celia* (UQP, 1997), says that to be an Aboriginal author it's important for people to have lived the experience.

> I find it a bit hard to imagine that anyone can really tell a story of an Aboriginal or Islander without having actually lived as one themselves [sic]. How can they talk about Aboriginal people and culture if they haven't actually done it? How can you possibly know what people feel and how they cope?[11]

Victorian novelist and publisher Bruce Pascoe and Wiradjuri poet Kerry Reed-Gilbert are clear about what defines an Aboriginal author for them: identity, descent and acceptance, the same lines followed by the Australia Council for the Arts. Pascoe says it includes "an Aboriginal heritage, provable family links and acceptance by the Koori community."[12] Reed-Gilbert adds that Aboriginal people have Aboriginal families, Aboriginal blood, and belong to their Aboriginal communities:

> Nobody can just pretend to be an Aboriginal author. Again we also have people whose skin is black and portray themselves as a Black person giving the wider community and the Black community the impression that they are an Aboriginal person when they're not [like Sykes and Johnson[13]].[14]

Cathy Craigie believes that an Aboriginal author's identity comes through in the writing, showing that the author has a grasp of the culture and society which they belong to/come from, and that it is written essentially for the Aboriginal reader, addressing Aboriginal dilemmas, situations and aspirations. She says,

> You have to be Aboriginal to do it, and your content has to have some sort of mention of Aboriginal culture. I think

that more importantly it's the way that you write it and it's the words that you use. It's gotta be something where you capture the essence of what being Aboriginal is about. The sense of humour, language patterns move in and out. It's showing that you are aware of your own culture.[15]

In contrast to many other writers' clear definition of what it means to be an Aboriginal writer, Melissa Lucashenko admits that Aboriginality is a hard thing to define, something of a continuum rather than 'you are or you aren't.' She believes that the 'acceptance' side of any definition of Aboriginality can cause problems:

I think it's something that you grow into, but at the same time as soon as you say that, all those full-blood people in the desert can point to us and say you're not Aboriginal because you haven't been through the lore, you haven't grown into it yet.
So an Aboriginal writer, I think you do have to write from the experience, but that experience is going to be widely different.[16]

Defining an Aboriginal literature and finding an Aboriginal literary discourse

Current writings by Aboriginal and Torres Strait Islander people belong within a cultural and historical continuity that predates the invasion whilst utilising, adapting and challenging the written genres and forms of the colonizing culture.[17]

David Unaipon is commonly thought to be the first Aboriginal writer in Australia with his book *Native Legends* (1929) and his articles for the *Daily Telegraph* in 1924. Unaipon in most contexts has been regarded as the earliest pioneer of Aboriginal writing and publishing, which suggests that Aboriginal written literature did not fully develop until the 1970s, 80s and 90s. But Penny van Toorn proposes that "Aboriginal people began using the technologies of alphabetic writing and print far earlier than the dominant literary historical narrative would suggest."[18] She points out that this writing and printing was used as early in fact as 1796 when Bennelong dictated a letter to Lord Sydney's steward. Van Toorn notes that letters, poems, essays, pamphlets, newsletters, newspaper articles, petitions, speeches and traditional stories written and printed by Aboriginal people have been overlooked as legitimate forms of literature and publishing.[19]

Indeed, non-Indigenous academic Stephen Muecke argues that even those considered to be "illiterate" – which constitutes the way a large number of particularly remote Aboriginal people are regarded – have always been reading and writing in the broad sense, but their forms of writing have simply been valued differently by other (mostly colonizing) peoples.[20] Muecke draws on Paddy Roe (from whom he recorded *Gularabulu: Stories from the West Kimberley* [1983]) as an example of someone who uses an "abstract signifying system of lines, dots, circles and so on" as a form of writing,[21] and asks "do we fail to call it writing because it is kept from white people?"[22] There is some consensus between van Toorn and Muecke that literature and publishing does not simply mean printed works in book form, but can range from dots and circles in the sand to letters, essays, articles, pamphlets and so on.

Jennifer Biddle also discusses the use of Aboriginal artwork as story-telling, particularly in the form of the art book *Kuruwarri: Yuendumu Doors* (1987), to highlight the contribution of art and written language as a means of communicating a particular story to the broadest possible audience.[23] The audiences include the Warlpiri peoples who can't read Warlpiri or English but can read the painted stories, those Aboriginal and Europeans who can read Warlpiri, and readers of English. This is truly a publishing achievement and indeed could be seen as trilingual as opposed to bilingual (if you consider the painted story as a form of writing).

Commentators and writers such as the late Judith Wright as early as 1988 were describing "Black writing" as "a literature in its own right."[24] With the dawning of this new discourse, came the rise of a new set of literary questions and issues. By whose standards would this writing be judged? Who would be most likely to review and assess such work? Most importantly for Aboriginal writers, Wright asked the questions:

> Do we go on talking from our critical heights, as though our standards are necessarily to be accepted even by those who have no cause to thank us for them? And do we continue to dismiss Black writers unless they somehow contrive to keep a lowly and conventional stand?[25]

Furthermore, by whom and how would this new literature be defined? At the outset it could be argued that any definition of Aboriginal writing should be coming from the writers themselves.

And while the diversity of Aboriginal Australia might make it difficult to define Aboriginal literature, there is some consensus amongst writers that it must at least be written by Indigenous people, and that there is something that stylistically marks Aboriginal writing.

Huggins and Bell find it relatively easy to define Aboriginal literature. Huggins sees it as something "[h]olistic, all-embracing, and written by an Indigenous person,"[26] while Bell defines it as a way of telling our side of the story, because we never had the opportunity before: "We were oral people, so literature wasn't something to worry about sixty years ago, but we've come a long way." In this way, Aboriginal literature can be defined and judged by writers in terms of what has driven its production and the way it reflects the real life experiences of Indigenous people.

Alexis Wright also considers the experience of the Aboriginal writer as something that affects the writing, creating a distinct literature because

> We see the world differently, our experience of the world differs from the rest of the population, and our linguistic expression will differ from what is accepted as standard English [sic]. If Aboriginal writing causes unease it is because it challenges non-Aboriginal perceptions of standard English [sic], or white concepts, values and ways of describing events, places, people etc.[27]

However, poet Lisa Bellear questions whether or not there is actually something that can be defined as Aboriginal literature. She says that if it does exist it's being primarily judged by non-Aboriginal people, the very ones Judith Wright suggested shouldn't be judging it. According to Bellear, these judges

> [c]ompare or validate the work of Indigenous people up to a standard which I would call substandard in many respects. Is it Aboriginal literature because it's written about an Aboriginal person? Or is it Aboriginal because it's written by an Indigenous person about Aboriginal characters? Or is it Aboriginal just because it's written by an Aboriginal person, even if it's about someone surfing down Byron Bay.[28]

Bellear, however, is quite adamant that she wouldn't describe as "Aboriginal literature" anything written by a non-Aboriginal person writing about Aboriginal culture.

Cathy Craigie also feels it's a difficult feat to define Aboriginal writing, but says at the very least it's got to be by Aboriginal writers and show all the essences of Aboriginal culture (which relates, in turn, to how one defines "Aboriginality"):

> The thing that binds us as Aboriginal people – [though] we have different languages and cultures, there's a general essence of what Aboriginal is and it's the way that you set things up. It's your thinking. I would expect Aboriginal people to understand land issues a lot easier [than Whites]. It's the content really, the way you handle the content.

Agreeing with Craigie, Melissa Lucashenko doesn't see Aboriginal writing as a separate genre, but more an issue of content, and says that in order for her to define Aboriginal literature she needs to consider the definition of Aboriginality.

> To me there are people who are biologically white, but culturally black and people who have lived in the communities for donkey's years and basically see the world through Black eyes. But they're not the people who are likely to write books, so that complicates it a bit. Aboriginal writing to me at the moment is a protest literature I suppose and it's centred around land and social justice and legal stuff.

Non-Aboriginal academic Kateryna Olijnyk Longley admits it's hard to sum up the body of Aboriginal writing coming out of Western Australia specifically. Noting writers Glenyse Ward, Jack Davis, Jimmy Chi and Sally Morgan, she says the writing "accommodates so many distinct cultural groups and literary (or anti-literary) approaches" and that "Aboriginal literature has done more than any other writing to change the direction of literary history in Western Australia over the last few years."[29]

Is there an Aboriginal style?

At the time of his outing as Wanda Koolmatrie, Leon Carmen claimed that his fraud was to show that there were no differences between Black and White writing, men's and women's.[30] After speaking with a number of Aboriginal writers, editors and readers, however, it's plainly obvious that his claim has no basis.

Throughout the history of Aboriginal Australia, most aspects of Aboriginal society, culture, religion and history were passed on to family and community via an Oral Tradition that included approximately 200 distinct Aboriginal languages spoken by 600 Aboriginal nations. This involved storytelling to pass on information over generations and this still exists today. Storytelling was the oral literature, the art form likened to dance, performance and visual arts which also pass on information. It is this storytelling or "oral" technique that contributes to a distinct Aboriginal style of writing.

The Oral Tradition is still very evident in Aboriginal writing today where many authors use 'Aboriginal English' out of respect for its speakers and in consideration for their Aboriginal readers. Rather than using Standard English (which they may not be trained in) or an Aboriginal language (which they may not be able to), many Aboriginal writers choose Aboriginal English, which is an Aboriginalisation of the English language that often needs some translation to non-Aboriginal audiences. The use of Kriol in Aboriginal writing (like that of Lionel Fogarty) is also common. Kriol is believed to have derived from the pidgin used to communicate between Aboriginal and non-Aboriginal people during the period of first contact.[31] There is a great difference between what is spoken and what is written in the Anglo world, but in Aboriginal society, they tend to be closer, with many writers wishing not to have manuscripts Anglicised (or "gubbarised"[32]) by editors, fixed on "correcting" Aboriginal English.

Kenny Laughton acknowledges what many writers also affirm that Aboriginal people tend to write how we speak: "so it's not the Queen's English or remotely Edwardian or Shakespearian, it's Blackfella lingo."[33] But Laughton also acknowledges that Aboriginal writers can "play the game" when required, being articulate in a variety of styles and writing what audiences want. He adds:

> We have also developed our own literary language in a sense, our slang some white linguists call, "Aboriginal English." I don't necessarily agree with this label as it only makes the white interpreters (who wrote on Aboriginal English) as the experts, once again. But I admit that we do use our own slang, and even though our language and tribal groups (whether you be bush or urban) are diversely different, we still link up through some of this common (equally recognisable) slang (i.e. *Koorie, bunji, gammon*, etc).

Alexis Wright also comments on the significant linguistic differences between Aboriginal languages and English,

Early colonial observers chose to denigrate Aboriginal languages as being like gibberish. In fact, Aboriginal languages have a great complexity which derives from the genius of our people to describe their complex relationships with each other and within their world.[34]

Wright gives an example of her own recording of oral literature for an anthology of land rights stories and essays for the Central Land Council published by IAD Press:

One exceptional memory man from the Tanami Desert region, wanted to do two tape recordings of the exact same story, one for himself for his particular local audience, and another one for me.

So we sat down in the spinifex one windy night and he went through his story in Warlpiri. It was about 40 minutes long. Then he went through it again as soon as the first tape was finished and told the exact same story, 40 minutes, and that was for me. He said he did not call himself boss, that is, the senior traditional owner, yet I believed he knew everything about his country. These are our great orators who can recall thousands of site names in their head, each with a sacred song, a Dreaming, and an interconnected sacred history over vast areas of land. And they might say to you, I cannot read or write, but I got it all along in my brains and I have to say it straight and the right way.[35]

Another example of the recording of oral literature done correctly can be witnessed in the highly regarded *Gularabulu: Stories of the Kimberley* by Paddy Roe and Stephen Muecke, first released in 1983. Muecke, as scribe, discusses the differences between the analysers of material and the story-tellers: one who considers material that needs to be studied in an academic sense, and one who needs a story to be told in a traditional sense. Understanding the significance of the storyteller, and he himself as the listener, Muecke says that to represent Roe's works honestly, the stories were presented in the text word for word, from taped recordings. Muecke also included Roe's hesitations as well as his own interventions to show the authenticity of the account to be in no doubt, explaining to the reader how he transcribed the storytelling and Roe's use of Aboriginal English. Muecke believes this was the first time that an Aboriginal narrative had been presented in its true form, explaining the common effects of editorial changes that had impacted on works in the past. He says:

> Presenting the stories as narrative art is a way of justifying
> a writing which tries to imitate the spoken word. When
> language is read as poetic, it is the form of the language
> itself, as well as its underlying content, which is important.
> Just as it would be unjustifiable to rewrite a poet's work
> into "correct" English (in other words to take away the
> poet's "licence"), so it would be unjustifiable to rewrite
> the words of Paddy Roe's stories.[36]

Muecke also explains that, while some parts of the text might
be difficult to understand, it is important not only to listen to the
language but the content of what Roe is saying: that as long as
Aboriginal people can speak out clearly like he does, then the culture will live on, even as times and people change.

Aboriginal speech patterns put into the written form is what
provides Aboriginal writing with character, passion, authenticity
and humour. An example of this is Alf Taylor's use of Aboriginal
English to great effect when the character Barney in his story "The
Wool Pickers" says:

> Um gunna take Auntie Florrie to dat French River Place,
> somewhere. And next we be goin' to see that Nyoongah
> bloke. You know, he was locked up in jail for twenty years
> an' come out to run his own country. Wass his name?[37]

Another great storyteller and an author whose writing is
largely based on the oral form, Ruby Langford Ginibi says Aboriginal writers choose Aboriginal English as a way of writing because

> We, Aboriginal people, come from an oral tradition, where
> our legends, and laws, were handed down by word of
> mouth, from generation to generation, it is we, who have
> always had to conform to the standards of those invaded,
> learn the Queen's English, so us Mob can write our stories
> so you Mob can comprehend what we are on about.[38]

Colin Johnson[39] believes that oral literature is often relegated
to the status of children's stories and hacked to pieces by editors
who do not pause to think why oral stories (commonly referred to
as "Dreamtime stories") even existed and what they signified.[40] He
points out that oral literature is important, though, as it "describes
Aboriginal life in Australia before invasion."[41] He also notes that

generally when Aboriginal oral literature has been collected and published,

> Little or no regard has been paid to how it was told, that is to the discourse of the story. Content was considered more important. Sometimes the very ones at fault have been academics, linguists who should have known better. Other whites were exploiters after a quick quid. They obtained a version of a story, then rewrote it for publication as a children's story.[42]

In his book on Aboriginal writing, *Writing from the Fringe*, Colin Johnson warns Aboriginal writers that if they write according to White styles, in White genres and with White theories, then they run the risk of being judged by White standards.

A number of Aboriginal writers suggest it's the language and the way it's used to tell the story that give their writing an Aboriginal style. Sandra Phillips, editor of books by Lisa Bellear, Jeanie Bell, Alexis Wright and Melissa Lucashenko, says there are obvious differences in language between Black and White writing; for example, "Jeannie Bell's sentences weave and flow rather than being manipulated to suit conventional sentence structure. They match the language to suit the style of communication."[43]

Melissa Lucashenko also notes the familiarity Aboriginal works have for her compared to non-Aboriginal works. She says, "It strikes a chord. Language, and the way people are socially, would tell me if an author is Aboriginal or not. The details could give it away." But she also adds that when you have Whitefellas who have lived a Black life then they could write a book that was, to her, for all intents and purposes, Aboriginal. Again, that would depend on how one defines Aboriginality. Lucashenko says:

> A lot of older white writing is about landscapes and it feels dry and false to me. More modern [Aboriginal] writing is more oral and is closer to what I call an Indigenous style. It's about standing back and noticing what people are doing and slotting it into an Indigenous context. The little details.

In terms of her own personal style Lucashenko says she can write in different styles including academic and 'street-style.' She adds "I think the style that's closest to my real style is short words, short sentences, very clear, very direct and fairly confronting but, again, acknowledging that it's a complex work."

Jackie Huggins who can and does write in many styles, admits there is a definite style when you read Aboriginal work compared to a non-Aboriginal work, "It's grammatical too, syntax, how we write. It can be the slickest writing, but you can still tell that it's Indigenous."

Kenny Laughton uses the contrast between White and Black writing to define an Aboriginal style saying that non-Aboriginal authors also have a distinct cultural advantage, having used the written form of recording language for hundreds of years longer than our writers:

> Our stories were an unwritten form. Translated and passed down through many generations by story telling and the corroborree. So in a sense, the art of writing as a means of saving or at least recording our language, culture, history, in comparison to say the European or Asian cultures, is a relatively new medium for Aboriginal people.

Kumbu-merri writer, lecturer and consultant in Aboriginal matters, Mary Graham offered the Australian Publishers' Association Residential Editorial Program in 1999 some basic differences between writing based on oral story-telling and European writing. These differences include:

> 1) A different logic between Aboriginal and non-Aboriginal thinking. All perspectives are valid and reasonable in Aboriginal society with no absolutes, where even contradictory things are negotiable.
> 2) There is a different sense of time for Aboriginal people, with the ´idea of beginning/middle/end being a foreign concept, meaning the Aboriginal view is not linear.
> 3) An individual is a member of a group, and while Europeans would say this leads to "conformity," Aboriginal people see this as not being isolated from their community.
> 4) Stories don't "belong" to an individual in Aboriginal society as they do in non-Aboriginal societies and it is against lore to tell someone else's story. And regardless of geography, all stories are traditional.
> 5) The place for authority is well defined in Aboriginal society and the older people in communities work out of a distinction between power and authority. Grey hair is a good thing, denoting authority, and it is a good thing to have children and grand-children.
> 6) Land is the basis of all life for Aboriginal people and

the relationship between land and people sets the tone for the relationship between people, and for this display of manners. All the creative process, culture, comes out of land itself.

7) Decolonisation is demystifying and defining Aboriginality as a new concept. There is a notion of universal "assumed knowledge" in our culture which means there is no necessity to describe.

8) Contradiction is an issue for the writer, that is, the editor should emphasise craft in editorial comments rather than the "utopian" idea of perfection. There is no utopia in Aboriginal culture. The pure/spontaneous thing is natural to an Aboriginal writer.[44]

Another example of Aboriginal style is given by Sandra Phillips who cites a manuscript she read as part of the David Unaipon Award,

I read it and said I think this is a non-Aboriginal woman. It can be quite easy to read something and figure it out. I have no doubt that it's not an Aboriginal person. It comes through in the language of the cover letter. And when people are Aboriginal they say I'm from here or there, this is who I am. That's the identifier. But you can't base statements like that on total credibility either, but that's part of the picture of the presentation. These are the sorts of things that a non-Indigenous editor mightn't pick up.

Cathy Craigie who is capable of changing styles in her writing says she prefers using Aboriginal English. So too, Alexis Wright, in an interview with Alison Ravenscroft, says she writes the way she speaks, which comes from her traditional land in the Gulf of Carpentaria. She adds that Aboriginal people generally need to be able to write their own work their own way, saying "We need to choose our own voices."[45]

Along with all the arguments which say that Aboriginal voices are distinctly different to White styles of writing – partly due to the use of Aboriginal English, and partly due to the content of the writing – it must also be recognised that within the editorial processes of Aboriginal publishing houses, new styles are actually being created. Two books released by Magabala Books in 1999 used the form of story-telling for the purposes of autobiography. *Jinangga* by Monty Walgar (as told to Cloud Shabalah) and *Holding up the Sky: Aboriginal Women Speak*, an anthology of nine women from around Australia, are written in the same style – short, simple sentences, occasional Aboriginal English, and little dialogue – with content based on experiences of Aboriginal people living in a variety of situations and locations. More noteworthy in this context is the anthology of women's writing whose nine stories are by women from such different locations as Broome, Beagle Bay, Perth, Yarrabah and northern New South Wales. The voice in each of these stories is so similar to the next that it is, at times, difficult to tell the authors apart.

In what genres do we excel?

Considering the number of published poets and autobiographers we have, it would be hard to ignore these as our main genres for writing, but as we move more into fiction, and even erotica, that is changing. Aboriginal writers are telling their stories through the printed word in poetry, fiction, autobiography and biography, essays, histories, short stories, plays and film scripts. But still we are categorised and known largely for life-writing.

Editors Josie Douglas and Marg Bowman from the Institute of Aboriginal Development Press in Alice Springs believe that when Aboriginal writing first began to emerge during the 1960s, poetry was the most popular genre:

> Aboriginal people were writing in a time of great political change and activism, land rights and the right to vote were all part of this era. Poetry at this time carried the voice of protest and was used as a political tool. Aboriginal poetry today still carries a political message. Even those themes that might normally be considered apolitical can't escape the political nature of Aboriginal peoples' experiences. Black poetry is a commentary on Black lives, showing the diversity and range of the Aboriginal experience.[46]

Regardless of why the poetry is being produced, non-Aboriginal Werner Arens says there is no way that you can by-pass the contribution that Aboriginal poets make to a "new consciousness in the White and Black community with regard to Australian self-image."[47] He cites the poetry of Kath Walker, Jack Davis and Kevin Gilbert over two decades as the force behind bringing public attention to the existence of "a second cultural tradition in Australia."[48] In *Writing from the Fringe*, Johnson sees the practicality of writing and publishing affecting the genres in which Aboriginal people appear, noting the costs of publishing a novel are far higher than running off short photocopied manuscripts of poetry at a community organisation.[49]

Although Jackie Huggins acknowledges that poetry is a popular genre with Indigenous writers, she points out that "The life-story, biography and autobiography will always be around because for most writers that's the first book that they write." Autobiography is a genre in which Aboriginal people throughout Australia are choosing to write, documenting their life experiences and expressing both their own anguish and the anguish of their fellows. Autobiographies are the history and textbooks of Aboriginal Australia.

This type of writing plays a number of roles, not only providing a vehicle for the author to learn to write about their own history, but also to educate and often entertain a wider audience who may have a narrow perspective on Aboriginal Australia, offering a first hand account of sometimes disturbing parts of Australian history. With much of her poetry based on real life experiences, Lisa Bellear feels that the genre of autobiography is a very important component of our culture "given that for 208 years we've been silenced and told that our stories aren't of worth."[50]

One of the most widely read autobiographies in Australia is Ruby Langford Ginibi's *Don't Take Your Love to Town* which has appeared on the NSW Higher School Certificate Curriculum for many years. She says that she decided to pick up a pen in 1984 to write her autobiography because she realised there was nothing taught in the school curriculum about Kooris:

> I thought if I wrote about my experiences as an Aboriginal person, it might give the other side, the "white side," some idea of how hard it is to survive between the Black and white culture of Australia, and they might become less racist and paternalistic towards our people.[51]

Some autobiographies cross into biographies as life-stories are retold to family members or trusted writers. Due to the profile of co-author Jackie Huggins, one of the more well-known biographies is *Aunty Rita*, a book of dialogue between mother and daughter and the first of it's kind. The story tells of Rita Huggins' forced removal from her traditional lands as a child, her resettled life on Cherbourg Aboriginal reserve under the Aborigines Protection Act, right through to the rise of Aboriginal political activism in the 1960s and her life in Brisbane.

Regardless of genre, 'rewriting history' can be an appropriate phrase for much of the work currently being penned by Aboriginal writers today. Aboriginal authors are rewriting the history books that have conveniently left out the facts around invasion, colonisation and attempted genocide. Aboriginal people today are documenting the history of a people misrepresented, or not represented at all in history books of the past. According to Langford Ginibi,

> We are writing our histories too. We are telling our stories, and saying the same things about our dispossession in the hope that people will understand us better. And the writing of our stories, our biographies, and autobiographies are our documentation of our histories and stories. From our Aboriginal perspectives, and they need to be read, and heard all over this great land, because for too long, we have had other people defining, and telling us who we are.[52]

In *Us Mob* Johnson agrees that so many Indigenous historical narratives are being written because he believes that while Indigenous people have no "true" past, they can have no "self."[53] He adds, "It is our [sic] past and only we can write it, for in a sense we need history and it is not 'ours' until we do the writing ourselves, giving importance to those stories which now matter to us."[54]

Although much Aboriginal history and real life experience is written in the non-fiction genres, there is a growing pool of fiction writers that touch on the politics of being Aboriginal and the realities of Aboriginal experiences in their novels. While we have a smaller pool of writers in the area of fiction than other genres, there is a strong core of published authors making names for themselves and their works can be found on university reading lists and course guides around the country.

Alexis Wright says that what she is doing in the novel as an Aboriginal writer is trying to make sense of her own world: "I care and I don't care about genres, discourse, standard English, expectations or assumptions, reality or chronology. If I challenge the lot it does not really matter because I have nothing to lose."[55] Unless she is asked to write otherwise, she says she chooses to write fiction because she feels she would fail if she tried to write factual history.[56] In writing *Plains of Promise*, for example, Wright says she tried to create a set of characters that are very real to her, and although a lot of the story comes from her own experience, the characters are not from her real life. Wright says fiction is the one way of saying all the things that need to be said to the reader, without exposing people from her traditional area to the kind of scrutiny that a conventional history book would have risked.[57]

As the pool of fiction writers grows, so does the pool of Aboriginal playwrights, who also include Aboriginal politics and experiences in their genre. Playwright Jack Davis believed that theatre offers an opportunity to use all the talents of speech and body movement present in Aboriginal oral literature and dance since time began. He was not surprised that his Aboriginal background was a great asset in theatre:

> The Nyoongah language was always full of humour and music. Theatre in a bush arena is the very essence of an Aboriginal corroborree and performances there are often full of brilliant dance and mime. There was and is great opportunity for theatre to draw upon the rich Aboriginal oral literature.[58]

Eva Johnson is another playwright who has made a huge contribution to the representation of Aboriginal women, and was the writer/director of the First National Black Playwrights Conference in Canberra in 1987. She is the author and co-director of the play "Tjindarella" which debuted at the First Aboriginal Women's' Arts Festival in Adelaide in 1984. The play examines Aboriginal oppression and highlights the effects of government policy on the forced removal of children from their parents and culture.

Kooemba Jdarra Indigenous Performing Arts in Queensland has also been very successful with its production of *The 7 Stages of Grieving* performed by Australian Film Industry Award winner Deborah Mailman. The story of an 'Aboriginal Everywoman,' the play has been staged in Sydney, Melbourne, Tasmania, Canberra, Western Australia and Brisbane. *The 7 Stages of Grieving* was also published by Playlab Press and the publication includes the script, reference material, support articles and the national tour program.

Katherine Brisbane, co-founder and publisher of Currency Press, the main publisher of Australian plays, said in her paper at IDEA '95 – 2nd World Conference of Drama/Theatre and Education,

> "Bran Nue Dae" in 1989 was a turning point in the short history of Aboriginal writing for theatre. Twenty years of evolution: in writers, political activists, actors, dancers, singers and song-writers, preceded it... Encouraged by the public statements [of the 60s], individual voices began to be heard. Poetry and song came first; drama followed.[59]

Brisbane now feels that the most important new Australian voice in drama, and one that will in due course be widely heard in other countries, is the Aboriginal one.[60]

Just as the theatre provides a mechanism for appealing to large audiences because of its entertainment value, so too do children's books by Aboriginal authors and illustrators. These books are increasingly used in education, to teach young people (and indeed older people with literacy problems) about Aboriginal society and culture and in particular about Aboriginal creation stories. Perhaps the more marketable Aboriginal works are, in fact, those in the area of children and juvenile literature because of the large educational market. Well-known names from various states and territories and Aboriginal nations grace the covers of many award-winning children's books.

Although better known for his political poetry, Lionel Fogarty also writes children's stories and published *Booyooburra: A Story of the Wakka Murri* in 1993. Fogarty says:

> My own initiative to write this story was to bring truth to the children's eyes and truth to the children's minds. With a little bit of information or a little tiny bit of a story from back then, you can bring it into the reality of today, because those stories are thousands and thousands of years old, and are still the essence of knowledge today.[61]

Authors like Narelle McRobbie (*Who's That Jumbun in the Log*) use Aboriginal words and illustrations to get messages across to children. She says her love of writing short stories for children has been furthered by her commitment to keep the language alive. McRobbie says it was her mother (to whom the book is dedicated) who instilled traditional language into her thoughts.[62]

Other writers whose family background and fluency in language affected their work include the late Daisy Utemorrah whose first collection of stories *Do Not Go Around the Edges* won the Australian Multicultural Children's Book Award in 1992 and was also short listed for the Children's Book of the Year. In 1994, Margaret Dunkle published *Black in Focus: A Guide to Aboriginality in Literature For Young People*, which focuses on books with Aboriginal themes from 1960 onwards. Nearly 1000 titles by Aboriginal and non-Aboriginal authors were culled to 300 books with Aboriginal themes appropriate for young people.

Short stories are continuing to be a form utilised by Aboriginal writers. In the anthology *Across Country* (ABC Books, 1998), names such as Herb Wharton, Alf Taylor and Alexis Wright give strength and credibility to this collection compiled by non-Indigenous editor Kerry Davis whose 'specialities' include "Indigenous literature."[63] What you'll find in *Across Australia* is thirty short stories by eighteen Indigenous writers from across Australia except Tasmania, which is a noticeable gap. *Across Country*, unlike glossy *Indigenous Australian Voices*,[64] not only showcases established writers such as Bruce Pascoe, Herb Wharton and Alexis Wright, but also provides a forum for many new and emerging writers to showcase their work.

Although Aboriginal writers are clearly writing across all genres, the question of whether or not there is an "Aboriginal genre" or "Aboriginal discourse" as such is not as clear. Sam Cook (ex-Magabala staffer) says she finds it difficult to categorise Aboriginal writing as she does not agree with pigeonholing Indigenous publications into Western genres. She notes:

> Our works are so much more. For example most of the titles considered children's books should also be considered art books and even cultural literacy resources. I see no reason why we cannot extend the definition of the genres to accommodate our differences.[65]

Aboriginality and writing

Ray Coffey, publisher at Fremantle Arts Centre Press (FACP), says the number of autobiographical works, family and community histories by Aboriginal writers is evidence that through personal testimony there is an obvious attempt to establish and project a sense of Aboriginal identity.[66]

Kerry Reed-Gilbert, whose poetry in *Black Woman, Black Life* is heavily influenced by her identity, is clear about the role of Aboriginality in writing. She says "Aboriginal identity is who we are as writers, as people. We live our lives as the Indigenous people of this land, we write as Indigenous people of this land."

Kenny Laughton maintains that it is important to retain our Aboriginality in our writing, believing that we have a moral obligation to be role models and prove that "we as Aboriginal people can not only achieve but mix it with the best of them, in any field, be it sport, work or writing." Like other Aboriginal writers referenced, Alexis Wright is adamant that she doesn't want her Aboriginality separated from her writing as it is. She says, "What's producing the writing? Without it I wouldn't be able to write the way I do."[67]

The concept of Aboriginality is certainly a difficult thing to grasp for contemporary Australians, indeed, sometimes even for Aboriginal people themselves, especially those who have been denied access to family, culture and community due to government policies of the past. The effects of the differing experiences of Aboriginality, though, are nevertheless evident in writings by Aboriginal people, regardless of genre.

The way in which Aboriginal people have been categorised by race in terms of where they fit into literature is no different than the way in which they have been defined in sports, history, the arts and politics. Although many would like to be regarded and critiqued for their writing, rather than their race, 'Aboriginal author' is also a cementing of identity for the writer, and a categorisation that doesn't offend most. Most writers are proud of their identity as well as their ability to write in a profoundly White world, because, in the words of Ruby Langford Ginibi "we are reclaiming our history, our heritage, and our identity, and that's very important to our cause."[68]

As to whether or not publishers are more wary since the Mudrooroo/Sykes controversies[69], Ray Coffey, speaking for FACP, says they probably aren't. As a publisher of only Western Australian writers, Coffey says it is perhaps easier for them to check on the credentials of writers who present as Aborigines, "We are perhaps more easily able to determine whether an individual is known and recognised by the local Aboriginal community as being Aboriginal."

Post-Colonial – NOT!

In terms of the academic world, the literature of African countries, Australia, Bangladesh, Canada, Caribbean countries, India, Malaysia, Malta, New Zealand, Pakistan, Singapore, South Pacific Island Countries and Sri Lanka are often defined as "post-colonial literatures." Ashcroft, Griffiths and Tiffin suggest,

> The term "post-colonial" is used generally to describe all cultures affected by the imperial process from the moment of colonisation to the present day. It is also considered as the most appropriate term for the new cross-cultural criticism which has emerged in recent years and for the discourse through which it is constituted.[70]

They go on to say that the idea of "post-colonial theory" is a reaction to equate European theory with what they term as post-colonial writing.[71] But it might also be suggested that the term "post-colonial" is simply a term used to describe much contemporary writing.

In terms of defining Aboriginal writing as "post-colonial" literature, it appears that there are two distinct views. First, that of the literary establishment who use the term as a way of describing a genre in which Aboriginal people write; and second, that of most Aboriginal writers who see the term implying that colonialism is a matter of the past and that decolonisation has taken place, which of course is not the case. In this way, most writers do not even consider the term in relation to their writing at all (which makes this discussion difficult).

As comments by writers below show, the term "post-colonialism" is meaningless to Aboriginal people, bearing in mind the political, social and economic status we currently occupy. Kathryn Trees in a joint paper with Colin Johnson asks the questions:

> Does post-colonial suggest colonialism has passed? For whom is it "post"? Surely not for Australian Aboriginal people at least, when land rights, social justice, respect and equal opportunity for most does not exist because of the internalised racism of many Australians.
>
> In countries such as Australia where Aboriginal sovereignty, in forms appropriate to Aboriginal people, is not legally recognised, post-colonialism is not merely a fiction, but a linguistic manoeuvre on the part of some "white" theorists who find this a comfortable zone that precludes the necessity for political action.
>
> Post-colonialism is a "white" concept that has come to the fore in literary theory in the last five years as Western nations attempt to define and represent themselves in non-imperialist terms.[72]

Unlike some other Pacific Nation writers who proudly accept the term "post-colonial,"[73] claiming to write from a post-colonial experience, there are few, if any Aboriginal Australian writers who agree with or use the term at all, least of all in relation to their writing. Its relevance to Aboriginal people appears to be non-existent. As high numbers of Aboriginal people continue to be incarcerated and die in prison, still experience infant mortality rates the same as Third World nations, and continue to need government assistance in attaining housing, education and basic health care, it is apparent that colonisation, as Aboriginal people interpret it, is very much alive. This is further exemplified by the current Liberal Government's desire to deny Native Title, and its failure to acknowledge the damaging effects of government policies that led to the 'Stolen Generations.'

Sandra Phillips quite strongly believes that we are still colonised and that it makes those in the literary and publishing community feel better to think we're post-colonial. She adds,

> But if only they'd realise the way in which they carry themselves in society today still is colonial. They take an ownership stand, saying if we didn't colonise these people they wouldn't be able to create this stuff.

Jackie Huggins is offended by the term post-colonial, preferring the term "neo-colonial" but feels that, along with the term "post-modernism," they are all just yuppie buzzwords. "[They] convolute the whole process of writing that says there isn't a colonial mentality still in existence. In Queensland for sure you can see it. I think because we are so close to a certain Member of Parliament here it's exacerbated unusually."[74]

Herb Wharton acknowledges the term but says he doesn't worry too much about or agree with a lot of the things academics say:

> When they're describing Australian literature, there's no cut-off date for the history of Australia. The literary history or the recorded history. 1788 is when Europeans came. But Australian history and its literature and stories were there all the time.[75]

Cathy Craigie, like myself, thinks it's hard to believe there is any such thing as "post-colonial" when you are the people who've been colonised.

> We're still in Aboriginal time, Murri time, we're still in there doing the same things. For me it's a continuation of a culture that's thousands and thousands of years old. It's not something that you cut off because white man has come in.

For Craigie the term post-colonial only fits the White system, rather than acknowledging our own time frame. She explains "My definition of time is endless, its past, present and future."

In contrast, both Lucashenko and Laughton agree that their writing reflects the effects of being colonised. Lucashenko who was born in 1967 says that everything in her life, including her writing, is touched by or has risen out of colonialism, not being able to grow out of anything traditional. She dissects the issue of post-colonialism.

> What's post-colonialism? Then you have to ask what's colonialism?, which is the process of coming in and taking people's land and sovereignty away from them. The process of actually taking that has almost ended, but it hasn't quite ended because of Mabo and Wik where it's politically still going on, and psychologically, because people in the bush are much closer to that stuff I think, than people in the city, so to them they are far more in the colonial period than we are. In some senses, people have discovered how to be Black living in Redfern, living the urban lifestyle, and that's sort of edging towards post-colonialism to me. I'm not saying that we're not oppressed, I'm saying that what I define as a colonial era is ending and now the oppression is still there, but the circumstances of our oppression are changing.

Although not accepting the use of the term, Kenny Laughton can see why Aboriginal writing has to be called post-colonial.

> Let's face it, prior to the arrival of white man, our history, everything about us was recorded by mediums other than the written word. But our ancestors were prolific storytellers, they must have been; for these stories to be passed on from generation to generation, for hundreds of thousands of years. So the "post-colonial" label is one that would sit comfortably with the anthropologists and the linguists and the historians, maybe even with some of our Aboriginal "academics"... But I don't necessarily accept it. Not as an Aboriginal author, especially knowing the depth, the intricate knowledge, and the elaborate ceremonies that were the blue prints for the Dreamtime generational stories. Our first form of written history may be classed as "post-colonial" but our stories could almost be described as "post-history."

In her book *Literary Formations: Post colonialism, Nationalism and Globalism* (1995), Anne Brewster says "post-colonialism" may be useful when describing certain aspects of post-invasion culture in Australia (such as the relationship between Australia and the United Kingdom or the West), but as a discourse it has not been scrupulous in distinguishing between the very different formations of colonisation and the decolonisation in 'settler' and Indigenous cultures.[76]

Brewster understands fully the irrelevancy of the term post-colonialism to Aboriginal people generally, and writers specifically, and says that through her own studies she realised that "the discourses of post-colonialism and feminism diverged from that of Aboriginality."[77]

Muecke agrees saying "Australia seems to be caught in a post-colonial syndrome, because, unlike America, independence has not been fully achieved either historically, through war for instance, or symbolically: the Fourth of July."[78] And while some advocates of the definition like Pacific Islander writer Albert Wendt write out of what they say is the experience of being colonised,[79] it is hard not to agree with Bruce Pascoe who says that, "All our writing is influenced by the stories and culture which have developed for 200,000 years. Colonial we aren't. Colonised we are."

Excerpted from "Dhuuluu-Yala (Talk Straight): Publishing Aboriginal Literature in Australia," a PhD thesis in Communication and Media at the University of Western Sydney, Nepean, 2000

Notes

1. M. Annette Jaimes, (1992) *The State of Native America: Genocide, Colonisation and Resistance,* (Boston: South End Press) 127.

2. cited in Lorna Lippman, (1991) *Generations of Resistance: Aborigines Demand Justice*, 2nd ed. (Melbourne: Longman Cheshire) 29.

3. Tony Birch, (1993) "'Real Aborigines' – Colonial Attempts to Re-Imagine and Re-Create the Identities of Aboriginal People," *Ulitarra*, 4: 13.

4. Marcia Langton, (1993) *Well I Heard It On The Radio And I Saw It On The Television*, (Sydney: Australian Film Commission) 28-29.

5. Nellie Green, (2000) "Chasing an Identity, An Aboriginal perspective on Aboriginality," *The Strength Of Us As Women: Black Women Speak*, (Canberra: Ginninderra Press) 47.

6. ibid., 51.

7. cited in Lippman, op.cit., 88.

8. Sonja Kurtzer, (Winter 1998) "'Wandering Girl': Who Defines Authenticity in Aboriginal Literature?" *Southerly*, 58(2): 20.

9. ibid., 21.

10. Jackie Huggins, (April 1993) "Always Was Always Will Be," *Australian Historical Studies*, 25(100): 462.

11. Jeanie Bell, personal interview, 15 January 1998. All other quotes from Bell are from this source unless otherwise indicated.

12. Bruce Pascoe, responses to questionnaire, 22 November 1997. All other quotes from Pascoe are from this source unless otherwise indicated.

13. Colin Johnson (aka Mudrooroo) and Roberta Sykes have both been called into question regarding their Aboriginality by the communities from which they say they belong, sparking debate amongst Aboriginal communities nationally about impostures, people who pose as Aboriginals for the purpose of establishing careers in publishing and academia, etc.

14. Kerry Reed-Gilbert, responses to questionnaire, 28 September 1997. All other quotes from Gilbert on this chapter are from this source unless otherwise indicated.

15. Cathy Craigie, personal interview, 9 October 1997. All other quotes from Craigie are from this source unless otherwise indicated.

16. Melissa Lucashenko, personal interview, 30 January 1998. All other quotes from Lucashenko are from this source unless otherwise indicated.

17. *Report on Strategies for the Further Development of the National Aboriginal and Torres Strait Islander Arts and Cultural Industry: Main Report.* A Report to ATSIC by Arts Training Northern Territory. ATSIC, Canberra, 1994, 255.

18. Penny van Toorn, (1996) "Early Aboriginal Writing and the Discipline of Literary Studies," *Meanjin*, 4: 754.

19. van Toorn, op.cit., 754.

20. Stephen Muecke, (1984) "Always Already Writing," *Reading the Country: Introduction to Nomadology*, Krim Benterrak, Stephen Muecke & Padde Roe, (Fremantle: Fremantle Arts Centre Press) 61.

21. ibid., 63.

22. ibid., 62.

23. Jennifer Biddle, (1991) "Dot, Circle, Difference: Translating Central Desert Paintings," *Cartographies: Poststructuralism and the Mapping of Bodies and Spaces*, (Sydney: Diprose, R & Ferrell, R. Allen & Unwin) 28. Unfortunately, Biddle is more concerned with what defines bilingualism in her discussion, than the actual expression being presented in visual, Warlpiri and English forms. Regardless of how many Europeans speak, or rather don't speak Warlpiri, Biddle is off-base in her reading of what has been described as a "bilingual dreaming book," failing to see that in this context the artists and owners of the intellectual property of the stories have been generous in allowing their stories to be told for three audiences. Biddle however is more concerned with the translations of Warlpiri stories (and indeed every reproduction of Central Desert Arts), highlighting that her academic training leads her to focus heavily on a linear analysis of how these paintings are translated and by whom, rather than what these paintings are saying and by whom.

24. Judith Wright, (1991) "The Writer As Activist," *Born of the Conquerors: Selected Essays*, (Canberra: Aboriginal Studies Press) 132.

25. Judith Wright, op.cit., 132.

26. Jackie Huggins, personal interview, 10 December 1997. All other quotes from Huggins are from this source unless otherwise indicated.

27. Alexis Wright, "Language & Empire: The Empires Of The East Have Crumbled Into Dust, But The English Language Remains," a paper presented at the Brisbane Writers' Festival, 7 September 1997.

28. Lisa Bellear, personal interview, 5 June 1997. All other quotes from Bellear are from this source unless otherwise indicated.

29. Kateryna Olijnyk, Longley (June 1991) "Directions," *Australian Book Review*, 131: 30.

30. Leon Carmen (15 March 1997) on *A Current Affair*, cited in Debra Jopson's article, "Writing Wrongs," *Sydney Morning Herald*, 38.

31. J.M. Arthur, (1996) *Aboriginal English: A Cultural Study*, (Melbourne: Oxford University Press) 235.

32. Term coined by Ruby Langford Ginibi.

33. Kenny Laughton, e-mail to the author, 17 October 1998. All other quotes from Laughton are from this source unless otherwise indicated.

34. Alexis Wright, "Language and Empire," op.cit.

35. ibid.

36. Paddy Roe and Stephen Muecke, (1983) *Gularabulu: Stories of the Kimberley*, (Fremantle: Fremantle Arts Centre Press) iv.

37. Taylor Alf, (1998) "The Wool Pickers," *Across Country*, (Sydney: ABC Books) 187.

38. Ruby Langford Ginibi, (2000) "My Mob, My Self," *The Strength Of Us As Women: Black Women Speak*, (Canberra: Ginninderra Press) 18.

39. See Note # 13.

40. Mudrooroo, (1995) *Us Mob: History, Culture, Struggle: An Introduction to Indigenous Australia*, (Sydney: Angus & Robertson) 94.

41. Colin Johnson, (1990) *Writing from the Fringe: A Study of Modern Aboriginal Literature*, (South Yarra: Hyland House) 6.

42. ibid., 143.

43. Sandra Phillips, personal interview, 5 June 1997. All other quotes from Phillips are from this source unless otherwise indicated.

44. Mary Graham, (1999) "Indigenous Writing and Editing," *APA Residential Editorial Program Report*, 27-28.

45. Alison Ravenscroft, (1998) "Politics of Exposure: An Interview with Alexis Wright," *Meridian*, 17(1): 76.

46. Josie Douglas and Marg Bowman, (July 1997) "New Publisher for Black Poetry," *Five Bells*, 4(6): 9.

47. Werner Arens, (1983) "The Image of Australia in Australian Poetry," *Australian Papers: Yugoslavia, Europe and Australia*, ed. `Mirko Jurak, Faculty of Arts and Science, Edvard Kardelj University of Ljubljana, 229.

48. ibid.

49. Johnson, *Writing from the Fringe*, op.cit., 28.

50. Lisa Bellear on ABC Radio National's "Women Out Loud," 19 March 1997.

51. Ruby Langford Ginibi, *The Strength of Us As Women*, op.cit., 17.

52. ibid., 18.

53. Mudrooroo, *Us Mob*, op.cit., 178.

54. ibid.

55. Alexis Wright, "Language and Empire," op.cit.

56. Alexis Wright, "Breaking Taboos" a paper given at the Tasmanian Writers' and Readers' Festival, September 1998.

57. Ravenscroft, op.cit. 75.

58. Keith Chesson, (1998) *Jack Davis: A life story*, (Melbourne: Dent) 197.

59. Katherine Brisbane, "The Future in Black and White: Aboriginality in Recent Australian Drama," published in Currency Press – The Performing Arts Publisher catalogue.

60. ibid.

61. "Lionel Fogarty talks to Philip Mead" *Jacket Magazine*, http://www.jacket.zip.com.au/jacket01/fogartyiv/html

62. Narelle McRobbie, (1996) *Who's That Jumbun in the Log,* (Broonme: Magabala Books) 30.

63. Kerry Davies Publishing Services, *Register of Editorial Services 1998*, Society of Editors (NSW).

64. An anthology written for American tertiary students and published by Rutgers University Press, New Jersey, 1998.

65. Sam Cook, email to the author, 2 October 1999.

66. Ray Coffey, email to author, 12 August 1999. All other quotes from Coffey are from this source unless otherwise indicted.

67. Ravenscroft, op.cit., 78.

68. Langford Ginibi, The Strength of us as Women, op.cit. 19.

69. see Note # 13.

70. W.D. Ashcroft, (1989) Gareth Griffiths & Helen Tiffin, *The Empire Writes Back: Theory and Practice in Post-Colonial Literatures*, (London: Routledge) 2.

71. ibid., 11

72. Kathryn Trees, (1993) "Postcolonialism: Yet Another Colonial Strategy?," *Span*, 1(36): 264-265.

73. Albert Wendt, personal interview, 12 June 1997.

74. Jackie Huggins, personal interview, 10 December 1997. The MP referred to by Huggins is Pauline Hanson of the One Nation Party.

75. Herb Wharton, personal interview, 10 December 1997.

76. Anne Brewster, (1995) *Literary Formations: Post-colonialism, Nationalism, Globalism,* (Melbourne: University Press) 19.

77. ibid.

78. Stephen Muecke, (1992) *Textual Spaces: Aboriginality and Cultural Studies.* (Kensington: UNSW Press) 10.

79. Albert Wendt, personal interview, 12 June 1997.

Aboriginal Text in Context

Greg Young-Ing

Portrayal of "The Other"

From the 15th to the mid 19th century, the vast majority of explorers, missionaries, anthropologists, and literary writers made reference to Aboriginal Peoples as an inferior vanishing race in a manner which is degrading and offensive to most Aboriginal Peoples. These writings convey little information about Aboriginal cultural reality.

In *Indians of Canada*, for example, which was for decades considered to be the authoritative anthropological text, originally published in 1938, Diamond Jenness begins in the first paragraph, "When Samuel Champlain in 1603 sailed up the St. Lawrence River and agreed to support the Algonkian Indians at Taboussac against the aggression of the Iroquois, he could not foresee that the petty strife between these two apparently insignificant hordes of savages would one day decide the fate of New France."[1]

Much of the literature written by explorers, missionaries and anthropologists provided little insight into the cultural realities of Aboriginal Peoples, yet it influenced the intellectual foundations for European-based society's perception of Aboriginal Peoples as basically under-developed. It has been argued by Aboriginal intellectuals, such as Ward Churchill and John Mohawk, that the common perception was also characterized, consciously or subconsciously, by Darwinian concepts that can be taken to suggest Aboriginal Peoples are located somewhere on an evolutionary scale between primates and homo-sapiens.

Later, imposters such as Grey Owl and Long Lance, came to have considerable notoriety lecturing, writing and publishing while masquerading as Aboriginals. Generally, these writers displayed a less condescending and more positive attitude toward Aboriginal Peoples; although their work tended to reinforce the stereotypical image of Aboriginal Peoples as glorified remnants of the past, *á la* Rousseau's concept of "the Noble Savage." As noted by Robert Berkhofer in *The Whiteman's Indian*, "Although each succeeding generation [of writers] presumed its imagery based more upon the Native Americans of observation and report, the Indian of imagination and ideology continued to be derived as much from polemical and creative needs of Whites as from what they heard and read of actual Native Americans or even at times experienced."[2] A review of the literature would reveal that high profile Canadian writers, such as Farley Mowat and Stephen Leacock, conveyed many of the perceptions created by explorers and missionaries.

Beginning in the 1980s, writing by non-Aboriginal academics has created another body of texts. Some of these writers must be credited with increasing public awareness in recent years; however, while much of this body of work has observational and analytical value, it cannot express Aboriginal cultures and worldviews, nor can it express Aboriginal Peoples' unique internal perspective on contemporary Aboriginal political and cultural issues. Although this body of work is predominately well-intentioned, some Aboriginal writers, such as Howard Adams, Lee Maracle and Leroy Littlebear, have stated that it tends to reduce the emotionally, historically and culturally charged issues to dry information laden with legalized and/or academic jargon. As stated by Adams, "Academia is slow to re-examine what has been accepted for centuries... These myths have been so deeply ingrained in the peoples' psyche that even Aboriginals will have to go to great lengths to rid themselves of colonial ideologies."[3]

As further observed by the Creek/Cherokee author Ward Churchill, "the current goal of literature concerning Indians is to create them, if not out of the whole cloth, then from only the bare minimum of fact needed to give the resulting fiction a ring of truth."[4] Here Churchill expresses a view commonly held by many Aboriginal Peoples – as well as many mainstream historians and academics – that the portrayal of Aboriginal Peoples has improved slightly, but there is still a persistence of subtle inappropriate stereotypes and faulty academic paradigms.

The paramount purpose of literature focussing on a specific cultural group should be to present the particular culture in a realistic and insightful manner with the highest possible degree of verisimilitude. As Franz Boas argued in his progressive anthropological concept of "ethnocentrism," this purpose can ultimately only be achieved through a perspective of a culture from the inside. Jacques Derrida calls the ethnocentrism of the European science of writing in the late seventeenth and early eighteen centuries a symptom of the general crisis of European consciousness, and states further that, recognition through assimilation of "the Other" can be more interestingly traced... in the imperialist constitution of the colonial subject.[5] Indeed, the vast majority of the body of literature on Aboriginal Peoples tends to view them as "the Other" and thus fails to achieve an internal cultural perspective. This failure has been a long-standing concern of Aboriginal Peoples and other marginalized groups and was identified by progressive anthropologists like Boas in the mid 20th century and by members of the Canadian literary establishment, such as Atwood, who wrote in 1972, "The Indians and Eskimos have rarely been considered in and for themselves: they are usually made into projections of something in the white Canadian psyche."[6]

Although increased cultural awareness and the concept of ethnocentrism throughout the 1980s and 1990s has led to a marked improvement in the contemporary literature on Aboriginal Peoples, there is still a significant body of literature being produced that contains some of the old stereotypes and perceptions, and lacks respect for Aboriginal perspectives.

Aboriginal Editorial

The need for Aboriginal editorial guidelines in many ways parallels the editorial advances that have been made in the late 20th century in writing about African Americans and women, and the development of concepts such as "Black History" and "Herstory." One predominant assertion made by Aboriginal writers, editors and publishers is that the experience of being Aboriginal is profoundly different from that of other people in North America. Many Aboriginal authors have cited cultural appropriation and misrepresentation through literature and lack of respect for Aboriginal cultural protocol as significant problems in Canadian publishing. Aboriginal Peoples have frequently taken the stance that they are best capable and morally empowered to transmit information about themselves. However, whereas it must be acknowledged that there are established genres of writing and reporting on Aboriginal subject matter, Aboriginal Peoples would at least like to have an opportunity to have input into certain aspects of how they are written about.

Aboriginal Peoples, along with various historians, academics and other cultural groups, have argued that it is important for any national and/or cultural group to have input into the documentation of its history, philosophies and reality, as a basic matter of cultural integrity. In some respects, Aboriginal Peoples need to "tell their own story" and/or exercise some authority over how they are represented, even more so than other national and cultural groups, because of the way in which they have been misrepresented by various disciplines, which have presented literature in a manner predominately inconsistent with, and often in opposition to, Aboriginal cultural concerns.

Establishing Culturally Appropriate Editorial Guidelines

The primary purpose of Aboriginal editorial guidelines should be to ensure the highest possible editorial standards, while at the same time developing and employing Aboriginal-based editorial practices and concerns. A culturally based editorial process may establish and incorporate some specific guidelines which do not necessarily follow established European-based editorial rules and practices. In an Aboriginal style guide certain unique editorial guidelines need to be developed and established in order to respect cultural integrity and complement the emerging distinct Aboriginal literary voice. Aboriginal writers, editors and publishers find themselves in a situation where, through their work, they are developing and defining an emerging contemporary Aboriginal literary voice. Similar to the situation that Aboriginal authors found themselves in during the 1980s within the literary process, Aboriginal editors and publishers are attempting to establish an Aboriginal-culturally based methodology within the editing and publishing process.

Some of the practices that are being implemented (or adopted) in editing texts are:

- utilizing principles of the Oral Tradition within the editorial process;
- respecting, establishing and defining Aboriginal colloquial forms of English (a developing area of study that is termed "Red English");
- incorporating Aboriginal traditional protocol in considering the appropriateness of presenting certain aspects of culture; and,
- consulting and soliciting approval of Elders and traditional leaders in the publishing of sacred cultural material.

More specific examples of how Aboriginal editors and publishers can develop culturally appropriate practices will be discussed throughout this paper; although it should be noted that, as a discipline, Aboriginal editorial and publishing methodology is in its initial stage of development.

Adherence to Aboriginal Cultural Protocol

Aboriginal Peoples have a distinct ethos based on a unique identity which stems from their histories, cultures and traditions. Aboriginal Peoples also have several responsibilities placed upon them through internal cultural imperatives which include telling the truth, honesty with one another and mindfulness of any impact on the community. Through consciousness of Aboriginal history and heritage comes the ultimate responsibility of being the link between one's ancestors and future generations, a cultural precept referred to by some Native American writers as "the time-space continuum."

It is crucial for those writing about Aboriginal Peoples to have a clear understanding of how Aboriginal Peoples perceive and contextualize their contemporary cultural reality. Over the past 500 years, Aboriginal societies have undergone attempted genocide, colonization and constant technological revolution, introduced by another society. This has coincided almost exactly with the time period that Western Society underwent its "500 years of print culture." Yet, even under these difficult circumstances, Aboriginal Peoples have dealt with the imposition of legislation and institutions, and the introduction of new technologies; moreover, they have survived, evolved, and developed with the foundations of their unique cultures intact.

Aboriginal Peoples have adapted into their various unique and distinct contemporary forms by adhering to two important cultural principles: 1) that incorporating new ways of doing things should be carefully considered in consultation with Elders, traditional leaders and community; and, 2) if it is determined that a new technology or institution goes against fundamental cultural values and/or might lead to negative cultural impact, then it should not be adopted. These principles exist, in one variation or another, in most First Nations and Aboriginal groups dating back to ancient times.

In many cases throughout the contact period, when repressive legislation and/or institutions were imposed on Aboriginal Peoples, Aboriginal institutions went underground giving the outward appearance that they had been undermined. The reemergence of various forms of traditional governments and spiritual institutions, such as the Potlatch and the Longhouse, are testimony to this phenomenon.

In other cases, Aboriginal Peoples found ways to incorporate traditional institutions and aspects of culture with new mediums into the contemporary context. The view that new mediums, such as text, print and new technologies can be integrated into Aboriginal cultures and can support Aboriginal political and social initiatives is consistent with Western theorists such as Lewis Mumford who has stated that "Technology is responsive to the ideological and cultural situation into which it is introduced." He has further stated that "culture can control the development of its tools."[7] The predominant mainstream perspective has tended to view Aboriginal cultures and the modern world in opposition to one another. Yet Aboriginal Peoples have shown through their adaptation that their dynamic cultures do not remain encapsulated in the past, static and resistant to development.

It is important for editors and publishers to understand how contemporary Aboriginal Peoples view themselves relative to their cultures and history, because several editorial problems and misrepresentations through literature stem from inappropriate perceptions of cultural positioning. Indeed, a vast number of writings on Aboriginal Peoples reflect the common mainstream perception that Aboriginal culture is static and must exist in some past state to be authentic. Aboriginal Peoples themselves, however, wish their cultures to be perceived as dynamic in interaction with the modern world and existing in a continuum between past and future generations of Aboriginal Peoples.

The Aboriginal Voice

The creation and/or expression of culture by Aboriginal Peoples, through any traditional medium or any contemporary medium or any combination thereof, constitutes an expression of what can be referred to as the "Aboriginal Voice." Drawing from a blend of traditional and contemporary sources such as oral history, traditional storytelling technique, inanimate, animal and spirit characters from legends, contemporary existence, literary technique, or other mediums such as film or multimedia, the contemporary Aboriginal Voice is a unique mode of cultural expression.

Throughout the past three decades, Aboriginal authors have developed and expressed the Aboriginal Voice by creating forms of literature which now stand out as a distinct culturally-based contemporary bodies of work within the literary canon. These important bodies of work are the most culturally authentic literary expression of Aboriginal reality, although it has often been overshadowed by non-Aboriginal writers who continue to develop a separate body of literature focussing on Aboriginal Peoples, or in the least using them as background material. Nevertheless, the significance of Aboriginal literatures is beginning to be acknowledged by the Canadian literary and publishing establishments, after years of marginalization, lack of understanding and access.

The Development and Politics of Aboriginal Patois

As early as the late 19th century, the so-called "Indian humorists" in the United States, such as the Creek author Alexander Posey, began writing in a form of Aboriginal patois which was then referred to as *Este Charte*. An American writer of the time made note of the *Este Charte* utilized by Creek writers and made the statement, "To write or speak 'correctly broken English' is almost impossible for anyone who isn't born with it."[8] Later, in the late 1960s, as Native American academics such as Daniel Littlefield began to trace the development of Aboriginal patois right up to contemporary Creek authors, such as Louis Littlecoon Oliver and Joy Harjo, the term "Red English" was created.[9] In his 1979 study *American Words* the Native American author Jack Forbes wrote, "We can find ways to Indigenize this language."[10]

Today "Red English" is sometimes referred to as "Rez English" in Canada and is commonly utilized as a literary technique by numerous Aboriginal writers such as Jeannette Armstrong, Lee Maracle, Louise Halfe and Maria Campbell. Jeannette Armstrong's Canadian bestseller novel *Slash*, for example, begins as follows: "School started that morning with old Horseface hollering at everybody to line up. Boy, it was cold. My ears hurting. I shoulda took my toque, I guess."[11]

The renowned Metis author Maria Campbell uses the phenomenon of Aboriginal patois in her most recent book, *Stories of the Road Allowance People*, in which she writes:

> "Dah stories der not bad you know
> jus crazy
> Nobody knows for shore what hees true
> I don tink nobody he care eeder
> Dey jus tell dah stories cause Crow
> he makes damn good storytelling
> Some mans der like dat you know."[12]

Stories of the Road Allowance People is indeed one of the most puristic examples of Aboriginal patois published to date. In her introduction Maria Campbell writes, "I am a young and inexperienced storyteller compared to the people who teach me. And although I speak my language I had to relearn it, to decolonize it, or at least begin the process of decolonization... I give them (the stories) to you in the dialect and rhythm of my village and my father's generation."[13]

In the foreword to *Stories of the Road Allowance People,* Ron Marken points out that academics like J.A. Cuddon have missed the point of cultural patois in stating that "Poetry belonging to this tradition is composed orally... As a rule it is a product of illiterate or semi-literate societies."[14] On the contrary, Marken argues, "The accents and grammar you will hear in this book are uncommon, but do not mistake them for unsophistication... These stories and poems have come through a long journey to be with us from *Mitchif* through literal translations through the Queen's Imperial English and back to the earth in village English... Our European concepts of "voice" are hedged with assumptions and undermined with problems. Voice equals speech."[15]

Aboriginal patois in its various forms is a cultural expression of how Aboriginal Peoples speak informally amongst themselves and communicate within their communities. As such it should warrant further research and receive a similar linguistic recognition/legitimacy recently being afforded to various forms of African American colloquial speech and the various forms of patois developed in the Caribbean and around the world.

The Salience of Aboriginal Literature

The many vast pools of information held by each individual First Nation or distinct Aboriginal group have been transmitted over centuries through the Oral Tradition and comprise unique bodies of knowledge with distinct cultural content. Furthermore, the Oral Tradition has often worked in conjunction with various physical methods of documentation, such as dramatic productions, dance performances, petroglyphs and artwork, namely birch bark scrolls, totem poles, wampum belts and masks.

Thus, according to Aboriginal tradition, the Oral Tradition is the primary mode of information transmission and documentation, and the Aboriginal Voice is the mode of expression. In as much as it is possible, it could be said that the Oral Tradition is the foundation of Aboriginal publishing, and the contemporary Aboriginal Voice is likewise the foundation of contemporary Aboriginal literature. The value of Aboriginal storytelling and the words of the Elders – even when spoken in the English language – are also important aspects of the Aboriginal Voice.

Although much of it still remains unwritten, Aboriginal Voice contains highly meaningful and symbolic "worlds" populated with fantastic, inanimate, animal, human and spirit characters who act out some of the most fascinating tales in world literature today. The body of natural scientific knowledge encompassed in the Aboriginal Voice also contains valuable paradigms, teachings and information that can benefit all of the world family of nations. Indeed, sectors of the scientific and academic establishment have recently come to the realization that Aboriginal knowledge is an integral part of the key to human survival.

Aboriginal literature has had to struggle through a number of impeding factors, including cultural and language barriers, the residential school system, ethnocentrism in the academic establishment, competition from non-Aboriginal authors, estrangement in the publishing industry, and a lack of Aboriginal controlled editing and publishing. Under these conditions it is not surprising that in the Canadian publishing industry Aboriginal literature has gone from being virtually non-existent to currently being relegated a marginal position. An important *raison d'être* for Aboriginal editorial should be to support and promote the Aboriginal Voice.

Aboriginal controlled editing and publishing is a solution to many of the problems which have held back and continue to hold back Aboriginal Peoples in the publishing industry. By incorporating cultural sensitivity, it could eliminate many of the problems that have been discussed in the body of this paper. Furthermore, it has the potential to make writing and publishing a fluid process under the influence of Aboriginal Peoples, so that the possibility of the writer going through an alienating process to get published is avoided. Most importantly, Aboriginal editorial direction produces the highest possible level of cultural integrity and the most authentic expression of the Aboriginal Voice within the parameters of the contemporary publishing industry.

Notes

1. Diamond Jenness, (1963) *Indians of Canada*, 6th ed. (Toronto: University of Toronto Press) 1.

2. Robert Berkofer, Jr., (1979) *The Whiteman's Indian: Images of the American Indian from Columbus to the Present*, (New York: Vintage Books) 71.

3. Howard Adams, (1995) *A Tortured People: The Politics of Colonization*, (Penticton: Theytus Books Ltd.) 33.

4. Ward Churchill, (1992) *Fantasies of the Master Race: Literature, Cinema and the Colonization of American Indians*, (Boulder: Common Courage Press) 38.

5. Gayatri Chakravorty Spivak, (1994) *Can the Subaltern Speak?*, *Colonial Discourse and Post-Colonial Theory: A Reader*, (New York: Columbia University Press) 89.

6. Margaret Atwood, (1972) *Survival: A Thematic Guide to Canadian Literature,* (Toronto: McClelland& Stewart Inc.) 91.

7. Ron Woodward, (1996) *Defining Technological Determinism: The Role of Technology in Society*, (unpublished) 7.

8. Jace Weaver, (1997) *That The People Might Live: Native American Literatures and Native American Community*, (New York: Oxford University Press) 89.

9. Jack Forbes, (1979) *American Words: An Introduction to Native Words Used in English in the United States and Canada*, (Davis, CA: University of California) 78.

10. Jeannette Armstrong, (1988) *Slash*, (Penticton: Theytus Books Ltd.) 15.

11. Maria Campbell, (1995) *Stories of the Road Allowance People*, (Penticton: Theytus Books Ltd.) 19.

12. ibid, 2.

13. J.A. Cuddon, (1992) *The Penguin Dictionary of Literary Terms and Literary Theory*, 3rd ed. (Toronto: Penguin Canada) 659.

14. Ron Marken, (1995) "Foreword," in *Stories of the Road Allowance People*, (Penticton: Theytus Books Ltd.) 5.

15. ibid, 5.

CONTRIBUTORS

Janice Acoose is a writer/scholar/producer/activist who has utilized print, video, radio, and television to reflect the beauty, strength, and power of First Nations and Metis peoples. Her roots stem from the Sakimay [Saulteaux] First Nation and the Marival Metis colony. Born in Broadview, Saskatchewan, she was culturally nourished in both the Saulteaux and Metis ways. Currently, an Associate Professor with the Saskatchewan Indian Federated College, Janice received critical attention for *Iskwewak – Kah' Ki Yaw Ni Wahkomakanak: Neither Indian Princesses Nor Easy Squaws* (Toronto: Women's Press, 1995). She is now pursuing her doctorate in English. As both professor and student of Indigenous literatures, she aspires to empower Indigenous students through critical reading and writing in English while simultaneously advocating for the retention of Indigenous languages. Through her studies in mainstream university she strives to ensure that First Nations and Metis cultures are acknowledged, represented, honoured and celebrated.

Kateri Akiwenzie-Damm is an Anishnaabe writer of mixed ancestry from the Chippewas of Nawash First Nation at Neyaashiinigmiing, Cape Croker Reserve on the Saugeen Peninsula in southwestern Ontario. Her poetry has been published in *my heart is a stray bullet* (Kegedonce, 1993), and *bloodriver woman* (absinthe chapbooks, 1998), and various anthologies, journals, and magazines in Canada, the U.S., Aotearoa/New Zealand, Australia and Germany. Currently, she is completing work on a CD of spoken word poetry and music; finalizing publishing arrangements for the collection of erotica by Indigenous writers she compiled and edited; writing a collection of short stories and a collection of poetry; and working on various multidisciplinary and publishing projects. Last year Kateri co-edited *skins: contemporary Indigenous writing* (Kegedonce), an international anthology of fiction by Indigenous writers. In March 2001, she was elected to the National Caucus of the Wordcraft Circle of Native Writers and Storytellers.

Laura Ann Cranmer is from the Nam'gis First Nation, which is part of the Kwakwaka'wakw Nation in BC. Laura is mother of four children, Jake, Nan, Josh and Ems, and grandmother of one little lightening boy, Seth. She is currently birthing her thesis, a play that concerns itself with themes of colonization, identity and healing, for her MA in Curriculum Studies at the University of Victoria. Laura combines her passion for healing with writing and teaching. She is currently on faculty in the First Nations Studies Department at Malaspina University-College in Nanaimo, B.C.

Jonathan R. Dewar is a SSHRC Doctoral Fellow in literature at the University of New Brunswick in Fredericton. His dissertation is an exploration of themes of connection to culture, authenticity, positionality and imposture in contemporary Canadian Aboriginal literature and criticism, specifically the role of literature as a site of (re)connection for persons of mixed-blood heritage. He writes from his position as a Huron-Wendat/Scottish/French Canadian and currently lives in Iqaluit, Nunavut.

Dr. Anita Heiss is from the Wiradjuri Nation of western New South Wales (NSW), Australia but was born and raised in Sydney. She is an author, poet, activist and social-commentator. In 2000 Anita completed her PhD on publishing Aboriginal writing in Australia through the University of Western Sydney, Nepean. Anita is the author of a juvenile novel *Who Am I? The diary of Mary Talence* (Scholastic, 2001), a satirical social-commentary *Sacred Cows* (Magabala, 1996) and a poetry collection *Token Koori* (Curringa Communications, 1998) and has been published widely in anthologies, journals and newspapers. Anita is well respected in the Indigenous arts and literary communities and has been writer-in-community in regional NSW and Western Australia. She is called upon regularly to be a representative of Indigenous writers nationally through her role as Deputy Chair and holder of the Indigenous Portfolio at the Australian Society of Authors.

Rauna Kuokkanen is a Sami woman from the river Deatnu, Samiland (Northern Scandinavia). Currently she lives in Musqueam territory, at the University of British Columbia, where she is working on her PhD on Indigenous philosophy and epistemologies. Prior to that, she was involved in Sami politics both locally and internationally.

Randy Lundy is of Cree, Irish and Norwegian ancestry. Born in Northern Manitoba but a long-time resident of Saskatchewan, he attended the University of Saskatchewan where he earned an honours BA and an MA, both in English Literature. Randy is also a poet whose work has appeared in literary journals from coast to coast. His first collection of poetry, *Under the Night Sun*, was published in 1999 by Coteau Books. He is currently an Assistant Professor of English at the Saskatchewan Indian Federated College in Regina, Saskatchewan.

Geraldine Manossa is a member of the Bigstone Cree Nation of Wabasca, Alberta. She is an MA candidate at the University of Lethbridge with her defense scheduled in the early part of 2002. She is a graduate from the En'owkin International School of Writing, and was also a student at the Banff Centre for the Arts-Aboriginal Dance Program. She recently finished a dance residency through Dancer's Studio West where she premiered her lasted work titled, *The Telling* and remounted, *Nimihitowin*.

Neal McLeod is from the James Smith Cree First Nation in central Saskatchewan. Currently he teaches Indian Studies at the Saskatchewan Indian Federated College and is completing his PhD with the Canadian Plain Studies at the University of Regina. His distinctive iconography, informed by Cree narrative memory, has fused several elements together, including the work of Norval Morrisseau; figurative studies from his training at the Umeå Konsthögskola - Academy of Fine Arts at Umeå, Sweden; and American Abstract Expressionism. In addition to his academic work and painting, Neal also writes poetry and makes short digital films with Tim Fontaine.

Dr. David T. McNab is a Metis who, as a public historian, has worked on Aboriginal Land and Treaty Rights issues for more than two decades. He is currently a Claims Advisor for Nin.Da.Waab. Jig, Walpole Island Heritage Centre, Bkejwanong First Nations and an Honorary External Associate in the Frost Centre for Canadian Studies and Native Studies at Trent University. He also teaches as a Conjoint Professor in the PhD Programme in the Department of Native Studies at Trent University, in the Canadian Studies Programme at University College, University of Toronto, as well as in the Public History Graduate Programme at the University of Waterloo. In addition to more than forty articles published in scholarly journals, he has edited and published two books, *Earth, Water, Air and Fire: Studies in Canadian Ethnohistory* (1998) and *Circles of Time: Aboriginal Land Rights and Resistance in Ontario* (1999). Both were published by Wilfrid Laurier University Press, with which he is now General Series Co-Editor of the new Aboriginal Studies Series.

Daniel David Moses is a Delaware, born at Ohsweken on the Six Nations lands along the Grand River in southern Ontario, Canada. A poet, playwright, dramaturge and editor, he holds an Honours BA in General Fine Arts from York University and an MFA in Creative Writing from the University of British Columbia. He currently lives in Toronto where he is an associate artist with Native Earth Performing Arts. His plays include *Coyote City* (a nominee for the 1991 Governor General's Literary Award for Drama), and *The Indian Medicine Shows*, which won the 1996 James Buller Memorial Award for Excellence in Aboriginal Theatre. He is also the co-editor of Oxford University Press' *An Anthology of Canadian Native Literature in English*. His most recent publications are *Sixteen Jesuses* (poetry), *Brebeuf's Ghost* (drama), both Exile Editions, and new editions of the plays *Almighty Voice and His Wife,* Playwrights Canada Press, and *Coyote City*, with "City of Shadow" included in *Necropolitei, Imago.*

Brenda Payne is of mixed European and Aboriginal heritage from the Cree and Metis Nations. She received an MA in English Literature from the University of British Columbia this past spring (2001). She has since returned to her hometown of Prince George, BC, where, with the guidance and support of her family and community, she and her partner are enjoying their experiences as new parents to their daughter Colby. Brenda also works part-time at AIDS Prince George as an HIV/AIDS educator, facilitating workshops that aim to break down the barriers of racism, homophobia and discrimination, which she finds challenging and rewarding. She is interested in theories of race and ethnicity and the shared experiences of those who are of "mixed" heritages and their exploration of the fluid nature of identity. She is also interested in narratives that give voice to journeys of grief and loss, healing and recovery.

Armand Garnet Ruffo is from Northern Ontario and is a member of the Biscotasing branch of the Sagamok First Nation. His work is strongly influenced by his Anishnaabe heritage. He now lives in Ottawa where he teaches in the Department of English Language and Literature (and is the former Director of the Centre for Aboriginal Education, Research and Culture) at Carleton University. His poetry collection *At Geronimo's Grave* (2001) and creative biography *Grey Owl: The Mystery of Archie Belaney* (1997) were both published by Coteau Books. His first collection of poetry, *Opening In the Sky,* was published by Theytus Books (1994). In addition to writing for the theatre, he has had poetry, fiction, and essays on Aboriginal literature published in journals and anthologies both in Canada and abroad.

Greg Young-Ing is a member of Opasquiak Cree Nation in The Pas, Manitoba and has an MA from the Institute of Canadian Studies, Carleton University, and an MA in Publishing from Simon Fraser University. His articles and poems have been published in the *Canadian Journal of Native Education, Paragraph Magazine, Fuse Magazine, Perception Magazine, Quill and Quire, absinthe, The Globe and Mail, and* the *Australian Journal of Canadian Studies.* He is a former member of The Canada Council Aboriginal Peoples Committee on the Arts and a member of the B.C. Arts Board. He is presently the Managing Editor of Theytus Books, the first Aboriginal publishing house in Canada. His first collection of poetry *The Random Flow of Blood and Flowers* was published by Ekstasis Editions in 1996.